The kitchen at Paxton House, a reconstruction by Peter Brears.

A New and Easy
Method of Cookery

(1755)

Elizabeth Cleland

A FACSIMILE EDITION

with an introduction
by

PETER BREARS

THE PAXTON TRUST
PROSPECT BOOKS
2005

This facsimile edition first published in Great Britain in 2005 by the Paxton Trust, Paxton House, Berwick upon Tweed, TD15 1SZ and Prospect Books, Allaleigh House, Blackawton, Totnes, Devon TQ9 7DL.

The edition used as the basis for the facsimile was first published in 1755 by the author Elizabeth Cleland in Edinburgh.

BRITISH LIBRARY CATALOGUING IN PUBLICATION DATA:
A catalogue entry for this book is available from the British Library.

ISBN 1-903018-39-0

Typeset in Adobe Garamond by Ben Morrow.
Printed and bound by the Cromwell Press, Trowbridge, Wiltshire.

Contents

Foreword, *by John Malden*   vii

Introduction, *by Peter Brears*   ix

Concordance of Recipes   xxvii

A New and Easy Method of Cookery, Elizabeth Cleland   xxxiii

AFTER THE FACSIMILE

Index   xxxvii

Foreword

This volume has been reproduced to coincide with the restoration of the original kitchen at Paxton House, built between 1758 and 1763 for Patrick Home of Billie to a design of John Adam. The house contains important collections of Chippendale and Trotter furniture, portraits and a Grand Tour library which, together with 80 acres of parkland and woods, were passed on to the Paxton Trust in 1988 by John Home Robertson with assistance from the National Heritage Memorial Fund.

The Home family of Wedderburn have played a dominant role in the history of the Scottish Borders, and have been responsible over the years for many great houses in the area – Wedderburn Castle, Paxton House, Caldra, Linthills and Milne Graden. In the extensive family archive, now deposited in the National Archives of Scotland, is one of the few copies of Elizabeth Cleland's *A New and Easy Method of Cookery*, first published in 1755 'chiefly intended for the Benefit of the Young Ladies who attend her School'. Among those young ladies was Christine Home, eldest daughter of Alexander Home of Jardinefield who, in 1755, was sent to Wedderburn Castle to look after her ageing grandmother who had recently had a paralytic stroke.

The restoration of the Paxton kitchen by the Paxton Trust, under the direction of Peter Brears, who has also written the introduction to this volume, was made possible by the generosity of the Morton Charitable Trust, and the use of the original of this volume has been made possible by the courtesy of John Home Robertson MSP.

John Malden, Director,
The Paxton Trust

Introduction

Published in Edinburgh in 1755, Elizabeth Cleland's *New and Easy Method of Cookery* is one of our most important sources regarding the culinary history of mid-eighteenth-century Scotland.[1] Her's was not the first recipe book to be published here, that honour going to *Mrs McLintock's Receipts for Cooking and Pastry-work,* Glasgow, 1736, but it is by far the most extensive.[2] Within over two hundred pages, it includes almost seven hundred recipes covering every aspect of food preparation, from traditional broths to the most fashionable of desserts. This made it one of the most successful Scottish cookery books of its period, second extended editions being separately printed by C. Wright & Co., by W. Gordon and Wright in Edinburgh, and by a London printer in 1759, a third edition by R. Fleming and W. Gray appearing in 1770.[3] As its title states, it was chiefly 'intended for the benefit of the young ladies who attend [Elizabeth Cleland's] school' which she presumably held at her house in the Luckenbooths adjacent to St. Giles at the head of Edinburgh's High Street.

In 1755, the social and economic life of this capital city was slowly beginning to revive after a hundred and fifty years of decline. This period had seen the departure of its royal court in 1603 and its

---

1.   A search through Edinburgh City and the National Archives has provided no information about Elizabeth Cleland. J. Gilhooly, *A Directory of Edinburgh 1752* (Edinburgh University Press, 1988), gives a Mrs Cleland at Cleland's, Stonelaw's Close, near the Tron Church. This address is too far down the High Street to be described as 'her house in the Luckenbooths'. William Gordon and Charles Wright were booksellers in James Court and Parliament Close, respectively, and John Bruce, the printer, was in Gosford's Close. All these addresses are near the Luckenbooths.
2.   V. Maclean, *A Short-title Catalogue of Household and Cookery Books published in the English Tongue 1701–1800* (London, 1981) 93–4.
3.   *Ibid.* 27.

parliament in 1707, the massive financial losses of the disastrous
Darien expedition to Panama, and the disruption of the 1715 and '45
Jacobite campaigns. It remained a major centre of social life and
culture however, with every modern amenity, including a university,
schools, infirmary, library, playhouse, concert and assembly rooms.
There too were professionals offering legal, medical, publishing and
architectural services, craftsmen offering numerous high quality
goods, and shops the widest range of both everyday and luxury
goods. This mass of activity was still constrained within the high
medieval walls and gates of the Old Town, since the glories of the
New Town lay years in the future. To the informed visitor,
Edinburgh's most notable features were the multi-occupancy buildings, often from six to fourteen storeys in height, and the volleys
from chamber pots which rained down from them, leaving pedes-
trians no option but to wade through the piles of excrement. The
houses of the nobility in the Canongate and Cowgate were considered paltry and mean by London standards, but they provided
essential accommodation for the landed families wishing to enjoy
the city's numerous facilities.[4] It would be these families that
provided the bulk of Elizabeth Cleland's pupils, since it would be
considered essential that their daughters should have a sound culinary education. If they married well, their knowledge would enable
them to order their households' meals with style and taste, while if
they had to earn their own living, it would qualify them to serve as
efficient housekeepers in major houses. It is interesting to note that
first editions of *A New and Easy Method of Cookery* have been found
in the library at Wedderburn Castle, and also in Sir Walter Scott's
library at Abbotsford, a clear indication of the gentry status of Mrs
Cleland's clients. In 1755, Anne Rutherford, daughter of the
Professor of Medicine at the University of Edinburgh, was still
living in her parental home in College Wynd, Cowgate, only a short
walk from the Luckenbooths where Mrs Cleland was then operating

4.   J.G. Dunbar, *Sir William Burrell's Northern Tour 1758* (Phantassie,
     1997) 77–8.

her school of cookery. We may reasonably assume that she attended Mrs Cleland's classes here, and bought her recipe book in preparation for her marriage in April 1758 to Walter Scott senior, Writer to the Signet, who lived a short way up Cowgate, in Horse Wynd. Over the following years, she kept his house, and bore him twelve children, the first six of whom died in infancy. Then followed Robert, John, Anne and, in August 1771, Walter, who was to become one of the greatest Scottish writers and patriots, and the foremost author of his age. It is interesting to realize that the recipes printed here were probably the very ones which nourished Sir Walter Scott in his formative years.[5]

In the eighteenth century, there were three very distinctive culinary traditions operating in Scotland. At the highest level came the cooking of the great noble families, who required the very finest of international cuisine. Their cooks were their best paid and most respected servants, autocrats of extensive kitchen departments, and men of great taste and education. Joseph Florence, French chef to three Dukes of Buccleuch was typical of this élite tradition, his painting by John Ainslie, now at Drumlanrig, being one of the most impressive and memorable of all servant-portraits.[6] Through his master, he became a friend of Sir Walter Scott, creating *Potage à la Meg Merrilies de Dercleugh* for him after the publication of *Guy Mannering*. J. Rozea, cook to the Earl of Hopetoun at Hopetoun House, demonstrated superb levels of skill and his knowledge of the classics in his *Gift of Comus or, Practical Cookery* published in Edinburgh in 1753.[7] Only two of the proposed twelve parts were ever printed, and in their 160 pages they got no further than preparing the stocks on which the subsequent dishes would depend. Only nobles with bottomless purses could afford such gastronomic excellence, and very few recipes from their cooks ever found their way into lesser kitchens.

5.   Maclean, *op. cit.* 28; *Dictionary of National Biography.*
6.   G. Waterfield & A. French, *Below Stairs, 400 Years of Servants' Portraits* (London, 2003) 73–5.
7.   Maclean, *op. cit.* 28.

Next came the cookery of the gentry and merchant classes, usually supervised by an experienced female cook or cook-house-keeper, or even the mistress of the house. This was the tradition which Mrs Cleland knew best, one which was extremely practical, wholesome and varied, including both everyday dishes and more luxurious ones for special occasions. Its kitchens, utensils and recipes will be discussed later, based on the information provided in her text.

The remaining type of cookery was that used by the country's working population, its agricultural, fishing, weaving and industrial communities. Economically limited, they made the very best use of locally available ingredients, fuels and utensils. These restrictions gave rise to considerable ingenuity, however, thus producing a highly individual tradition of true Scottish cookery, one of the most interesting of all Europe's national cuisines. Anyone wishing to read more on this theme should refer to F. Marian McNeill's *The Scots Kitchen* of 1929, and the numerous works of Professor Alexander Fenton.[8]

Scottish Gentry Kitchens

By the end of the seventeenth century, classical Palladian architecture was already well established in lowland Scotland, especially in Lothian. Here, architects such as James Smith and Sir William Bruce were building elegant country houses and villas complete with pedimented facades rising above basements which incorporated most of the domestic offices. At Auchendinny, finished in 1707, the kitchen occupied a large room in the vaulted basement, while the bakehouse was set in one of the flanking wings. It was soon realized that there were great advantages in moving the kitchen department away from the residential block, where its noise, smells, fire-risk and constant comings and goings would cause minimal disturbance to

8. F.M. McNeill, *The Scots Kitchen* (London & Glasgow, 1929; 2nd ed., 1963); A. Fenton, ed. with Eszter Kisbán, *Food in change: Eating habits from the middle ages to the present day* (J. Donald, 1986); and with Janken Myrdal, *Food & Drink & Travelling Accessories* (J. Donald, 1988).

the owners. It was for this reason that William Adam placed the kitchens at Arniston, Gorebridge, in a block to the east of the entrance court, a symmetrical block to the west housing the stables, both being linked to the main house by service corridors.[9] It would be in kitchens of this type that many of Elizabeth Cleland's pupils would expect to carry out their supervisory or practical duties.

A good example of an almost contemporary kitchen still survives in its original condition at Paxton House, Berwickshire, designed by John Adam and built for Patrick Home in 1758.[10] In the original design, the kitchen was a modest 16ft square room in the basement of the main house, its only ancilliaries being a 6ft by 13ft larder and a 9ft square scullery. On further consideration, it was decided to build on a much grander scale, with a suite of kitchen offices housed within a large west wing. At its heart, lay an 18ft by 27ft kitchen, almost double the size of the original proposal, and now rising up through two storeys. To each side lay a larder, a scullery, and the cook's bed-sitting room, while to the rear there was a bakehouse with a 6ft diameter bread oven, a brew-house and a gyle house where the ale cooled, and access to the back yard with its coal houses, game larder &c. Every fixture was of the highest quality. The main fireplace wall in the kitchen, for example, was faced with finely-cut red sandstone blocks which formed architectural surrounds to a row of charcoal stoves, a roasting hearth, and a flanking pastry oven and boiling-copper. To complete the architectural impact, all the plastered walls were painted a matching stone colour, lined out in white to give the impression of a completely stone-faced interior. Access to the main house was by means of a curving corridor, doorways pierced through its side walls providing a constant cross-draught which effectively carried off all

9. For an introduction to the architecture of the region, and the houses mentioned here, see C. McWilliam, *Buildings of Scotland, Lothian* (London, 1974) 55 *et seq.*
10. John Adam's original plans are currently housed at Paxton House, Berwickshire.

kitchen smells. In this kitchen, we can see all the culinary plant required to cook Mrs Cleland's recipes.

The Oven

The pastry oven is a 3ft diameter domed masonry-lined recess set into one corner of the kitchen. In use, faggots of burning sticks were thrust into it, so that their flames could heat its dome, before being drawn up a flue just outside its iron door. Once sufficiently heated, judged either by experience or by noting how long it took to scorch pieces of writing paper placed on its floor, the embers were raked out, dropping through a slot in its threshold. After an oven-mop or 'fruggin' had removed the finer ashes, an oven-peel was used to insert hoops or frames filled with cake mixtures, tin plates set with macaroons, cutlets or pastries, tin pans of Naples biscuits, Marlborough cakes &c, or white iron (tinplate) pastry pans of apples and so forth.[11] By the mid-eighteenth century, the use of earthenware and stoneware baking vessels was also well established in Scotland, these being known both as pans and as cans. The shallower, broader examples were used for potting or pastry-making, their meaty contents being covered with either coarse or puff paste.[12] Rather deeper ones were suitable for puddings and pies, deep ones for stewing, and the tallest, those with very narrow mouths, for jugging hare.[13] Descriptions of them being 'brown-glazed', 'well-glazed' and 'earthen' suggest that they had been made at one of the local potteries, such as Prestonpans, eight miles to the east of Edinburgh.[14] The 'small white tart-pans' used for potted beef &c, were much more likely to be of fine Staffordshire white salt-glazed stoneware. This beautiful ovenproof pottery, would also have been

11. Mrs Cleland, pp. 75, 156, 158–163, 173. The references in succeeding notes (up to note 37) are to the pages in the present facsimile which mention examples of the utensils used by Elizabeth Cleland.
12. e.g. 77, 107, 109, 110.
13. e.g. 48, 53, 78, 102, 119, 125.
14. e.g. 41, 173, 51.

used for making Mrs Cleland's 'white stone bowl', her fluted 'Turk's-cap' or turban mould, the 'shaped Mold that has Holes in it' for egg-cheese, and the 'cups' used for custards.[15] The 'Galleypots' in which marmalade and apple jelly were sealed would most probably have been made of tin-glazed earthenware, or its humbler local earthenware equivalent, while the 'Stone jars' in which pickles were sealed down under bladders were probably from the South London brown salt-glazed potteries.[16]

The Stove

Wherever good-quality cookery is being practised, the cook requires a practical, steady source of heat set at about table-height, just like our modern gas and electric stoves. From the seventeenth century or earlier, charcoal stoves fulfilled this function. As the restored set at Paxton shows, they were formed by setting iron firebaskets a few inches deep into the top of a fireproof bench. Charcoal from bunkers beneath was then shovelled in and ignited, the draught rising through their bottom grates soon producing a glowing mass of radiant and convected heat, ideal for stewing, frying and preserving. In order to raise the pans to a convenient height and to prevent them stifling the fires, each firebasket was further provided with a low triangular trivet made of wrought iron. If extra grates were required, small portable versions were available. Known as chafing dishes, these had bowl-shaped bodies fitted with firebars across their bases, a dish below to collect their ashes, and three knobs above their rims to support the dishes in which rump steaks or Scotch rarebits were gently stewed.[17]

The various copper vessels used on the stove, the chafing dish or the hob are described as stewpans (cylindrical, tinned inside, with a lid and iron handle), saucepans (the same, but pot-bellied) and goblets (cast-iron cooking pots). However, it is not so straightforward

15. e.g. 118, 136, 150, 178, 182.
16. e.g. 116, 165, 178, 182.
17. e.g. 52, 152.

as this, since mid-eighteenth-century Scots cooks used a different terminology from their English counterparts. The celebrated 'J. Rozea' cook to the Dukes of Montrose and Roxburgh and, in 1753, to the Earl of Hopetoun at Hopetoun House, made this distinction quite clear: 'you must have a sauce-pan and cover, which in Scotland is called a goblet-pan, and what the English calls a stewpan, they name it a sauce-pan. The above is meant, that my readers in Scotland may remember this distinction.'[18] For even smaller quantities, there were open-topped, iron-handled pans cast in brass or bell-metal, along with skillets, which had three integral legs and long handles cast in Bath metal, a bronze-like alloy of around 20 per cent tin and 80 per cent copper.[19]

Other more specialized vessels included tea kettles, teapots, long, lidded and internally-tinned fish kettles, shallow, circular preserving pans, and a sugar boiling pan, the last two being untinned since they were for higher-temperature use when boiling syrups and the like.[20] The frying pans required for some of the recipes must have been very large, since they had to be capable of holding four pounds of sliced beef or a whole turbot. They probably resembled the frying pan rescued from the Cowdray House fire of 1793, which has a slightly concave base, deep, flaring sides, and a long iron handle.[21]

The stove was also useful for grilling or broiling, the steaks or meat being supported above the charcoal on a grid-iron, rather like that of a modern barbecue. In Scotland, this grid was known as a brander, hence the term 'brander' meaning to grill food using this utensil.[22] The wafer-irons specified by Mrs Cleland were large iron tongs, their heads being discs measuring some four inches in

18. e.g. 3, 6, 14, 168; J. Rosea, *The Compleat Cook, Market Woman and Dairy Maid* (London, 1756) 71.
19. e.g. 167, 168, 181.
20. e.g. 23, 138, 145, 146, 179, 186.
21. e.g. 1, 22. This frying pan is now in the museum in the kitchen tower at Cowdray House, Midhurst, Sussex.
22. e.g. 35, 71. See also A. Warrack, *Chambers Scots Dictionary* (Edinburgh, 1979) 50.

diameter by under half an inch in thickness, their inner faces bearing boldly engraved patterns.[23] In use, both sides were buttered and heated over the stove, and then a spoonful of lightly spiced and rosewater-scented batter clamped tightly between them. This rapidly expanded, sending out jets of perfumed steam as it baked to a pale buff colour. After about half a minute, the tongs were opened and the wafer, still flexible, was rolled around a finger until it formed a cone-shape, which soon dried to perfect crispness. These were frequently filled with thick cream, the predecessor of the ice-cream cone.

The Roasting Range

The roasting fireplace at Paxton is typical of its period, measuring some seven feet by three, with a six-foot-high arched opening. An inventory of 1820 appears to list its original fittings:[24] a built-in grate 4 feet 5 inches long with two contractors (plates which adjusted the length of the fire) and key and two common cranes (to hang pots from) 12s 6d; a plate iron fender 4 feet 6in, 2s; a poker, tongs and shovel 3s 6d; ... a smoke jack with one chain (to turn the spits) £1 15s; 5 spits and two racks (to hold them in front of the fire) 7s 6d; an iron dripping pan and stand (to catch the juices falling from the meat) 4s; two double skewers (to hold the meat firmly on the spits) 1s 6d; two balance skewers (to balance the meat, so that it turned evenly) 1s; twelve single skewers and a hanger (on which they were stored) 1s; one tin basting spoon (to ladle the fat from the dripping pan over the meat, to keep it moist) 6d; a tin drudge, (a small cylindrical pot with a pierced domed cover, used to shake seasoned flour over roasting meats in order to produce a savoury froth or coating) 3d; and an iron kitchen screen 3ft 10in square on castors 12s 6d. This

23. e.g. 152.
24. 'Inventory and Valuation of the Furniture, Paintings, Books and Others in the House of Paxton in the parish of Hutton and County of Berwick that belonged to the deceased George Home Esquire at the time of his death which happened on the Tenth day of February 1820', Paxton House.

screen was an open-fronted cupboard, its shelved interior lined with brightly-polished tinplate, which stood just behind the roasting meat. Here it reflected the radiant heat back on to the joint, helping to keep the kitchen cool, and also acted as a 'hostess trolley' in which food could be kept piping hot ready for serving.

The roasting range could also be used for cooking other dishes by radiant heat. At its simplest, this could mean holding the frying pan before the fire, in order to cook the upper sides of pancakes and fried eggs.[25] Where more control was required, especially for grilling downwards (impossible with a stove), or giving a flash of fierce heat to finish a cold dish, a salamander would be thrust into the heart of the range's glowing coals. Here its head, a thick disc of iron, would soon become red hot, so that, by gripping its long handle with thick cloths, the cook could quickly brown the surfaces of custards or burnt creams, the Georgian version of crème brulée. If no salamander was available, Mrs Cleland recommended using a red-hot shovel instead.[26]

The two cranes swivelling over the fire would have had a number of adjustable pot-hooks hanging from their arms, for the roasting fire was ideal for heating the large vessels used for making stocks and simmering large joints. Those mentioned by Mrs Cleland include sheet-brass kettles, with iron rims and handles, and sheet-copper pots and pans similar in design, but pot-bellied, lidded, and with tinned interiors. Her 'broad gravy pan' was probably of this type.[27] Once the meat had been put in, boiling water for fresh meat, or cold water for salt meat, and brought up to boiling point, it began to throw off a grey, foamy scum, which would spoil the clarity and quality of the broth. A skimmer with a round, pierced sheet-brass head mounted on a long iron handle was therefore used to remove it before it had any opportunity of boiling back into the stock. When the meat had cooked to tenderness, an iron meat fork enabled it to be lifted out

25. e.g. 121, 127, 129.
26. e.g. 136, 138, 140.
27. e.g. 1, 2, 7, 170.

onto its dish and allowed to rest before going to the table. If gravy or broth was being made, however, it would be allowed to cook down to 'strings' or 'tavers', the Scots word for rags.[28]

Other utensils mentioned by Mrs Cleland include chopping knives for mincing foods or flattening steaks, penknives for paring fruit, marble or wooden mortars for pounding meats, fruits and other things to smooth pastes, moulds for sweetmeats, and scallop shells for baking oysters and lobsters.[29]

Kitchen Textiles

Textiles played an important role in Mrs Cleland's kitchen. Linen napkins were used to dry slices of eel before frying, for example, and flannels for cleaning walnuts as they were being pickled.[30] The coarsest straining cloths were bags woven from strong horsehair twine, in which apple pulp was pressed when extracting cider, smaller versions made from coarse canvas being similarly used when squeezing currants or gooseberries for wine-making. Squares of the same canvas were used for rapidly separating the liquid and solid contents of any mixture. Known as strainers, they could also have fairy butter pressed through them, to fall in attractive moss-like lumps on to supper-plates.[31] Finer cloths and flannels were more effective for clarifying liquids by slow filtration, some being sewn into cone-shaped jelly bags, although the same effect could be achieved by tying a large square to the four legs of an upturned chair or frame, and placing the collecting-bowl on the underside of the seat.[32] If dry materials were to be sieved, a piece of fine linen or horsehair cloth was stretched across a wooden hoop to form a 'searce' or 'hair-sieve'. In these, powdery foods could be readily shaken to remove all lumps &c, while semi-solids could be worked through

28. e.g. 6, 144, 186; A. Warrack, *op.cit.* 600.
29. e.g. 35, 52, 69, 99, 120, 177, 178, 186.
30. e.g. 28.
31. e.g. 153, 171, 199, 201.
32. e.g. 67, 138, 109, 171.

using the back of a spoon, to produce the smoothest purées.[33]

The combination of strength, flexibility and porosity offered by textiles made them ideal for containing foods. If whole spices or colouring materials were bound in scraps of linen or muslin, for example, they could be retrieved from stews and liquid foods at the end of the cooking process, without the need for straining.[34] Cloths were also indispensable for boiling puddings, both large squares and cylindrical bags having their interiors buttered before being filled, tied up, and plunged into a boiling pot. When apple dumplings were to be boiled, they were arranged at intervals within a long roll of cloth, which was tied between each dumpling, forming them into a chain which could be readily lifted into and out of the boiler. Even when puddings began to be boiled in basins, rather than cloths, a buttered cloth was still necessary to hold them in place, and to prevent the entry of water, which would have made them unpleasantly soggy. Cloth, in the form of broad tapes, broad netting, or squares tied at each end like a Christmas cracker, was also used to bind joints of meat or fish for boiling and roasting. They had the advantage of keeping the joints in their original form, rather than cutting deeply into them, like the modern trussings of twine.

When hanging up salt beef, in order to dry it for preservation, it was useful to enclose it within a canvas bag, for this not only kept it clean, but also prevented bluebottles from laying their eggs on it, and turning it maggoty.[35]

Scots Weights & Measures

Following the 1707 Act of Union, the combination of largely regional weights and measures used in Scotland was officially replaced by standard British ones. However, as with metrification today, the old measures continued in everyday use for a considerable time. In Mrs Cleland's recipes, the weights appear to be the standard

33. e.g. 107, 125, 147, 186.
34. e.g. 181, 199.
35. e.g. 52.

pounds and ounces with which we are still familiar, but volumes are a different matter, since they retained Scots measure. The Scots gallon was nearly three imperial gallons, about twenty-four pints, and the Scots pint some four imperial pints, for example. The chopin or half-pint frequently employed in these recipes is therefore a quart or two imperial pints, the mutchkin one imperial pint, and the gill a quarter of an imperial pint.

Food of the Scottish Gentry

Today it is impossible to think of Scottish food without conjuring up images of its great national delicacies. Many of these are attributed to the influence of France during the centuries of social, economic and political co-operation between the Scots and the French, the Auld Alliance. In the sixteenth century, Mary of Lorraine married James V and introduced the perfection of French civilization to Scotland, while Mary Stuart's childhood in France brought in Italian influences current in the contemporary French court. As a result, Scotland obtained the haggis or *hachi* (hash), petticoat tail shortcakes or *petit gasteau* (little cakes) and gigots or *gigot* (legs of lamb &c). Other foods owed their origins to native Scottish ingenuity. In the late eighteenth century, for example, Janet Keiller invented the world's first orange marmalade.[36]

Given this great culinary tradition, we should expect Mrs Cleland's book to be bristling with Scottish dishes, but it isn't. Certainly there is Scots barley broth and a Scots collops – actually an English dish of scotched (hacked or sliced) veal.[37] There is not a trace of haggis or a petticoat tail, and the marmalade is unlike anything we would recognize as such today. There must be good reasons why a major Scottish cookery book should appear neither Scots nor French, but massively English in its content. To understand why this should be, we must first debunk the Auld Alliance as a culinary

36. C.A. Wilson, *The Book of Marmalade* (London, 1985) 65–6;
    F.M. McNeill, *op. cit.* 235.
37. e.g. 7, 62, 147.

influence. The haggis, for example, was as much an English as a Scottish dish, appearing in English recipe books from 1420, and so popular in the seventeenth century that Gervase Markham's *English Housewife* of 1660 actually says that of its 'goodnesse it is in vain to boast, because there is hardly to be found a man that does not affect [like] them'.[38] It was only in the eighteenth century that the haggis fell out of fashion in England, and became recognized as a characteristic Scottish dish. The French word *hachi* has nothing to do with haggis, being centuries later in origin, and quite different in meaning. The word gigot certainly is of French origin, but it has been used by English cooks since at least the 1520s, so that its Scottish use is most probably from English sources.[39] As for short-cakes, these first appear in *The Good Huswifes Handmaid* published in London in 1594, and were cut in 'petticoat tails', which exactly describes their shape around 1800.

If we look for real evidence for the origins of gentry cookery in Scotland, we must discover which books were being bought and read by its ladies. They were neither Scots nor French, but English, as we can see from manuscript accounts. The Foulis family of Ravelston, for instance, bought Gervase Markham's works in 1680, along with the Countess of Kent's *Choice Manuall* of 1633, Robert May's *Accomplisht Cook* of 1660 (with its five haggis, one skink, and fifteen French recipes) and *The Closet of Sir Kenelm Digby Opened* of 1696; while Lady Grisell Baillie owned the English translation of Massialot's *Court and Country Cook* of 1702 and Henry Howard's *British Cook's Companion* of 1729.[40] This reliance on English sources is hardly surprising, since this country had published some ten cookery books in the sixteenth century, and forty in the seventeenth.[41] These had

38. See *Oxford English Dictionary,* 'Haggis'.
39. Society of Antiquaries, *Royal Household Ordinances* (London, 1790) 174.
40. U.A. Robertson in P.A. Sambrook & P. Brears, *The Country House Kitchen 1650–1900* (Stroud, 1996) 230.
41. These numbers are based on entries in A.W. Oxford, *Notes from a Collectors Notebook* (London, 1909).

included many individual French recipes, along with whole volumes dedicated to them, such as La Varenne's *The French Cook* of 1653, M. Marnette's *The French Pastery Cooke* of 1656, *Archimagirus Anglo-Gallicus* of 1658, *The English and French Cook* of 1674 and Vincent La Chapelle's *The Modern Cook* of 1733.[42] It is from sources such as these that dishes in the French mode were introduced into polite Scottish kitchens.

There was also a great influx of English dishes, particularly from the most popular London cookery books. Mrs Cleland certainly had access to Eliza Smith's *Compleat Housewife* of 1727, copying seventeen of her recipes, especially those for cakes such as Shrewsbury, Marlborough, Whetstone and plumb cakes. She copied a further thirty-seven from Hannah Glasse's *Art of Cookery Made Plain and Easy* of 1747, demonstrating just how English recipes were readily absorbed into the Scottish repertoire through the teaching in Mrs Cleland's cookery school.

Even though Mrs Cleland did not think of many of her dishes as being especially national in character, and so only gave three a 'Scots' prefix, her book shows clear indications of its Scottish origins.[43] The large number of broths and soups, for example, the wide range of oatmeal dishes, the long run of venison recipes, and one of the earliest recipes for tablet, are all essentially Scottish. A further seventy years were to pass before the country's cookery, along with most aspects of its gentry culture, were subjected to a massive re-branding exercise inspired and driven by Sir Walter Scott. In culinary terms, the propaganda for Scottish national cookery was led by Mrs Christine Isobel Johnstone, wife of Sir Walter's publisher. Her *Cook and Housewife's Manual* published in Edinburgh in 1826 [44] under the pseudonym of Mrs Margaret Dods of Cleikum Inn, St. Ronan's is as

---

42. *Ibid.* 69, 73, 83, 99.
43. Elizabeth Cleland's only 'Scots' recipes are for Scots barley broth, 7, white Scots collops, 62, and Scots flummery, 147.
44. M. Dods, *The Cook and Housewife's Manual* (Edinburgh, 1826, new editions, 1827, 1828, 1829 and 1988).

much fictional nationalist journalism as recipe book. Where Mrs Cleland recognized three Scots dishes, Meg Dods discovered a further twenty-five, along with a whole chapter of twenty-nine additional 'Scotch' national dishes of particular importance. In fact, many of these are as much, if not more English than Scottish. White puddings, liver puddings, roast pig, pig's cheek, fried tripe, black puddings, sheep's head broth and plumb porridge are universal throughout the British Isles, yet here they are chosen for their supposedly Scottish origins. Regrettably, this practice of Scottish-ification has continued to develop, even the scholarly Marian McNeill could not help adding *Scots fashion* to Elizabeth Cleland's decidedly English Hedge Hog and Floating Island in her *Scots Kitchen* of 1929.[45] She also continued the Scotch marmalade myth, even though the English had been making it from the late sixteenth and early seventeenth centuries, and had developed the modern variety by the 1760s.[46] One of the great values of Elizabeth Cleland's book, and a sound reason for publishing this new edition, is that it gives us a true picture of the state of Scottish gentry cookery in the mid-eighteenth century, before it was subjected to romantic re-interpretation.

Although the recipes in *A New and Easy Method of Cookery* are overwhelmingly English in character, they include a number of Scots terms, some of which are now virtually unknown to cooks in both countries. With regard to fish, for example, maids are now called skate or thornback, sperling as smelt, and cabbolow as salted cod. Similarly draucht are sheep entrails, haricles are pluck, and midrit, the heart and skirts of a bullock, while a blade is a cabbage or kail leaf, and a bake, a small biscuit.[47]

With regard to the recipes, they required a wide range of ingredients, including all manner of game, meat, fish, vegetables and home-grown fruits and nuts, all of which were readily available

45.   E. Cleland, 148, 146; F.M. McNeill, *op. cit.* 172, 174.
46.   C.A. Wilson, *op. cit.* 47–8, 62.
47.   A. Warrack, *op. cit.* 17, 35, 68, 144, 149, 345, 357, 554.

in the fertile lowlands and the fishing ports of their eastern and western coasts. Scottish farming and market-gardening were already of the highest standard, while excellent Scots beef had been a major export to England for a hundred and fifty years. The main imported items included oranges, lemons and limes, sweet and bitter almonds, sugar and treacle, rice, sago, millet and vermicelli, and dried fruits such as currants, raisins and prunes. Except for medicinal use, only a restricted number of spices were in regular use: allspice (Jamaica pepper), caraway, cinnamon, cloves, coriander, ginger, mace, nutmeg and black and white pepper. All these ingredients are fairly predictable, but there are some surprises too, this being one of the few recipe books which gives directions for cooking ox or cow's eyes.[48] French cuisine has its *yeax de veau farcis*, stuffed calves eyes, but Elizabeth Cleland removed the iris and lens, blanched the remainder, then thin-sliced them and stewed them in a savoury sauce.

Other recipes of particular interest include one for Yorkshire pudding which is virtually unique in boiling it for three hours, rather than cooking it under the meat. She was well aware of the usual method, however, for both her clary cake and tansy were to be cooked 'in a Dish in the Dripping-pan when Meat is roasting'.[49] Her directions for making patties in patty-pans are also quite useful, since these are omitted from most other contemporary publications. Some patties were made by lining the pans with pastry, some topped with 'cross Bars' similar to those of traditional fruit pies, while others had puff-paste lids with holes cut in them, presumably to allow steam to escape as they were being baked. For more decorative effects, patties, tarts and Florentines (shallow pies) were covered with lids of 'carved Puff paste', sometimes pre-baked ready to place over the finished patty.[50] These successors to the 'cut-laid tarts' of the seventeenth century remained popular well into the eighteenth

48. E. Cleland, 74.
49. *Ibid.* 112, 121, 125.
50. *Ibid.* e.g. 133, 134, 124.

century, designs for them being published in Edward Kidder's *Receipts of Pastry and Cookery* of *c*.1720.

Although the *New and Easy Method of Cookery* is an interesting record of early Georgian Scottish gentry cookery, it should not be used solely as an historical record. Even today, it remains an eminently practical cookery book, one which gives instructions for making hundreds of delicious dishes which should present few problems for anyone with basic culinary skills. Obviously the medicinal recipes should not be tried, but all the others will produce good quality dishes providing the widest range of flavours, textures and aromas which are well worth reviving. It will be best to use free-range eggs of the smallest size, and an oven temperature of 180°C, 350°F, Gas Mark 4 for initial trials, varying these in the light of experience. In this way Elizabeth Cleland's book may regain its intended purposes: an interesting addition to the library, and a source of inspiration in the kitchen.

Peter Brears,
Leeds 2004

Concordance of Recipes

In common with most writers of eighteenth-century cookery books, Elizabeth Cleland took a number of her recipes from those of other popular writers of the day. Although a comprehensive comparison with all cookery books published in the first half of the eighteenth century is practically impossible, it is clear that Mrs Cleland had access to Eliza Smith's *Compleat Housewife* of 1727 and Hannah Glasse's *Art of Cookery* of 1747. Both of these were extremely popular. Smith's work, with over five hundred recipes, went through eighteen editions up to 1773, while Glasse's, with over nine hundred and sixty recipes, went through twenty editions, with numerous reprints through to the 1840s. The recipes that were drawn from these two authors were not fully transcribed in *A New and Easy Method of Cookery*, but were condensed, presumably due to considerations of space. Even so, the use of identical quantities, methods and phrases makes their origins perfectly obvious. There is also a number of alterations perhaps made in the light of practical experience. Eliza Smith's plumb cake has 'four pounds of eggs weighed', for example, while Elizabeth Cleland revises this to thirty-four eggs with half the whites. Other changes appear to be mistakes, as when the cloves in Eliza Smith's mushroom-powder are increased in quantity from four to forty – thus transforming a flavoursome relish into a powerful oral anaesthetic quite capable of numbing the mouth completely!

Although not reprinted here, the second edition of Elizabeth Cleland's book includes 'NECESSARY DIRECTIONS Whereby the Reader may easily attain the useful Art of Carving.' This too appears to come from Eliza Smith (15th ed., pp. 394–6), who may have got her's from Robert May (1685 ed., pp. 82–4), who probably got his from a late medieval manuscript source. It reproduces full medieval English carving terms and instructions, even for heron, crane and swan, birds which hardly ever appeared on mid-eighteenth-century tables. Presumably these were added to give the book an additional air of authority and style.

Cleland		Glasse	Smith
9	An Eel soup	77	
9	Onion soup	77	
21	To bake a Turbot	88	
27	To roast a Cod's Head	87	
40	To stew Collops	96	
43	To make Veal Hams	129	
44	Beef Hams	129	
50	To make Escarlot Beef	50	
52	To boil a Rump of Beef the *French* way	20	
54	A Shoulder of mutton in Epigramme	24	
57	To stew a Neat's Tongue whole	23	
62	To stew a Knuckle of Veal	19	
62	Lamb with Rice	62	
64	To roast a Ham, or Gammon of Bacon	64	
66	A Pig in Jelly	66	
68	To make *Bologna* Sausages	68	
68	To fry Sausages with Apples or Potatoes	68	
93	To dress a wild Duck with Lemmon Juice	40	
95	To dry a Goose	42	
96	To dress Partridges a la Braize	47	
98	A Pupton of Pigeons	98	
98	Pigeons boiled with Rice	98	
100	A stewed Pheasant	48	
101	To roast Snipes or Woodcocks	49	
101	To roast Larks	49	
119	A boil'd Apple Pudding	112	
124	A Florendine of oranges or Apples	113	

Cleland		Glasse	Smith
125	To make a White Pot	79?	
127	Rice Pancakes		136
131	A Paste of Drippings	75	
142	Ratafia Cream	144	
148	To make Flummery Caudle		192
155	To toast Cheese	97	
155	To make Wigs	141	
156	Wigs another Way		174
157	Shrewsbury Cakes		177
157	Almond Cakes		177
157	Drop Biscuits	140	
158	Marlborough Cakes		179
158	Whetstone Cakes		182
159	A Plumb Cake		183
159	To ice a great Cake	138	
159	A rich Nun's Cake	139	
162	Thin *Dutch* Biscuits		179
164	A Cake to eat hot		172
171	Mushroom Powder		86?
179	White Plumbs		201
179	Damsons	154	
180	Mulberries		220
185	Currants in Jelly		208
189	Green Apricocks		230

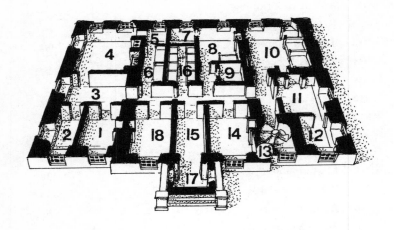

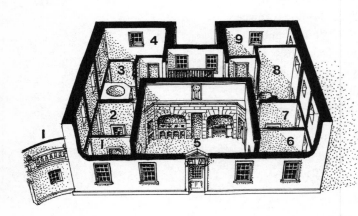

Cut-away views of John Adam's plans for Paxton House, 1758 (drawn by Peter Brears).

Above: The house as a single block with all services at basement level.

KEY

1.—Latter-meal Room; 2.—Larder; 3.—Servants' Hall; 4.—Kitchen; 5.—Scullery; 6.—Men-servants' Bedrooms; 7.—Housekeeper's Store; 8.—Housekeeper's Room; 9.—Housekeeper's Closet; 10.—Nursery; 11.—Dry Laundry; 12.—Woman house; 13.—Stair to Dining Room; 14.—Butler's Pantry; 15.—Ale Cellar; 16.—Wine Cellar; 17.—Empty Bottle Store; 18.—Second Table Room (Upper Servants' dining room).

Below: As built, with the kitchens in a separate wing, linked to the main house by a quadrant corridor.

KEY

1.—Passage to main house; 2.—Larder; 3.—Bake House; 4.—Meal Girnal (store); 5.—Kitchen; 6.—Cook's Bed-sitting Room; 7.—Scullery; 8.—Brewhouse; 9.—Malt Girnal (store).

A NEW AND EASY METHOD OF COOKERY

The Facsimile

A
NEW AND EASY
METHOD
OF
COOKERY.

TREATING,

I. Of GRAVIES, SOUPS, BROTHS, &c.

II. Of FISH, and their SAUCES.

III. To Pot and Make HAMS, &c.

IV. Of PIES, PASTIES, &c.

V. Of PICKLING and PRESERVING.

VI. Of Made WINES, DISTILLING and BREWING, &c.

By ELIZABETH CLELAND.

Chiefly intended for the Benefit of the Young LADIES *who attend Her* SCHOOL.

EDINBURGH:

Printed for the Author by W. GORDON, C. WRIGHT, S. WILLISON and J. BRUCE: And sold at Her House in the *Luckenbooths.*

M. DCC. LV.

THE CONTENTS.

CHAP. I.

Of Gravies, Soups, Broths and Pottages.

Pag.

TO make a ftrong Broth for Soups or Sauces   1

To make brown Gravy for Soups   ib.

White Gravy for Soups or Sauces   2

A good Stock for Fifh Soups ib.

A Vermicelli Soup   ib.

To make a Craw-fifh or Lobfter Soup   ib.

A Veal Soup with Barley   3

A green Peafe Soup   ib.

A brown Pottage Royal   ib.

Rice Soup   4

Barley Pottage   ib.

A Pottage, forced Pigeons with Onions   ib.

To make Plumb Broth   5

To make Spring Soup   ib.

Pottage of Chervil the *Dutch* Way   ib.

Jelly Broth for confumptive Perfons   ib.

To make Soup de Santé the *French* Way   6

To make a Summer Pottage ib.

To make meagre Broth for Soups with Herbs   7

To make *Scots* Barley Broth ib.

A Calf's Head Soup   ib.

To make Mutton Broth   ib.

To make another Barley Broth 8

A Purfiain Soup   ib.

A Cucumber Soup   8

To make Soup meagre   ib.

An Eel Soup   9

An Almond Soup   ib.

Onion Soup   ib.

A general Cullis for Fifh   10

A Veal Cullis   ib.

Green Cullis for Soups or Sauces   11

To make a brown Soup   ib.

To make a white Soup   ib.

To make Peafe Soup   12

To make Onion Soup   ib.

Afparagus Soup   ib.

To make Hodge Podge   13

To make a green Peafe Soup ib.

A very good Peafe Soup   ib.

To make a Pottage the *French* Way   14

To make Pottage of chopped Herbs   ib.

A Fifh Broth   ib.

An Oifter Soup   15

To make Calves Feet Broth ib.

Broth of Roots   ib.

To make Cake Soup   16

A Pottage of Goofe Giblets ib.

A Muffel Soup   17

A Peafe Soup with Herbs in it ib.

To make Peafe Pottage   ib.

A Turnep Soup   ib.

A Hare Soup   18

CHAP. II.

Of dreffing all Kinds of Fifh, and their Sauces.

TO ftew Carp or Tench 18

To drefs a Cod's Head 19

To make Oifter, Lobfter or Shrimp Sauce   19

To

CONTENTS.

	pag.
To roaſt or bake a Salmon	19
To pickle Salmon	ib.
A Turbot, or any flat Fiſh in Jelly	20
To broil Salmon	ib.
To farce Slices of Salmon	ib.
To haſh Salmon	21
To fry Salmon	ib.
To bake a Turbot	ib.
To fry a Turbot	22
To fouſe a Turbot	ib.
To ſtew a Turbot	ib.
To cramp Cod the Dutch Way	ib.
To ſtew Soals, or any flat Fiſh	ib.
To boil a Turbot, or any flat Fiſh	23
To roaſt or bake a Pike	ib.
To make Oiſter Loaves	24
To dreſs a Pike with Oiſters	ib.
To fouſe a Pike	25
To boil a Pike	ib.
To fry a Pike	ib.
To bake Plaice, or any flat Fiſh	26
To ſtew Soals	ib.
To boil Mallets, or ſtew them	ib.
To pickle Smelts	ib.
To roaſt a Cod's Head	27
To ſtew Cod	ib.
To broil a Cod	ib.
To dreſs a Cod's Tail	28
To ſtew Carps à la Royale	ib.
To boil Carps	ib.
To dreſs Eels with white Sauce	ib.
To dreſs Eels with brown Sauce	29
To fry Eels	ib.
To dreſs Eels à la Daube	ib.
To roaſt a large Eel	30
To bake Tench	ib.
To roaſt Tench	ib.
To fry Tench	ib.
To crimp Scate	31
Flounders with Sorrel	ib.
To boil Flounders or Plaice	31
To broil Flounders or Plaice	ib.
To ſtew Plaice or Flounders	32
To dreſs Cabbolow	ib.
To pot Salmon, Trouts or Eels	ib.
To pot Lobſters or Scollops	33
To fricaſey Oiſters, Cockles or Muſſels	ib.
To butter Crabs or Lobſters	ib.
To make Caper Salmon	ib.
To keep Salmon in Pickle for a Year	34
To ſtew Haddocks or Whitings	ib.
To pot Herrings	ib.
To pickle Oiſters, Scollops, Cockles or Muſſels	ib.
To ſcollop Oiſters or Lobſters	35
To ſtew Eeels	ib.
To make a Fricaſey of Oiſters	ib.
To make forc'd Meat for Fiſh	ib.
To fry Soals	36
A good Way to dreſs Lobſters	ib.
Lobſters the Italian Way	ib.
To dreſs Crabs	37
To make Water Sokey	ib.
To ſtew Trouts	ib.
To fouſe Trouts	ib.
To fry Lobſters	ib.
To ſtew Crabs	38
To boil a Piece of Sturgeon	ib.
To roaſt a Piece of Sturgeon	ib.
To fry Sturgeon	ib.
To fry Sperlings	39
To ſtew Sperlings	ib.
To boil Mackarel	ib.
To pickle Mackarel	ib.
To broil Mackarel	ib.
To fry Maids	ib.
To boil Gurnets	40
To fry Whitings	ib.
To ſtew Scollops	ib.
To make a Collar of Fiſh	ib.
To ſtew a Pike	41

CHAP.

CONTENTS.

CHAP. III.

To pot and make Hams, &c.

pag.

To pickle Tongues 42
To make Hams or Bacon ib.
To boil Hams ib.
To make Mutton Hams 43
Another Way to make Mutton Hams ib.
To make Veal Hams ib.
Beef Hams 44
To roaft an Ox or Sheep's Heart ib.
To roaft a Haunch of Venifon ib.
To roaft a Shoulder, or any Joint of Venifon ib.
To roaft Venifon that has been falted or baked 45
To boil Venifon ib.
To ftew Venifon ib.
Venifon in Blood ib.
To drefs Venifon à la Royale in Blood 46
To recover Venifon, when it ftinks ib.
Venifon in Avet ib.
A Civet of Venifon ib.
To keep Venifon all the Year ib.
To boil a Haunch of Venifon 47
To broil Venifon ib.
To make Venifon Sokey ib.
To roaft a Fillet of Veal ib.
To roaft a Shoulder of Veal with farcing Herbs 48
To ftew a Knuckle of Veal ib.
To broil a Shoulder of Veal ib
To roaft a Calf's Head 49
A Calf's Head Surprife ib.
To boil a Calf's Head ib.
Beef à la Daube ib.
To make Efcarlot Beef 50
Beef la Vinaigre ib.
To roaft a Tongue and Udder ib.
Ox Tongues à la Mode ib.

pag.

To collar Beef 50
To ftew a Rump of Beef 51
To make *Dutch* Beef ib.
Beef Staiks with Oifter Sauce 52
To make hung Beef ib.
To boil a Rump of Beef the *French* Way ib.
To ftew a Rump of Beef 53
To grillard a Breaft of Mutton ib.
To make Mutton Cutlets ib.
To roaft a Collar of Mutton 54
To roaft a Leg of Mutton with Oifters ib.
A Shoulder of Mutton in Epigramme ib.
Carbonaded Mutton 55
To boil Sheeps Tongues with Oifters ib.
To roaft a Calf's Head with Oifters ib.
To drefs Calves Feet 56
Cakes of Beef to be fried or brandered ib.
To force the Side of a Surloin of Beef ib.
A Neat's Tongue the *Polifh* Way ib.
To fry a Neat's Tongue 57
To ftew a Neat's Tongue whole ib.
To bake Ox Cheeks ib.
To roaft a Leg of Mutton with Cockles ib.
To pot Beef ib.
To make Beef Ollops 58
To make Veal Collops ib.
To make Forc'd-meat Balls 59
Another Sort of Forc'd-meat Balls ib.
Another Sort of Forc'd-meat Balls ib.
To make Veal Fricandoes ib.

To

C O N T E N T S.

pag.

To force a Leg of Mutton or Lamb   60
To make a Mutton or Lamb Hafh   ib.
To make minc'd Collops   ib.
To make Beef Collops   ib.
Entry of Sheeps Trotters forced   61
Veal Olives   ib.
Another Way   ib.
To ftuff a Rump or Round of Beef   62
White *Scots* Collops   ib.
To ftew a Knuckle of Veal   ib.
Lamb with Rice   ib.
To make a Calf's Head Hafh   63
To make a Lamb's Head Hafh   ib.
Another Way to drefs a Lamb's Head   64
To ftew a Lamb's Head   ib.
To drefs any Sort of Liver   ib.
To roaft a Ham, or Gammon of Bacon   ib.
To roaft Pork without the Skin   65
To roaft a Breaft of Pork   ib.
To broil Pork Steaks   ib.
To drefs a Pig the *French* Way ib.
A Hog's Head Cheefe Fafhion 66
Pork Brawn   ib.
In Imitation of Brawn   ib.
A Pig in Jelly   ib.
To drefs a Loin of Pork with Onions   67
To roaft a Quarter of young Pig Lamb Fafhion   ib.
A Pig Rolliand   ib.
To make *Bologna* Saufages   68
To fry Saufages with Apples or Potatoes   ib.
Oifter Saufages   ib.
Oxford Saufages   ib.

pag.

A Soufe for Brawn   69
To make Saufages   ib.
Pigs Petty-toes   ib.
To roaft a Pig's Haflet   ib.
To make a Ragoo of Tripes 70
To drefs a large Pig's Feet and Ears   ib.
To make a Ragoo of Mufhrooms   ib.
To make a Ragoo of Kidneys ib.
To ragoo a Breaft of Veal   ib.
A Ragoo of Lambs Stones and Sweet-breads   71
To ragoo a Neck of Veal   ib.
To ragoo Venifon   72
A Ragoo of Livers   ib.
To ragoo a green Goofe   ib.
A Ragoo for a Duck à la Braife   ib.
To ragoo Pigeons   ib.
A Ragoo of a Calfs Head   73
To make a Ragoo of Onions ib.
A Ragoo of ftuffed Cucumbers   ib.
To fry Tripe Ragoo   ib.
To roaft Tripe   74
Tripes the *Polifh* Way   ib.
To boil Tripes   ib.
A Ragoo of Palates and Eyes ib.
A Ragoo of Sheeps Tongues and Sweet-breads or Kernels   75
A Ragoo of Truffles and Morels   ib.
Brain Cakes   ib.
Veal Cutlets   ib.
To mince Fowl, Veal or Lamb   76
To fry Veal Sweet-breads   ib.
To farce Veal Sweet-breads ib.
Rolled Fricandoes of Veal   77
To roaft a Calf's Liver   ib.
To broil any Sort of Midriff ib.

C H A P.

CONTENTS.

CHAP IV.

To make Pies and Pasties, &c.

	pag.
TO make a Venison Pasty	77
A Mutton Pasty, as good as Venison	78
A Pigeon Pye	ib.
A Lamb Pye	ib.
A Veal Florendine	ib.
A Chicken Pye	79
A Calf's Foot Pye	ib.
An Eel Pye	ib.
A Goose Pye	80
A Trout Pye	ib.
A Mutton Steak Pye	ib.
A Lobster or Shrimp Pye	ib.
An Oister Pye	ib.
A Skirret Pye	81
Minced Pies	ib.
An Apple Pye	ib.
A Beef Steak Pye	28
A Goose-berry Pye	ib.
A Hare Pye	ib.
A Giblet Pye	ib.
A Lark Pye, or any small Birds	83
A Muirfowl or Partridge Pye	ib.
A Partridge Pye	84
A Pye of Mutton and Potatoes	ib.
A Pye of Kernels and Artichokes	ib.
An Apple Pye with Potatoes	85
An Apple Pye with Chesnuts and Almonds	ib.
A white Fricasey of Lamb	ib.
White Fricasey of Mushrooms	ib.
To fricasey Tripes or Cow-heels	86
White Fricasey of Chickens	ib.
Fricasey of Rabbets	ib.
Brown Fricasey of Chickens or Rabbets	87
To fricasey Kernels and Oisters	ib
A white Fricasey of Cows Palates	ib.

	pag.
A white Fricasey of Lambs Stones, Kernels and Cockscombs	88
A white Fricasey of Oisters	ib.
To fry Chickens, Lamb or Veal	ib.
A white Fricasey of Skirrets or Parsnips	ib.
To stew Chickens with Pease and Lettices	89
Boiled Ducks and Onions	ib.
To boil a Turkey or Fowl with Sellery	ib.
Or this Sauce for Hens or Chickens	90
To roast a Pig	ib.
To make a white Fricasey Sauce for boiled Fowls, Chickens or Turkeys	ib
To make a Mutton Haricot	91
To roast Chickens in Paste	ib.
Chickens and Sellery	ib.
Chickens farced with Oisters	ib.
Chickens with Gravy forced	92
Chickens Royal	ib.
Chickens with Tongues, Colliflowers and Greens	ib.
To boil Chickens and Asparagus	ib.
To roast young Turkeys	93
Ducklings à la Mode	ib.
Stoved Ducks the *Dutch* Way	93
To dress a wild Duck with Lemon Juice	ib.
To stew Ducks wild or tame	94
To dress Ducks with Oisters	ib.
To roast a green Goose	ib.
To dress a Goose with Onions or Cabbage	ib.
To souse a Goose	ib.
To dry a Goose	95
To boil a Goose	ib.
To boil the Giblets	ib.

To

CONTENTS.

pag.

To roaft a Goofe 95
To roaft Partridges 96
To drefs Partridges à la Braife ib.
Partridges with Oifters 97
To hafh Partridges ib.
To roaft Pheafants ib.
To boil Pheafants, Partridges, Chickens or Quails ib.
A Pupton of Pigeons 98
Pigeons boiled with Rice ib.
To ftew Pigeons ib.
To fry Pigeons 99
To broil Pigeons ib.
To boil Pigeons ib.
To do Pigeons à la Daube ib.
Pigeons ftoved with Cabbage Lettice 100
Pigeons difguifed ib.
A ftewed Pheafant ib.
To roaft Growfe, or what is called Muir-fowl ib.
To roaft Snipes or Woodcocks 101
To ftew Larks or any other fmall Birds ib.
To roaft Larks ib.
Curlews ib.
Quails ib.
Plovers 102
To ftew Plovers ib.
A jagged Hare ib.
To roaft a Hare ib.
To roaft a Hare another Way 103
To roaft a Hare with the Skin on ib.
To hafh a Hare ib.
To mince a Hare ib.
To boil Rabbets 104
Boiled Rabbets with Saufages ib.
To ftew Rabbets the French Way ib.
To collar Salmon ib.
To collar Pork 105
To collar a Pig ib.
To collar a Fore-quarter of Lamb, or a Breaft of Veal ib.
To collar Cow-heels 106

pag.

To collar a Calf's Head 106
To make a very good Collar of a Hog's Head ib.
To collar Eels ib.
To pot a Cow's Head 107
To pot Pigeons ib.
To make Liver Puddings 108
The proper Sauces for wild Fowl ib.
To pot Woodcocks or Snipes ib.
To pot a Hare 109
To pot a Calf's Head ib.
To pot Beef ib.
To pot Tongues 110
To pot Venifon ib.
To pot Beef or Venifon in Slices ib.
To pot Salmon the Newcaftle Way 111
To pot a Pike ib.
To make Marrow Pafties ib.
To drefs a Veal or Lamb's Ear, properly called Kidneys ib.
To make Blood Puddings 112
Yorkfhire Pudding ib.
Plumb Pudding ib.
Almond Puddings in Lemon or Orange Skins ib.
Peafe Pudding 113
To make an Almond Pudding ib.
To make a Citron Pudding ib.
Rice Pudding 114
Another Way to make a Rice Pudding ib.
To make a Potatoe Pudding ib.
To make a Sagoe Pudding 115
To make an Apple Pudding ib.
To make a Goofeberry Pudding ib.
Tanfy Pudding ib.
Marrow Pudding 116
Oatmeal Pudding ib.
Four-hour Pudding ib.
Bread Pudding, ib.
Flour Pudding 117
A boiled Rice Pudding ib.
A Sewet Pudding ib.
An Oatmeal Pudding ib.

A

CONTENTS

	pag.
A Cuſtard Pudding	118
An Orange Cuſtard or Pudding	ib.
A Lemon Pudding	ib.
A Carot Pudding	ib.
A yellow Pudding	119
A Barley Pudding	ib.
A boil'd Apple Pudding	ib.
An Orange Pudding	120
A Lemon Pudding	ib.
A Pudding of whole Rice	ib.
To make Clary Cake	121
Pancakes	ib.
Cuſtard Pancakes	ib.
Pancakes	ib.
To make Apple Dumplins	ib.
To make fried Pan Puddings	122
Pancakes	ib.
To make French Fritters	ib.
Apple Fritters	ib.
Potatoe Fritters	123
Currant Fritters	ib.
To make Barm Dumplins	ib.
Hard Dumplins	ib.
Another Way to make Apple Dumplins	123
A Florendine of Oranges or Apples	124
An Almond Florendine	ib.
To make a plain Tanſy	ib.
To boil a Tanſy	125
A Pipin Tanſy	ib.
To make a white Pot	ib.
Another Sort of white Pot	126
A Rice white Pot	ib.
Pancakes Royal	ib.
Common Pancakes	ib.
Iriſh Pancakes	127
Rice Panckaes	ib.
Oatmeal Pancakes	ib.
Chopped Apples in ſmall Pancakes	ib.
Criſp Pancakes	128
To make a Clary Amulet	ib.
To poach Eggs and Spinage	ib.
Eggs with Cabbage Lettice	ib.

	pag.
To butter Eggs	129
Fried Bacon and Eggs	ib.
To make an Amulet	ib.
Eggs and the Juice of Sorrel	ib.
A pretty Diſh of Whites of Eggs	130
Eggs poached in Cream	ib.
Oiſters or Cockles fried with Eggs	ib.
To make Puff Paſte	ib.
Paſte for any raiſed Pies	131
Another Sort of Paſte	ib.
A Paſte of Drippings	ib.
Cold Water Paſte for Paſties	ib.
Paſte for Tarts	132
To make Apple Tarts	ib.
Gooſeberry Tarts	ib.
Prune Tarts	ib.
Cheſnut Tarts	133
Sweet-meat Tarts	ib.
Gooſeberries for Tarts	ib.
Peach Tarts	ib.
Raſpberry Tarts	134
To make Orange Tarts	ib.
To make Orange Cheeſecakes	ib.
To make Cheeſe-cakes	ib.
To make Potatoe Cheeſe-cakes	135
To make Egg Cheeſe-cakes	ib.
To make Almond Cheeſe-cakes	ib.
To make Almond Cuſtards	136
To make Cuſtards of Rice	ib.
To make Cuſtards	ib.
Orange Cuſtards	137
Another Sort of Almond Cuſtards	ib.
To put Sweet-meats of all Colours in Jelly	ib.
To make a Trifle	ib.
To make burnt Cream	138
To make Jelly of Hartſhorn	ib.
To make Calves Feet Jelly	ib.
To make Blamong	139
To make Leech Cream	ib.
To make whipt Sillabubs	ib.
To make Orange Cream	140
To make Lemon Cream	ib.

Maids

CONTENTS.

pag.

Maids Cream 140
To make a Rhenish Wine Cream ib.
To make Currant Cream 141
Sack Cream ib.
To make yellow Lemon Cream ib.
Yellow Cream 142
Almond Cream ib.
Ratafia Cream ib.
To make Steeple Cream 143
To make Strawberry or Rasp-berry Cream ib.
To make Codlin or Goose-ber-ry Cream ib.
To make a very pretty red Cream ib.
To make Cream deloutee ib.
To make Rice Cream 144
Clouted Cream ib.
Sack Cream 145
To make Tablets ib.
To make a Crokain ib.
To make a floating Island 146
Solid Sillabubs ib.
To make Sillabubs from the Cow ib.
A Jelly Posset ib.
A Sack Posset, or what is called the Snow Posset 147
To make Oat-meal Flummery ib.
To make Scots Flummery ib.
To make West Country Flumme-ry 148
To make a Hedge Hog ib.
To make Flummery Caudle ib.
To make Hartshorn Flummery 149
To make a Calf's Foot Flumme-ry ib.
A Sack or Ale Posset ib.
A Sack Posset without Cream or Eggs ib.
A very good Posset 150
To make an Oat-meal Posset ib.
Egg Cheese ib.

pag.

Cheese Loaves 150
Almond Puffs 151
Pudding Puffs ib.
Lemon Puffs ib.
Orange Loaves ib.
To make Wafers 152
Dutch Wafers ib.
To make a Hen's Nest ib.
To make a Caudle for sweet Pies 153
To make Fairy Butter ib.
To make a Slipcoat Cheese ib.
To make Cream Cheese, as at Newport 154
To make a good Cheese ib.
To make a thick Cheese 155
To make a Welsh Rabbet ib.
To toast Cheese ib.
To toast Cheese another Way ib.
To make Wigs ib.
A Plumb-cake or Bun 156
Wigs another Way ib.
To make Bath Buns ib.
Shrewsbury Cakes 157
Almond Cakes ib.
Drop Biscuit ib.
Marlborough Cakes 158
A Seed-cake ib.
Another Sort of little Cakes ib.
Whetstone Cakes ib.
A Seed-cake very rich ib.
A Plumb Cake 159
To ice a great Cake ib.
A rich Nun's Cake ib.
Sugar Biscuits 160
A Diet Loaf ib.
Saffron Cakes ib.
Ratafia Biscuits 161
Short-bread ib.
A Seed-cake ib.
To make Biscuits 162
White Cakes ib.
Thin Dutch Biscuits ib.
Quince Cakes 163
York Cakes ib.
Naples Biscuits ib.

Macaroons

CONTENTS.

	pag.		pag.
Macaroons	163	To make Buns	164
Ginger-bread	164	A Cake to eat hot	ib.
Dutch Ginger-bread	ib.	A common Breakfast Cake	165
Poor Knights of *Windsor*	ib.	*Bath* Cakes	ib.

CHAP. V.

Of Pickling, and Preserving, &c.

General Rules to be obser-
ved   165

To pickle Samphire   166

To pickle Elder Flowers when they are green, and before they are blown   ib.

Walnuts   ib.

Walnuts green   167

Mushrooms   ib.

Onions   168

Red Cabbage   ib.

Cucumbers, or Kidney Beans ib.

Cucumbers in Slices   169

Mangoes   ib.

Colliflowers   ib.

Colliflowers red   ib.

Asparagus   170

Plumbs like Olives   ib.

Sellery   ib.

Codlins like Mangoes   ib.

To make Goose-berry Vinegar   171

Mushroom Powder   ib.

To codle the right Codlin with Cream   ib.

To keep Fruit for Tarts   172

Damsons or small Plumbs for Tarts   ib.

To make a Pupton of Apples ib.

To make Black Caps   173

To bake Apples   ib.

To stew Apples in Halves   ib.

To preserve Apples for Tarts, or Torts for a Year   ib.

To make a Caudle for Apple or Gooseberry Torts   174

To preserve Goose-berries green   ib.

To preserve Pears   174

To preserve Raspberries whole   174

To make Raspberry Jam   175

To preserve the green admirable Plumb   ib.

To preserve Gooseberries whole   176

To scald Fruit for present Use ib.

To make white Quince Marmalade   ib.

To preserve Apricocks   177

Red or white Currants whole ib.

Pears red   178

To make Marmalade of Oranges   ib.

To preserve Gooseberries for Tarts   ib.

White Plumbs   179

Damsons   ib.

Green Plumbs   180

Mulberries   ib.

Jelly of Gooseberries   ib.

To preserve Gold Pipins red 181

To make Marmalade of Plumbs, or any Fruit   ib.

Syrup of Nettles   ib.

Syrup of Maiden Hair   182

Jelly of Apples the Colour of Amber   ib.

Gooseberry Jam   ib.

To preserve Cherries   ib.

To make Currant Jelly   183

Conserve of Roses   ib.

Clear Pipin Jelly   ib.

Jelly of Pipins with Slices   184

To colour Jellies   ib.

A fine Way to dry Cherries ib.

Currants preserv'd in Bunches   185

Currants

CONTENTS.

pag.

Currants in Jelly 185
To preserve Raspberries liquid ib.
Raspberry Cakes 186
Raspberry clear Cakes ib.
To preserve green Amber Plumbs 187
Green Mogul Plumbs 188
Yellow Amber Plumbs ib.
Green Grapes ib.
Green Apricocks 189
Apricock Chips ib.
Jam Apricocks ib.
Green Walnuts 190
Mulberries liquid ib.
Another Way ib.
To preserve *Seville* Oranges in Quarters or in Sticks ib.
Oranges preserved in Slips 191
Red crisp Almonds or Prawlings ib.
White Citrons 192

pag.

To make clear Quince Cakes 192
Marmalade of Apricocks ib.
Marmalade of Apples 193
Marmalade of Raspberries ib.
Marmalade of Quinces after the *Italian* Manner ib.
To make Quiddany of Pipins of an Amber or Ruby Colour ib.
Quiddany of all Sorts of Plumbs 194
Paste of ripe Apricocks ib.
Gooseberry Paste ib.
To make Ketchup 195
To keep Artichoke Bottoms the whole Year ib.
Syrup of Lemons and Oranges ib.
To preserve whole Oranges ib.
Angelica 196
Peaches in Brandy ib.
To dry Pears or Apples ib.

CHAP. VI.

Of made Wines, &c.

pag.

TO make Orange Wine 197
Raisin Wine 198
Vinegar ib.
Balm Wine 198
Metheglin 199
Currant Wine white or red ib.
Gooseberry Wine ib.
Elderberry Wine 200
Purging Ale ib.
To brew strong Ale and small Beer 201
Syder ib.

pag.

Ratafia 201
To distil cold Surfeit-water 202
To make Plague Water ib.
Shrub ib.
A fine Wash for Scurvy or Redness in the Face, ib.
Best Pomatum for the Lips 203
Eye-Water ib.
Sacred Tincture ib.
Stoughton's Drops ib.
Daffy's Elixir 204
Yellow Balsam ib

A NEW AND EASY

METHOD of COOKERY.

CHAP. I.

Of GRAVIES, SOUPS, BROTHS, and POTTAGES.

To make a strong Broth for Soups or Sauces.

TAKE a Hough of Beef, or any coarse Piece, and set it over the Fire, in four *English* Gallons of Water, skim it clean, season it with Salt, whole Black and *Jamaica* Pepper, Mace, Cloves, a Bunch of sweet Herbs, and six or seven Onions; boil it on a very slow Fire, for four Hours, then strain it, and keep it for Use.

To make brown Gravy for Soups.

Cut three or four Pounds of coarse Beef in thin Slices, put it in a Frying-pan, with a very little Piece of Butter, a sliced Carot and Turnip, and Onions,

A   with

with a Bunch of sweet Herbs ; cover it close, put it on a very slow Fire, fry it brown, but don't burn it ; then put to it some good Broth, then boil all together very well, and keep it for Soups or Sauces ; season it with Pepper, Salt, *Jamaica* Pepper, and Cloves.

White Gravy for Soups or Sauces.

TAKE a Knuckle of Veal, and boil it in six *English* Quarts of Water, till it is in Strings, then strain it ; but when it is half boiled, put in whole Mace, Pepper, Cloves, and Salt, so keep it for Use. You make Gravy of Mutton the same Way.

A good Stock for Fish Soups.

PREPARE Scate Flounders and Eels, lay them in a broad Gravy Pan, with a Sprig of Thyme, Parsley and Onions, season them with Pepper, Salt, Cloves and Mace ; then pour in as much Water as cover them ; boil them on a very slow Fire for an Hour, then strain it off : If it is for brown Soup or Sauces, put in the Skins of the Onions, and a brown Crust of Bread, with dried Mushrooms ; keep the Gravy Pan close covered.

A Vermicelli Soup.

TAKE three *English* Quarts of good Broth, put in it two Ounces of Vermicelli, and a Bit of lean Bacon, stuffed with Cloves ; put two Chickens or a boiled Fowl in it : You may make Rice Soup the same Way, but boil the Rice first in Water, then in Broth ; half an Hour boils the Vermicelli.

To make a Craw-fish or Lobster Soup.

LET your Stock be as in Page first, take as many as will fill your Dish, then take out the Sand-bags out of
the

the Tails, and all the woolly Parts that are about them; put them in a Sauce-pan with your Soup, with Crumbs of Bread, and a little Butter; peel an Onion, ſtuff it with Cloves, and boil all the Shells in the Fiſh Stock, before you put in the Tail, and take them out when they are well boiled; ſtrain your Stock before you put in the Fiſh or any Seaſoning.

A Veal Soup with Barley.

YOUR Stock muſt be with a Fowl, and a Knuckle of Veal, ſeaſoned only with Mace, then ſtrain all off; put in half a Pound of fine Barley; boil it an Hour; ſeaſon it with Salt; put the Fowl in the Middle, and juſt as you ſerve it up, put in chopped Parſley.

A green Peaſe Soup.

TAKE a Peck of young green Peaſe, put them in a Stew Pot, cover them with Water, put in a little Thyme, Parſley, Onion, Pepper, Salt, and a good Lump of Butter; then cover them, and let them ſtew a While; then cut four Cabbage Lettices in Quarters, with ſix Cucumbers, pared and ſliced, and a Handful of Purſlain; put them in the Soup, with a Piece of Butter, and more ſeaſoning; then fill your Pan with Water; the Soup will take Stewing two Hours; if the Liquor is too much waſted away in that Time, add a little more boiling Water to it; you may put Slices of fried Bacon in the Diſh, or a roaſted Fowl if you pleaſe.

A brown Pottage Royal.

SET a Gallon of ſtrong Broth over the Fire, with two ſhivered Palates, Cocks Combs, Lambs Stones ſliced, with Forc'd-meat Balls, a Pint of Gravy, two Handfuls of Spinage, and young Lettice minced; boil theſe together with a Duck, the Leg and Wing
being

being broke, and the Bones pulled out, and the
Breaſt ſlaſhed, and browned in a Pan of Fat; then put
the Pottage in a Diſh, and the Duck in the Middle; lay
about it a little Vermicelli boiled up in ſome ſtrong
Broth, with ſavoury Forc'd-meat Balls, and Sweet-
breads; boil the Duck in the Broth for half an Hour
before you diſh it.

Rice Soup.

TAKE a Quarter of a Pound of Rice, waſh it,
boil it in Veal Broth till very tender, with a little
Mace and a young Fowl; ſkim it very clean, and ſeaſon
it with Salt to your Taſte; then ſtir in half a Pound
of Butter, and a Mutchkin of Cream boiled up; then
ſtir it in the Soup; ſerve it up with the Fowl.

Barley Pottage.

LAY a Pound of fine Barley to ſteep in two Chopins of Cream, ſome Salt, Mace and Cinnamon; when
it is thick, ſweeten it to your Taſte.

A Pottage, forc'd Pigeons with Onions.

WASH and blanch them, take a Piece of Veal, a
little Suet, pound them, and ſeaſon it with Pepper, Salt,
Nutmeg, Lemon-peel, ſweet Herbs, Chives, Parſley,
and Muſhrooms, all chopped ſmall; mix all together
with Crumbs of Bread, and as many raw Eggs as will
wet it; put it in your Pigeons, and ſtop their Vents;
ſet them to boil in good Broth; take ſmall Onions,
boil them and drain them, then put them to the Pigeons; take the Cruſts of fine Bread in ſome of the
Broth, and put them in the Diſh under the Pigeons,
and pour the Pottage on them.

To make Plumb *Broth.*

TAKE a good Hough of Beef, and a Knuckle of Veal, put it in the Pot with fix *Scots* Pints of Water, boil it on a flow Fire; take up the Veal before it is too much, but boil the Beef to Pieces; if the Broth is too ftiff, put in a Pint of boiling Water; put in the Crumbs of two Penny Loaves, two Pounds of Currants wafhed clean, two of Raifins ftoned, one of Prunes, let all boil till they fwell; feafon it with Salt, Cloves, Mace, and Nutmeg, ftrain the Broth before you put in the Fruit.

To make Spring *Soup.*

TAKE twelve Lettices, cut them in Slices, and put them into ftrong Broth, get fix green Cucumbers, pare them, and cut out the Cores, cut them into little Bits, and fcald them in boiling Water, and put them into your Broth; let them boil very tender, with a Mutchkin of young Peafe and fome Crumbs of Bread

Pottage *of Chervil the* Dutch *Way.*

PUT into eight Chopins of good Broth a Knuckle of Veal, cut in Pieces the Bignefs of an Egg, don't let it boil too faft, but keep it fkim'd; feafon it with Pepper, Salt, Cloves and Mace, a Quarter of an Hour before you difh it; put in a good deal of Chervil chopp'd fmall, fome Forc'd-meat Balls, and fome Crumbs of Bread; let them boil well before you put them in, but not too much; fo difh it.

Jelly Broth for confumptive Perfons.

GET a Joint of Mutton, a Capon, a Fillet of Veal, put them in an Earthen Can clofe ftopt, with three
Quarts

Quarts of Water ; then put the Can in a Pot of Water, and when all the Flesh is boil'd to Rags strain it off for Use.

To make Soup de santé the French *Way*.

BOIL a Hough of Beef to Tavers on a very slow Fire ; skim it, and when there is only what will fill your Dish, strain it ; take three Pounds of Beef, cut in thin Slices, put it in a Pan with sliced Onions, Carots and Turnips in it, and a little Bit of Butter, till the Meat is brown, and the Pan dry ; then pour your Soup on it, boil it an Hour, skim it and strain it ; then get Chervil, Sorrel, Endive, Sellery, and Cabbage Lettices ; cut them, but not too small, half boil them in Water, drain them, then put them in a closs Goblet with your Soup ; boil them till the Herbs are tender ; season it with an Onion stuffed with Cloves, Pepper and Salt ; put in the Dish a boiled Knuckle of Veal, or a Fowl, two *French* Rolls, the Crust only, or toasted Bread.

To make a Summer Pottage.

TAKE a Hough of Beef, a Scrag of Mutton or Veal, chop them, and boil them gently in a sufficient Quantity of Water for six Hours, being covered close, then put in four Onions, and whole Pepper ; when the Meat is boiled to Rags, strain it, put in Cloves, Mace, and a Faggot of sweet Herbs, with Sorrel, Beets, Endive and Spinage, of each a Handful, shred grosly, boil it till they are tender ; put it in the Dish with roasted Pigeons, or Ducks, in the Middle of it, and small Slices of fried Bacon, toasted Bread cut in Dice, Sausages cut in little Bits ; in the Time of Asparagus, cut into Pieces the green Part, and boil them in it.

To

To make Meagre Broth for Soups with Herbs.

SET on the Fire a Kettle of Water, put in it some Crusts of Bread, and all Sorts of Herbs, green Beets, Sellery, Endive, Lettice, Sorrel, green Onions, Parsley, Chervil, with a good Piece of Butter, and a Bunch of sweet Herbs; boil it for an Hour and a Half, then strain it off; this will serve to make Artichoke or Asparagus, or *Soup de santé* with Herbs; season it with Salt, Pepper, Cloves, *Jamaica* Pepper; cut the Herbs grosly, and it will be a very good Soup, boiling a good Lump of Butter with the Herbs, putting toasted Bread in the Dish; but take out the Bulk of the sweet Herbs.

To make Scots Barley Broth.

BOIL a Hough of Beef in eight Pints of Water, and a Pound of Barley, on a flow Fire; let it boil to four Pints; then put in Onions, Pepper, Salt, and Raisins if you like them, or you may put in Greens and Leeks.

A Calf's Head Soup.

TAKE a Calf's Head, stew it tender; then strain off the Liquor, and put in a Bunch of sweet Herbs, Onions, Salt, Pepper, Mace, and some fine Barley, boil it till the Barley and Head is done; then serve it with the Head in the Middle.

To make Mutton Broth.

TAKE about six Pounds of Mutton, boil it in three *Scots* Pints of Water, with sweet Herbs, Onions, two or three Turnips, a Quarter of a Pound of fine Barley or Rice, Salt and Pepper; a little before you take it up, put in it a Handful of chopped Parsley.

To

To make another Barley Broth.

TAKE a Neck and Breaſt of Mutton, cut it to Pieces, put as much Water as will cover it ; when it boils ſkim it ; put in Barley, diced Carots, Turnips, Onions, a Faggot of Thyme and Parſley, Pepper and Salt, ſtove all well together ; you may put in a Sheep's Head, but firſt ſinge and ſcrape it, and ſoak it well in Water ; to make this green, put Beet Leaves, Brocoli, and green Onions, all ſhred ſmall.

A Purſlain Soup.

WHEN your Purſlain is young, cut the Sprigs off, but keep their whole Length; boil them in a Stew-pan, with ſome Peaſe-ſoup, and ſmall Onions ; when your Purſlain is boiled in good Broth, put a Cruſt of Bread ſoaked in Broth in the Diſh, then pour your Soup on it with the Purſlain ; ſeaſon it to your Taſte.

A Cucumber Soup.

PARE and ſlice them, not very thin, ſtew them in a little Butter, and put them in ſtrong Broth, ſeaſoned with Pepper, Salt and Onions; ſo ſerve them up.

To make Soup Meagre.

BOIL two or three Pounds of coarſe Beef in eight Chopins of Water, boil it to four ; then ſtrain it off; then fry Slices of Carots, Turnips and Onions, in clarified Butter ; drain them very well, put them in with Sorrel, Beets, Purſlain, Endive, Sellery, Cabbage-Lettice, of each a Handful ; cut them groſly, and put them all in the Soup, with Cruſts of Bread, a Bunch of Parſley, green Onions and Thyme ; ſeaſon it with Pepper
per

per, Cloves and Salt ; after you put in your Herbs and Greens, boil them till the Roots are enough ; boil the Roots and Sellery in it before you put in the reſt.

An Eel Soup.

TAKE Eels according to the Quantity of Soup you would have ; a Pound of Eels will make a Mutchkin of Soup : to every Pound of Eels add a Chopin of Water, a Cruſt of Bread, two or three Blades of Mace, whole Pepper, an Onion, and a Faggot of ſweet Herbs ; cover them cloſs, and let them boil till Half the Liquor is waſted ; then ſtrain it, and put Toaſts of Bread cut in Dice in the Diſh, then pour on your Soup ; you may put Forc'd-meat Balls made of Fiſh, or Bread, in it.

An Almond Soup.

YOUR Stock muſt be of Veal, blanch and beat a Pound of *Jordan* Almonds very fine, with the Yolks of ſix hard Eggs, putting a little cold Broth in as you pound them, then put in as much Broth as will fill the Diſh ; put it on the Fire, ſtir it often, then ſtrain it, off, and put in two ſmall Chickens, and ſome Slices of fine Bread, ſeaſon it with white Pepper, Mace and Salt, ſend it up hot.

Onion Soup.

TAKE Half a Pound of Butter, put it in a Stew-pan on the Fire, and boil it till it has done making a Noiſe ; then take ten Onions, pared and cut ſmall, throw them in the Butter, and let them fry a while, then ſhake in a little Flour, keep it ſtirring all the while, and let them do a little longer ; then pour in three Mutchkins of boiling Water, ſtir them round, cut ſmall the upper Cruſt of the ſtaleſt Penny Loaf you have, and put in it ; ſeaſon it with Pepper and Salt let

B

it boil ten Minutes, take it off the Fire, beat the Yolks
of two Eggs with Salt, a Spoonful of Vinegar, mix
them, then ſtir it into the Soup ; mix it well and diſh
it.

A general Cullis for Fiſh.

WASH and ſcale ſome Carps, and cut them in
Bits, put ſome Butter in a Pan, and place a good deal
of Slices of Onions, and the Bill of the Carp in it, put
it on a ſlow Fire, and when the Onions ſtick to the
Bottom, put in ſome Peaſe Soup ; put in a Sprig of
Thyme, Parſley, Chives, Pepper, Cloves, and Mace ;
you may put in it a Clove of Rockambole or Garlick, if you like it ; put a Lump of Butter into another Stew-pan, and put it on the Fire, with as
much Flour as will thicken it ; ſtir it till it is a light
Brown, then put a little of the Carp Liquor in by Degrees, keeping it ſtirring all the Time ; then pour all
together with Anchovies, dry Muſhrooms, and Lemon-peel, with the Juice of it, and two Gills of white
Wine ; you may put in Gravy if you pleaſe : This
Cullis will do for any Fiſh Soup or Cullis ; you may
make any Fiſh the ſame Way.

A Veal Cullis.

PUT in a Stew-pan a Piece of Butter, then cut
Slices of Veal and lay them in it, with ſome Slices of
a Carot, Turnip and Onions, and Slices of Ham if you
like it ; cover it cloſs, and when the Veal is brown take
it out, and ſhake into your Pan a little Flour, keep it
ſtirring with a Spoon till the Flour is brown ; then
put in ſome Broth by Degrees, keep it ſtewing all the
while ; if you have no Broth put in Water, put in as
much as you will want then : put in the Veal with a
Bunch of ſweet Herbs, whole Pepper, Mace, Onion
ſtuffed with Cloves, and ſome Lemon-peel, let it ſtew
well on a ſlow Fire, put in a Gill of white Wine, and
when

when it is a good Brown, and the Veal well boiled in it, ſtrain it off ; take off all the Fat, and you may uſe it with all Sorts of Entries.

Green Cullis for Soups or Sauces.

L E T green Peaſe be done without Liquor, then take Parſley, Spinage, and green Onions, of each a Handful ; blanch them, ſqueeze them well, and pound them, put in ſome Broth, with a Bit of Ham, an Onion ſtuffed with Cloves, ſome Slices of Veal, a Bunch of ſweet Herbs ; your Peaſe and Veal muſt be ſtewed before you put in the Broth ; and when clammy, put in the Broth and Juice of the Herbs, when all ſtews a while, take out the Meat, and pound the Peaſe, and then mix all together ; ſeaſon it with Pepper, Salt and Mace, put in more green Parſley and green Onions, boil all ; and when boil'd ſtrain it, it will ſerve in all green Soups and Sauces.

To make a brown Soup.

P U T in your Broth Pot a Hough of Beef, but firſt cut ſome of the beſt Pieces in thin Slices, ſkim your Pot, and let it boil very ſlow ; fry your Steaks a little brown, and when your Broth is boiled, put it to your Steaks, with a little ſweet Herbs, two or three whole Onions, whole Black, and Clove Pepper and Cloves ; before you put in your Ingredients, ſkim off all the Fat ; you may put in Vermicelli in your Diſh, or Sellery with toaſted Bread ; boil your Vermicelli and Sellery before you put it in your Soup ; ſtrain your Soup before you put it to your fried Collops ; put in your Broth by Degrees.

To make a white Soup.

B O I L a hind Leg of Lamb, Mutton or Veal, in Rags, then ſkim off all the Fat, ſeaſon it with Pepper,
Cloves

Cloves and Mace, (they muſt be all whole) two or three whole Onions, and a Bunch of ſweet Herbs; you may either whiten it with pounded Almonds or ſweet Cream; ſtrain it and ſalt it to your Taſte, ſend the Shank in it to the Table.

To make Peaſe Soup.

BOIL a Hough of Beef, with a Pound and a Half of Peaſe, till they are all diſſolved, then ſtrain it and put in it whole Onions and Spice, ſalt it to your Taſte, brown ſome Butter and Flour and mix with it: You may put boil'd Sellery cut in Dice in it, if you pleaſe. Take the whole Onions always out of every Thing; before it goes to the Table put Spearmint in it.

To make Onion Soup.

TAKE ſome of the Broth of a Hough of Beef, and boil in it a Dozen large Onions cut in Slices, with black and *Jamaica* Pepper, Salt, and a Bunch of ſweet Herbs; thicken it with brown'd Butter and Flour and Crumbs of Bread: Take out your Herbs before it goes to the Table; let there be ſome ſmall whole Onions boil'd in it.

Aſparagus Soup.

TAKE ſome of the Broth of a Hough of Beef, and green it with the Juice of Spinage, cut half a Hundred of Aſparagus, half an Inch long, and boil them in it, with black and *Jamaica* Pepper, an Onion ſtuffed with Cloves, and a Bunch of ſweet Herbs, thicken it with Flour and Butter, boil it well after you put in the Butter and Flour.

To make Hodge-podge.

BOIL a Neck and Breaſt of Mutton in three Quarts of Water, ſkim it well, then put in Turnips and Carots cut in Dice ; if they are old, boil them in Water firſt, when it is almoſt boil'd put in ſome Crumbs of Bread, two Onions, and a Chopin of green Peaſe, thicken it with brown'd Butter and Flour, put in it a brown'd Cruſt of Bread, Pepper and Salt ; you may put in Sellery or Endive if you pleaſe ; Brocoli or Aſparagus is very good in it, when you can't get Peaſe ; take out the Cruſt of Bread before you ſend it to Table.

To make a green Peaſe Soup.

BOIL a Peck of Peaſe into two Quarts of Water till they are all in Smaſh, keep out a Mutchkin of the youngeſt, put them in a little before you diſh them ; ſtrain and rub your Peaſe thro' a Search, then put it on the Fire again, and put a little Juice of Spinage in it, and a little Spearmint, Pepper and Salt to your Taſte, Half a Pound of Butter work'd in Flour, then your green Peaſe : Let it boil till you think it thick enough, and then ſerve it up. If you have a Mind to have it rich, inſtead of Water, put the Broth of a Hough of Beef, with a good white Gravy, in it.

A very good Peaſe Soup.

BOIL three Pounds of lean Beef in eight Chopins of Water, and three Pound of Peaſe, till the Meat is all in Rags, then put in two or three Anchovies, a Faggot of Thyme, Spearmint, Parſley, and Ginger, Pepper, Salt and Cloves, with ſome Onions ; then boil it for a while, and ſtrain it off in a clean Pan, then give it another Boil, ſtirring in it a good Piece of Butter. Fry ſome Forc'd-meat Balls, Bacon cut in thin Slices, and
Bread

Bread cut in Dice, with Spinage boil'd green and chopped small, with a Bit of Butter and Salt, and roll'd in Balls : Put all in the Dish, and pour the Soup boiling hot over them.

To make a Pottage the French Way.

TAKE hard Lettices, Sorrel, Chervil, Beets and Spinage, of each a like Quantity, or any other Herbs you like, as much as a Half Peck will hold pressed down ; pick, wash and drain them, put them in a Pot with a Pound of fresh Butter, and set them over the Fire, and, as the Butter melts, stir them down in it till they are as low as the Butter, then put in some Water ; season it with Pepper, Cloves and Salt, put in a Crust of Bread, and some Chives, and when it is boil'd, take out the Bread, and thicken it with the Yolks of three or four Eggs, take Care they don't curdle, beat them well, put Toasts of Bread in the Dish with it.

To make Pottage of chopped Herbs.

MINCE, very fine, Spinage, Chives, Parsley, Marigold-flowers, Succory, Strawberry and Violet Leaves, stamp them with Oat-meal in a Bowl, put chopped Greens in with it ; you may either put Broth or Water to them ; if Water, boil a good Piece of Butter in it ; put Sipets in the Dish, and pour it over them.

A Fish Broth.

CUT Carots, Turnips and Onions, in thin Slices, put them into a Stew-pan with a Lump of Butter ; when they are brown put to them some Fish Broth, made of either Carps, Eels, Haddocks or Scate, then put in Parsley, Thyme, Chives, and some dry Mushrooms ; season it with Pepper, Salt and Cloves ; boil it an Hour with a Crust of Bread in it.

An

An Oiſter Soup.

TAKE a Chopin of Oiſters, waſh them clean in their own Liquor, then ſtrain the Liquor, put to it two Gills of Water and one Gill of white Wine, a Sprig of Thyme and Parſley, a Shalot, a Bit of Lemon-peel, a few Cloves, a Blade of Mace, and ſome whole Pepper, let them ſtew gently for a little ; put a Quarter of a Pound of Butter into a Pan, flour it well, then let it fry till it has done hiſſing, keep it ſtirring; then take the Oiſters and dry them in a Cloth, and flour them, put them in the boiling Butter, and fry them till they are plump, then put in their own Liquor, with three Mutchkins of ſtrong Broth, keep it ſtirring all the Time : If your Soup is not brown, you may put Toaſts in the Diſh cut in Dice, and a *French* Loaf toaſted.

To make Calves-feet Broth.

BOIL the Feet in juſt as much Water as will make a good Jelly, then ſtrain it, and ſet the Liquor on the Fire, putting in two Blades of Mace, put in two Gills of Malaga, and Half a Pound of Currants, waſh'd and pick'd ; and when they are plump'd, beat up the Yolks of two Eggs, and mix them with a little of the cold Broth, and thicken it over a ſlow Fire, keeping it ſtirring all the while one Way : Seaſon it with Salt, Sugar, Nutmeg, boil in it the Rind of a Lemon, and juſt before you diſh it put in it the Juice of a Lemon.

Broth of Roots.

BOIL three Pounds of good white Peaſe ; when they are very tender, bruiſe them to a Maſh, put them into a Pot that holds ſix Chopins of Water, put it on the Fire for an Hour, ſtrain it off and rub the Peaſe thro' a Sieve ; then put it in a Pan with a Bunch of ſweet

Herbs,

Herbs, a fhred Carot, fix Onions, Parfley Roots, Sorrel, Chervil, Lettice, Endive and Sellery, a Handful of each : Seafon it with Salt, Pepper, Cloves, and *Jamaica* Pepper ; boil it very well, it will be very good to put in any Herb Soup, or for a Soup with toafted Bread in it.

To make Cake-foup.

TAKE a Hough of Beef, a Knuckle of Veal, ftrip off the Skin and Fat, then take all the mufcular and flefhy Parts from the Bones, boil the Flefh gently in three *Scots* Pints of Water, for fo long a Time till the Liquor will make ftrong Jelly ; try it if it is very ftrong before you ftrain it, by putting fome to cool ; ftrain it through a Sieve and let it fettle, then let it be put in white Stone Cups, as clear as you can from the Settling, and fet them in a Pan of cold Water, and put them on a flow Fire, and let the Water boil gently, till the Jelly is as thick as Glue ; take Care the Water does not go into the Cups, then let them ftand to cool, and then turn out the Glue upon a Piece of Flannel, keep them turned every eight Hours on a dry Place of the Flannel till they are quite dry ; then paper them in white Papers, and hang them up in a dry Place ; there muft be but one in every Paper : When you are going to make Ufe of them, boil an *Englifh* Quart of Water, and pour it on them, keeping it ftirring all the Time till it diffolves, it will make good Soup ; feafon it to your Tafte with Pepper, and put no Seafoning in the Glue ; you may carry it in your Pocket, it will be good for Gravy or Sauce.

A Pottage of Goofe Giblets.

SCALD and wafh them clean, and cut them in Pieces, feafon them with Pepper, Salt, Onions, and a Bunch of fweet Herbs, boil them in good Broth till they are very tender, with fome Crufts of

Bread

Bread in it; you may put green Peafe and fliced Lettices in it, take out the Herbs before you difh them.

A Muffel Soup.

GET a Pint of Muffels, fcald them and wafh them clean, put them in a Pan with three Mutchkins of ftrong Broth, and a Mutchkin of their own Liquor, a Bunch of fweet Herbs, an Onion ftuffed with Cloves, Pepper, Mace and Salt, put in Crumbs of Bread to thicken it, you may put a Gill of white Wine in it; boil it till it is fmooth, you may fqueeze in it a little Lemon Juice, fo ferve it up hot.

A Peafe Soup with Herbs in it.

BOIL two Pounds of Peafe in fix Chopins of Water till they are very foft, pour off fome of the Liquor, and rub the Peafe thro' a Sieve, ftill putting in fome of the Liquor to make them go through; then boil a Pound of Butter, and when it breaks in the Middle, put in an Onion and a little Mint cut fmall, Spinage, Sorrel, and Sellery cut grofly, let them boil a while, ftirring them often; then with one Hand fhake in fome Flour, while with the other you pour in the thin Liquor; then ftir all together, feafon it with Pepper, Mace and Salt, boil it for an Hour longer, then difh it : You may put in a little fweet Cream if you pleafe.

To make Peafe Pottage.

TAKE two Quarts of Peafe, put them into three Quarts of Water, feafon it pretty high with Pepper and Salt, boil them till they are enough, mix a Spoonful of Flour with Water, and put in a little Mint, a Leek, two Handfuls of Spinage, all cut fmall; put in Half a Pound of Butter, boil it and difh it.

A Turnip Soup.

PARE and cut in Dice twelve Turnips, which will make a Difh full, fry them in clarified Butter a light

C   brown,

brown, put them in two Chopins of good Gravy and the Crufts of fine Bread, let them drain from the Fat, boil them till tender : You may put a Fowl in the Middle.

A Hare Soup.

CUT your Hare in Quarters, and the reft in fmall Pieces, put it in a Stew-pot with a Crag or Knuckle of Veal; put in a Gallon of Water, a Bunch of fweet Herbs, let it ftew till the Gravy is very good, fry a little of the Veal and put in it to make it brown, put in Bread to thicken the Soup, or you may put in Rice, but boil it firft a little, or fine Barley, a Quarter of a Pound of either will do ; feafon it with Pepper, Salt, and Mace, with an Onion ftuffed with Cloves; take out the Herbs, Veal and Onion, before you difh it.

CHAP. II.

Of dreffing all Kinds of FISH, *and their Sauces.*

To ftew Carp or Tench.

WHEN they are catch'd put them in a Tub of Water, kill them and fave all their Blood, fcrape them, falt them well to take off the Slime, then wafh and dry them very well in a Cloath : If they are fmall, fry them firft, ftew them in a Mutchkin of Claret, and the fame of Gravy, a Piece of Butter work'd in Flour, Pepper, Cloves, Salt and Mace a whole Onion, a Bunch of fweet Herbs, and an Anchovy, if you have them; put Truffles, Morels, and Oifters in it, boil the Truffles, and Morels, fcald and pick the Oifters : Let your Sauce be boil'd, then put in your Fifh and ftew them a good while, but don't let them break :

break : If the Sauce wants it, put in Ketchup; the large ones put in without frying, and ftew them on a very flow Fire, there muft be more Claret and Gravy in thefe than the fried ones; brown the Butter and Flour that you put in them that are not fried.

To dreſs a Cod's Head.

IF you boil it, let your Water be boiling, put in it a Handful of Salt, a little Vinegar, and then put in your Fiſh, be fure the Water covers it ; if large, it will take an Hour to boil it ; if fmall, Half an Hour ; the fame Time bakes it, if the Oven is very hot : If baked, put Butter over and under it, the Sauce muſt be either Oiſters, Shrimps or Lobſters. Garniſh the Diſh with Parſley, Horſe-radiſh, and Forc'd-meat Balls, and ſliced Lemon.

To make Oiſter, Lobſter or Shrimp Sauce.

PICK your Oiſters clean and fcald them, ftrain their own Liquor and put it on them, then put Gravy if you have it, or a little Water in it ; put in it a good Piece of Butter worked in Flour, a whole Onion, the Rind of a Lemon, Pepper, Salt, Nutmeg, and the Juice of Half a Lemon, you may put in Ketchup if you have it. The Lobſters muſt be cut in Pieces, and white Wine in it.

To roaſt or bake a Salmon.

SCORE it on the Back, feafon it with Salt, Pepper, Mace and Nutmeg ; put grated Bread, the Grate of a Lemon, Parſley, Thyme, Salt and Butter in every Score, and in the Belly ; put it in a cloſe cover'd Pan in the Oven, with fome Butter on the Top and Bottom. You may give it either Oiſter or Lobſter Sauce, or plain Butter.

To pickle Salmon.

TAKE a whole Salmon, and fcrape it clean, don't waſh it, cut it in round Pieces two Inches thick, ftrew
Salt

Salt on it to purge out the Blood. Make a ſtrong Pickle
of Salt and Water, whole Pepper, Mace and Cloves,
with a Mutchkin of Vinegar and ſix Bay Leaves ; when
it boils put in the Salmon, and let it boil a Quarter of
an Hour; then take it out, and ſet the Pickle to cool,
ſkim all the Greaſe off it, then put in your Salmon
You may do large Trouts or Pikes the ſame Way ; if
your Salmon is very thick, it will take more boiling.

A Turbet or any flat Fiſh in Jelly.

WHEN your Fiſh is well clean'd, let it lye in Salt
two Hours, then waſh it and boil as much Water as
will cover it ; put in your Water Two-pence Worth of
Iſinglaſs, Salt, Cloves, Mace and Pepper, and a Gill of
Sherry, and one of Vinegar ; put in your Fiſh when
the Liquor boils, and when you think it is enough, take
it out and put on the Liquor again, and let it boil till it
jellies; then beat the Whites of three Eggs and put in
it, and give it four or five Boils more, then run it thro'
a Jelly Bag, put your Fiſh on the Diſh, and when it is
almoſt cold, pour it on, Lemon Juice being better than
Vinegar, and boil the Rind in it.

To broil Salmon.

BROIL ſome Pieces of Salmon, ſeaſoned with Pepper and Salt; for the Sauce, put Butter, and Duſt of
Flour, a green Onion, an Anchovy, a little Ketchup,
Oiſter Liquor, a Glaſs of white Wine, and the Juice of
a Lemon ; ſeaſon it with Pepper, Salt, Nutmeg, and
the Grate of a Lemon ; diſh your Salmon, and pour
your Sauce about it ; you may dip the Pieces of Salmon in melted Butter, and ſtrew on them Crumbs of
Bread and ſweet Herbs ſhred ſmall, before you broil it,
and the ſame Sauce.

To farce Slices of Salmon.

CUT Slices of Salmon an Inch thick, take off the Skins,
then mince ſome of the Salmon, with ſome Eels, Muſhrooms,

rooms, Chives and Parsley ; season it with Pepper, Salt, Nutmeg, Cloves and Lemon-peel, pound them with a Piece of Butter ; then put in it some Crumbs of Bread, and wet it with Eggs ; dip the Salmon in Butter, and lay the Farce all over them ; lay some Butter in a Dish, lay your Salmon in it, and cover it closs; put it in the Oven ; when baked, put it in the Dish, with either Oister, Lobster, or Cockle Sauce.

To hash Salmon.

HASH some Salmon in a Sauce-pan, dry it over the Fire till it grows white ; then mince small some Mushrooms, Parsley, Shrimps and Oisters, and mince them all together ; put some Butter in a Pan, with a little Flour ; keep it stirring till it is brown ; then put in the Salmon, give it a Turn or two on the Fire, season it with Salt and Pepper, and a little Juice of Lemon ; put in a little Broth ; serve it up hot.

To fry Salmon.

TAKE a Chine, or any other Part of Salmon, and cut it in Pieces, and fry them in clarified Butter or Beef Drippings, a little brown and crisp: For Sauce, put in the Sauce-pan some Claret, a Piece of Butter work'd in a little Flour, some Oister Liquor, the Juice of Lemon, and Nutmeg; put it on the Fire, and keep it stirring ; dish the Fish, and pour it over them.

To bake a Turbot.

LAY some Butter in a Dish, the Size of the Turbot, and put Butter all over it ; season it with Pepper, Salt, Cloves and Nutmeg, Crumbs of Bread, Lemon-peel, Chives, Parsley, a little Thyme, all shred small; flour it all over with it, bake it in the Oven a light brown, send it to the Table dry, with two Sauce-boats, one with Butter, the other with Oister Sauce.

To fry a Turbot.

SCORE your Turbot, flour it and fry it in clarified Butter, or good Beef Drippings; let it be boiling hot; then put it in, and fry it a good brown, then drain it; make the Pan clean, put in it Claret or white Wine, Anchovy, Nutmeg, and an Onion, ſtuffed with Cloves and a little Salt; then put in your Fiſh, and let it boil a good While; then put in a Piece of Butter, work'd in a little Flour, and ſome Lemon-peel, mix it well: Put your Fiſh in the Diſh, and pour the Sauce over it, but take out the Onion.

To ſouſe a Turbot.

BOIL it in Salt and Water, as much as will cover it, with a Mutchkin of Vinegar, Lemon-peel, Ginger, whole Pepper and Cloves; when boiled take it out, and when it and the Liquor is cold, put it in again with ſome Bay Leaves, and it will be fit to eat in two Days.

To ſtew a Turbot.

CUT it in Slices, and fry them; when they are half done, put them in a Stew-pan, with Claret, Lemon Juice, a ſliced Onion, Nutmeg, and a Bit of Butter; let the Fiſh ſtew till done; diſh it.

To cramp Cod the Dutch Way.

BOIL four Chopins of Water, and a Pound of Salt, ſkim it well; then put in the Slices of Cod; when it has boiled three Minutes it is done; then drain them well, and diſh them with raw Parſley about them; they muſt be cut very thin; they are eaten with Oil, Muſtard and Vinegar.

To ſtew Soals or any flat Fiſh.

SKIN your Soals, if they are large, on both Sides, and cut them in the Middle; if ſmall, leave them whole, and ſkin them of the black Skin, the other

Fiſh

Fifh is not to be fkinned, have a Pan full of clarified
Butter or Beef, or Beef Dripping, boiling hot; flour
your Fifh and put them in, fry them a light brown,
then put them to drain all the Fat from them; brown
a good Piece of Butter and Flour, and put to it fome
Gravy, Oifter Liquor, a Bunch of fweet Herbs, an O-
nion or two, Cloves, Mace, Pepper and Salt, half a
Mutchkin of Claret, the Juice of a Lemon, and a chopped Anchovy; when they are well mix'd together
put in your Fifh, and let them fimmer over a very
flow Fire; if it is not thick enough, work a Bit of Butter in Flour and put in it; half an Hour ftews them:
You may put Truffles and Morels in them; take out
the Herbs and Onions, garnifh your Difh with fliced
Lemon.

To boil a Turbot or any flat Fifh.

PUT in your Fifh-kettle as much Water as will cover the Fifh, a Handful of Salt, two Gills of Vinegar,
and a Stick of Horfe-radifh; put your Fifh in when the
Water boils; an Hour boils a Turbot; the fmall Fifh
lefs; you may give them Oifter, Lobfter, or Shrimp
Sauce: Garnifh the Difh with Parfley, fliced Lemon,
and Horfe-radifh; let your Fifh lye in Salt and Water
ten or twelve Hours before you boil it: If you foufe
your Fifh, you muft put in more Vinegar, Pepper,
Cloves, Mace, Salt, and Bay Leaves; take out your
Fifh, then boil your Liquor better, put in whole Ginger and Lemon-peel, it will make your Liquor better;
and when both is cold pour the Liquor on your Fifh:
It is to be eaten cold with Oil, Vinegar and Muftard, or
with fome of its own Liquor; you may put *French*
white Wine in it with Vinegar. You may foufe Pike
the fame Way.

To roaft or bake a Pike.

SCORE your Pike on the Back, rub it all over with
melted Butter; make a Stuffing of Crumbs of Bread,
Oifters,

Oifters, Lemon-peel, Parfley, Shalot, Thyme, fweet Mar= joram, and Anchovies, all fhred fmall; put in as much Beef Sewet finely chopped, as Bread; feafon it with Pepper, Salt, Cloves and Nutmeg; wet it with two Eggs, and lay a Lair of it in every Score, and put fome in the Belly: Strew on the Fifh Crumbs of Bread, Pep- per, Salt, the Grate of a Lemon and Nutmeg, roll it up in the Caul of Veal or Lamb, or a very thick butter- ed Paper; tye it to a Spit and flame it well with But- ter, or turn it round in a Difh, and put Butter about it. Put it in the Oven, and when done, drain all the Gravy from it, and make a Lobfter or Oifter Sauce for it; or you may take a little Gravy, a Piece of Butter work'd in Flour, an Onion ftuffed with Cloves, a Gill of red or white Wine, the Gravy that comes out of the Fifh, Oifter Liquor, and Ketch-up. Garnifh the Difh with fried Parfley, fliced Lemons, and fhred Beet-roots and Pickles.

To make Oifter Loaves.

GET five little *French* Loaves, cut a little round Bit out of the Top, and take out all the Crumbs, fry the Crufts, and boil them in clarified Butter: Take half a Hundred of large Oifters, fcald and wafh them very clean, crum the Pith of the Loaves, and put fome of it in the Oifters; ftrain the Liquor to them; put grated Lemon and Nutmeg, a good Piece of Butter, a little Pepper, ftir this in a Tofs-pan on the Fire till it is very hot; then ftir in a little white Wine, and a little Juice of Lemon, then fill your Loaves with it, let both be hot; put the Bit you cut cff the Top on it a- gain; you may make it without the Crumbs; thicken the Oifters with a little Cream and the Yolks of Eggs.

To drefs a Pike with Oifters.

SCALE and gut it, wafh it clean, cut it in Pieces, and put them in a Stew-pan with a Gill of white Wine, a Half Mutchkin of Water, Half a Gill of Vinegar, Parfley, Chives, Mufhrooms if you have them, and
Truffles,

Truffles, Morels, and blanch'd Oifters, with their own Liquor, a Piece of Butter work'd in Flour, Pepper, Salt, Mace and Nutmeg ; boil them all together, with a Bunch of fweet Herbs, and an Onion and Parfley muft be fhred.

To foufe a Pike.

PUT the Pike into as much Water as will cover it, with Bay Leaves, Pepper, Cloves, Mace and Salt : Let it boil till it is tender, that a Straw may run thro' it ; then take it up and put in the Liquor white Wine and Vinegar : When your Liquor is cold put in your Fifh. When it goes to the Table, garnifh it with pickled Barberries, Lemon and Parfley ; put fome of its own Liquor about it.

To boil a Pike.

THRUST the Tail of the Pike in its Mouth, boil as much Water as will cover it; put in it a Gill of Vinegar, the Juice and Rind of a Lemon, a Piece of Horfe-radifh, put a Stuffing of Forc'd-meat made of Fifh in the Belly ; and when the Water boils, put in your Fifh, and boil it with a quick Fire : For the Sauce, take a little of the Liquor it is boil'd in, an Onion ftuffed with Cloves, the Liver minc'd, a Bunch of fweet Herbs, Pepper, Mace and Salt, put in Oifters or Cockles blanched, and pour on Liquor, a good Piece of Butter worked in Flour, a little white Wine and Ketchup ; garnifh it with Pickles and fliced Lemon.

To fry a Pike.

CUT it in Slices, put in it Verjuice, Salt, Pepper, Lemon Juice, Chives and Bay-leaves; let it lye Half an Hour, then dip them in a Batter and fry them ; difh them garnifh'd with flic'd Lemons and Parfley : Make your Sauce of brown'd Butter and Flour, Oifter Liquor, Mufhroom Liquor, Gravy of Fifh or Flefh, Pepper, Salt and Mace, a little white Wine, and Lemon Juice.

D

To

To bake Plaice or any flat Fish.

CUT off the Heads, Tails and Fins; season them with Salt, Pepper, Nutmeg and Cloves, Parsley, sweet Herbs, Lemon-peel, Anchovies and Shalots, put Butter under and over them; strew on them Crumbs of Bread, bake them a fine Brown, cut all the Ingredients small; you may put in either Oisters, Cockles, or Shrimps, a Gill of white Wine, and the Juice of a Lemon. If the Dish is a handsome Dish you bake them in, you may send them to Table in it, if not, take Care in taking them out; you may send them, as they are baked, with either plain Fish Sauce, or Lobster, or Shrimp.

To stew Soals.

PUT your Soals in a Stew-pan, with two Gills of white Wine, whole Pepper, Mace, Lemon-peel and Salt; when they are half-stewed, put in a little Butter work'd in Flour, stir it till it is melted; then put in some Oisters and their own Liquor, keep them often shaking till the Fish is enough. Squeeze in a little Juice of Lemons: Garnish the Dish with Lemon, and fried Toasts of Bread.

To boil Mullets, or stew them.

BOIL your Water and Salt, just as much as will cover them; then put in your Fish, with Vinegar and Horse-radish; take them up and let them drain, boil some of their own Liquor, a Bunch of sweet Herbs, Onions, Pepper, Salt, Lemon-peel and Nutmeg, Ketchup, white Wine and Lemon Juice, thicken it with Butter and Flour; so serve them up, garnished with red Cabbage, scraped Horse-radish, and sliced Lemon.

To pickle Smelts.

YOUR Fish being washed and gutted, dry them in a Cloth; lay them in Rows, and put between every Row, Pepper, Nutmeg, Cloves, Mace and Salt, with the Powder of Cochineal, Salt-petre and Peter-salt; co-

cover

ver them with Bay Leaves, then boil as much Vinegar
as will cover them, and when cold pour it on them.

To roſt a Cod's Head.

SCORE it with a Knife, and ſtrew a little Salt on it,
and lay it in a Stew-pan before the Fire, with ſome-
thing behind it, throw away the Water that runs out of
it the firſt half Hour; then rub it over with a little
Butter, and ſtrew on it Nutmeg, Cloves, Mace and
Salt; turn it often and baſte it with Butter : If it is a
very large Head, it will take four Hours roſting; take
all the Gravy that runs out of it, and put more Gravy
to it, and a Glaſs of white Wine, three Shalots, a little
Horſe-radiſh, Pepper, Cloves, Mace, Salt and Nutmeg,
a good Lump of Butter worked in Flour, the Liver of
the Fiſh boiled, and chopped with Anchovies very
ſmall, ſome Oiſters and Shrimps; thicken it with the
Yolks of two Eggs, juſt as you're going to put it in the
Sauce-boat. Lay your Cod's Head on the Diſh, and
put ſmall fried Fiſh and Forc'd-meat Balls, Slices of
Lemons, Horſe-radiſh and Pickles over it, and ſend it up
very hot.

To ſtew Cod.

CUT the Cod in thin Slices, lay it in a Diſh with
a Mutchkin of Gravy, and two Gills of white Wine,
ſome Oiſters and their Liquor ; ſeaſon it with Pepper,
Salt and Nutmeg, and let it ſtew till it is almoſt enough,
then thicken it with a Piece of Butter roll'd in Flour,
let it ſtew a little longer : Put in the Juice of a Piece
of Lemon ; ſerve it up very hot.

To broil a Cod.

CUT the Cod in middling Pieces about an Inch
thick, flour it well, and put it on the Gridiron over
a ſlow Fire : The Sauce is a little Gravy, a Glaſs of
white Wine, an Anchovy, Pepper, Salt, an Onion
ſtuffed with Cloves, a Spoonful of Walnut Liquor ;
boil the Liver, chop it ſmall, and a Piece of Butter
rolled

rolled in Flour in the Sauce; you may put in Oifters, Shrimps or Mufhrooms; fee that your Fifh is well broil'd: Difh it, and put Parfley about it. Send your Sauce in a Boat.

To dreſs a Cod's Tail.

LOOSE the Skin that it may fall from the Flefh; take the Fillets out, and make it with more Fifh in Forc'd-meat, and fill up the void Spaces; then put the Skin upon the Tail again, rub it with Butter, and ftrew on it Crumbs of Bread, Pepper, Salt, and Lemon-peel, fweet Herbs fhred fmall: Then put it in the Oven, and bake it a light Brown. You may make a Ragoo for it, or give it any Fifh Sauce you pleafe.

To ſtew Carps à la Royale.

WHEN they are very clean, put them in Claret, Salt, Pepper, Lemon-peel, an Onion ftuffed with Cloves, Horfe-radifh, and a little Vinegar; cover them clofs, and let them ftew gently on a flow Fire for three Quarters of an Hour; then beat fome Butter, fome of the Liquor that the Fifh is ftewed in, with two Anchovies chopped fmall, and fome Oifters. Difh your Carps on Sippets, and pour the Sauce over them.

To boil Carps.

SAVE the Blood, then boil them in a good relifhed Liquor for half an Hour; make the Sauce of the Blood, Claret, and good Gravy, two Anchovies, two Shalots, whole Pepper, Cloves and Mace. Let all ftew together; thicken it with Butter rolled in Flour, grate Nutmeg in it, and a little Lemon Juice; falt it to your Tafte; drain your Fifh well: Difh them, and pour the Sauce boiling hot over them.

To dreſs Eels with white Sauce.

SKIN and cut them in Pieces, blanch them, then dry them in a Napkin; tofs them up in Butter, with

Salt,

Salt, Pepper, Cloves, Lemon-peel, and a Glaſs of white Wine : Toſs up likeways ſome Artichoke Bottoms, Muſhrooms and Aſparagus, with Butter and ſavoury Herbs : Thicken the Sauce with the Yolks of Eggs ; ſo ſerve them : Put Slices of Lemon and a little Juice in it.

To dreſs Eels with brown Sauce.

CUT your Eels in Fieces, toſs them up in clarified Butter and Flour ; then put to them a little Fiſh Broth, Chives and Parſley ſhred ſmall, ſome Muſhrooms and Capers, a Bunch of ſweet Herbs, an Onion ſtuffed with Cloves, Pepper and Salt. When well boiled, put in a Glaſs of white Wine, and the Squeeze of a Lemon, and the Yolk of an Egg with Butter. So ſerve it up hot.

To fry Eels.

SKIN them, bone them, and cut them in Pieces, and lay them in Vinegar, Salt, Pepper, Bay Leaves, ſliced Onions, for two Hours ; then drudge them with Flour, and fry them in clarified Butter. Serve them up dry with fried Parſley.

To dreſs Eels à la Daube.

MINCE the Fleſh of Eels, ſeaſon it with Salt, Pepper, Cloves and Nutmeg ; cut the Fleſh of another Eel into Lardoons ; then lay one Lair of them on the Skin, and another of the minced Fleſh, continuing ſo to do, till you have made it into the Shape of a Brick of Bread ; put the Skin about it, and wrap it up in a Cloth, and ſtew it in half Water and half red Wine ; ſeaſon it with Pepper, Salt, Cloves and Bay Leaf ; let it cool in its own Liquor, and when you are going to ſend it to Table, cut it in Slices.

To roaſt a large Eel.

WASH it in Salt and Water, cut off the Head, and flea off the Skin a little below the Vent ; gut it, wipe it clean with a Cloth, and give it three or four Scores with a Knife ; then ſhread ſome Parſley, Thyme, and ſweet Marjoram, with an Anchovy, and ſome ſcalded Oiſters ; mix them with Salt and Butter, and put them in the Belly of the Eel, and in the Scores; then draw the Skin over the Eel again, tye the Skin with a Pack-thread, to keep in the Moiſture ; faſten it to a Spit, and roaſt it leiſurely, baſte it with Water and Salt till the Skin breaks, then baſte it with Butter; make your Sauce of beaten Butter and white Wine, with three or four Anchovies chopped in it.

To bake Tench.

WHEN they are well cleaned, lay them in a Pan with Gravy, white Wine, and ſome Muſhrooms, An-chovies, and three or four Shalots, ſome Pepper, Cloves, Mace, Salt and Lemon-peel, with a Bunch of ſweet Herbs ; lay ſome Butter all over the Fiſh, then cover them very cloſs, and bake them an Hour ; then pour off the Liquor, and ſtrain it, only preſerving the Muſh-rooms ; then add to it a Spoonful of Lemon Juice, and thicken your Sauce with the Yolks of three Eggs, mix it by Degrees with the Sauce, lay your Fiſh in a hot Diſh, and pour the Sauce over them.

To roaſt Tench.

HAVING cleaned it well from the Slime, make a Hole as near the Gills as you can, ſtuff the Belly as full of ſweet Herbs as you can, then tye it to the Spit, and roaſt it ; mix Butter with Vinegar and Salt, and baſte it often ; give it what Fiſh Sauce you pleaſe.

To fry Tench.

SLIT them down the Back, drudge them with Flour and Salt, then fry them ; make the Sauce of Gravy
Muſh-

Mushrooms, Artichoke Bottoms, Truffles, Anchovies and Capers, all chopped small, and well stewed ; the Juice of a Lemon, and some Fish Cullis, or a Piece of Butter worked in Flour ; boil it very well ; send your Fish with Parsley on it, the Sauce in a Bowl.

To crimp Scate.

CUT the Fish the crofs Way into ten Pieces, Inch broad, ten long, more or lefs, according to the Size of the Fish, then boil it quick in Salt and Water ; put it dry on a Difh, and ftrew on it green Parsley ; if it is to be eaten hot, put in one Cup Butter and Muf-tard, and, in another, Butter and Anchovy ; send Oil and Vinegar to Table with it.

Flounders with Sorrel.

CUT three Scores on one Side of them, and lay them in a Pan with as much Water as will cover them, with a little Vinegar and Salt, boil them quick ; then boil four Handfuls of Sorrel picked, and chop it very fmall ; put it over the Fish, and pour half a Pound of melted Butter over it ; drain the Fish very well.

To boil Flounders or Plaice.

PUT Salt, whole Pepper, white Wine, Vinegar, and a Bunch of fweet Herbs into your Water ; let it boil apace before you put in your Fish ; let them boil till they fwim, then take them up and drain them ; take a little of the Liquor, put in it fome Butter work'd in Flour, two Anchovies and fome Capers ; beat it up thick on the Fire, then pour it in a Sauce Boat ; put Parsley and fliced Lemon on the Fish.

To broil Flounders or Plaice.

SPLIT them, put Parsley and green Onions cut in a Stew-pan, with Pepper, Salt, and a Lump of But-ter ; put in your Plaice or Flounders, and turn them two or three Times, to make them get a Tafte, with-out

out putting them over the Fire; then ſtrew them with Crumbs of Bread, and put them a broiling; when done, you may ſerve them up with any Sauce you pleaſe.

To ſtew Plaice or Flounders.

CUT them into, and place them in the Stew-pan, with as much Water as will cover them, put in a Blade of Mace, Salt, Lemon-peel, and a Spoonful of Lemon Juice, mix'd with Crumbs of Bread, Pepper, Nutmeg, Thyme, Parſley and Onion ſhred ſmall; then ſtew them on a ſlow Fire, lay the Fiſh in the Diſh, and pour it on them; or you may put them in the Pan with white Wine, Truffles, Muſhrooms, Parſley, Tnyme, Chives, the Melts, and a little Butter and Flour, ſtir and turn them, but don't break them, put in the Yolks of two Eggs, well beaten; to fry them, only drudge them with Flour, and fry them brown, and put fried Parſley over them when brandered; the Sauce is melted Butter and Vinegar.

To dreſs Cabbolow.

BOIL it in boiling Water till it fleaks, put it on the Diſh, and ſtrew a good deal of hard Eggs, chopped fine over it, or you may leave the Fiſh in Heaps, and the chopped Eggs in Heaps; you may dreſs any ſalt Fiſh the ſame Way: If it is too dry, ſteep it before it is boiled, and ſend a Bowl of Butter and Muſtard to Table with it.

To pot Salmon, Trouts or Eels.

CUT off the Heads and Fins, ſcrape and wipe them very clean, cut them in middling Pieces, ſeaſon them very well with Pepper, Cloves, Mace and Salt, put them in a Can, and put a good deal of Butter about them, cover them with coarſe Dough, made of Meal; put them in a ſlow Oven: The Salmon will take an Hour baking, the reſt but half an Hour; when they come out of the Oven, take them out of the Can, and let them drain well from the Liquor, and let both cool; then take all the Butter off the Can, and clarify

fy it with more Butter to cover your Fifh, put them
in fmall Pots, and pour the clarified Butter over it; you
may fend them to Table in the fmall Pots: If you find
they don't come eafy from the Bones, put them a while
longer in the Oven.

To pot Lobfters or Scollops.

LET your Lobfters be as whole as you can, take
them out of the Shell, and your Scollops quite whole,
put them in different Pots, and the lefs the Pots are,
the better; feafon them with Pepper, Salt, Cloves and
Mace, put a good deal of Butter on them, put them
in a flow Oven, and cover them; half an Hour bakes
them, as they were boiled before; when cold, put
clarified Butter over them.

To fricafey Oifters, Cockles or Muffels.

PICK them very clean, and ftrain a little of their
own Liquor on them, with Crumbs of Bread, and a
Piece of Butter work'd in Flour; feafon them with
Pepper and Mace, a little Salt and Nutmeg, the Grate
of a Lemon, a little white Wine, and the Juice of a
Lemon; don't put too much Flour among the Butter.

To butter Crabs or Lobfters.

PICK all the Fifh out of the Shell, put it in a
Sauce-pan with Crumbs of Bread, Nutmeg, a very little
white Wine, ftir it about, and when hot, put it in the
Shells, and fome Crumbs of Bread on it, brown it
before the Fire, and put the Juice of a Lemon in it,
or a Lemon.

To make Caper Salmon.

TAKE out the Chine, falt it twelve Hours, then
drain it well from the Salt and Blood, take an Ounce
of Salt-petre, and an Ounce of Peter-falt, and half a
Pound of Bay Salt; rub it very well for fix Days with
this, then hang it up to dry by a flow Fire.

E

To keep Salmon in Pickle for a Year.

CUT off the Fins, and chine it, falt it for twenty Hours on a Board, boil a Pickle of Salt and Water, that will bear an Egg, as much as you think will cover the Salmon ; when your Pickle is almoſt boiled, put in it an Ounce of Salt-petre, and an Ounce of Peter-falt, a Pound of Bay Salt, ſkim it well, and when it is cold, pour it from the Bottom, then put your Salmon in it ; a Lime Can is beſt to keep it in ; cut the Salmon in Pieces, as much as you think proper to boil at once.

To ſtew Haddocks or Whitings.

PUT them in the Pan, with a little Water, Pepper, Salt, Mace, chopped Paſley, Lemon-peel and Onion, a good Piece of Butter worked in Flour ; let them boil on a quick Fire. When you think they are enough, put in a little Wine, then take out the Fiſh, and thicken the Sauce with the Yolks of three Eggs well beaten ; take Care it does not curdle : When you put Butter and Flour in any thing, ſtir it till it diſſolves ; ſhread the Parſley.

To pot Herrings.

CUT off the Heads and Fins, put them in a Pan ; feaſon them with Pepper, Salt and Vinegar : If you put in a little Sherry in them, put the Juice of a Lemon inſtead of Vinegar : Cover them cloſs, and bake them in a ſlow Oven : They are to be eaten when cold. Eels may be done the ſame Way.

To pickle Oiſters, Scollops, Cockles or Muſſels.

WASH and pick them clean in their own Liquor, then ſtrain the Liquor, put them in it with whole Pepper, Cloves, Mace and Salt ; give them two or three Boils, then take them off, and eat them cold : A little of it is good in any Fiſh Sauce.

To

To *fcollop Oifters or Lobfters.*

SCALD the Oifters, put them in the Scollop Shells, put a little Butter in the Bottom ; feafon them with Nutmeg, the Grate of a Lemon, a very little Pepper, fome of their own Liquor, and a little white Wine : Put Crumbs of Bread over them ; then put them in a flow Oven. Cut the Lobfter in Dice, and do it the fame Way. You may do them before the Fire on a Brander.

To *ftew Eels.*

CUT the Tails and Fins if large, fkin them ; cut them three Inches long : Feafon them with Pepper, Salt and Cloves ; put them in a Stew-pan, with a little Gravy or Water, a Bunch of fweet Herbs, and two Onions : Cover them clofs, and let them ftew on a flow Fire. When the Fifh comes eafy from the Bone, they are done. Take out your Herbs, and put in Crumbs of Bread, and a little Butter worked in Flour, a Glafs of white Wine, and the Squeeze of a Lemon.

To *make a Fricafey of Oifters.*

PICK your Oifters very clean, put them on the Fire, and give them a Scald, fkim them and drain them clear from their own Liquor ; ftrain the Liquor, put it in a Sauce-pan with the Oifters, the Rind of a Lemon, an Onion ftuffed with Cloves, a Blade of Mace, a Piece of Butter worked in Flour ; when the Rawnefs is off the Flour they are enough, put Sippets in the Afhet under them : Take out the Onion and Lemon-peel, and put a little white Wine, and the Juice of a Piece of Lemon in them, Pepper and Salt ; thicken them with the Yolks of two Eggs.

To *make Forc'd-meat for Fifh.*

CHOP a large Haddock very fmall, and put as much chopped Sewet as Fifh, and as much Bread, and a few chopped Oifters ; feafon it with Pepper and Nutmeg,

meg, a little ſhred Parſley, Onion, Salt and Lemon-peel; wet it with an Egg or two, ſo roll it in ſmall Balls, flour your Hands as you are rolling them; fry them in Butter a light brown, they will ſerve any Sort of Fiſh.

To fry Soals.

FLEA them, and drudge them with Flour, and get a Pan almoſt full of clarified Butter, or good Drippings of Beef; when it is boiling hot, put in the Soals and fry them a good Brown on both Sides; drain them very well from the Fat, put criſped Parſley and Slices of Orange over them. Or, you may give them a Sauce made thus: Take two Gills of Gravy, the ſame of Claret, an Onion ſtuffed with Cloves, Mace, and a little Salt or Anchovy Liquor; brown ſome Butter and Flour, and ſtir it in by Degrees, with chopped Morels, and Forc'd-meat Balls; you may put fried Oiſters in it, and a little Oiſter Liquor: Send it in a Sauce Boat.

A good Way to dreſs Lobſters.

PARBOIL your Lobſters, break the Shells, pick out all the Meat, cut it ſmall, take the Meat out of the Body, mix it fine with a Spoonful of white Wine, put it in the Stew-pan with the reſt; cut the Tail in long Pieces, put in a Piece of Butter and a Gill of white Wine, ſome Crumbs of Bread, a little Pepper, Salt, Nutmeg, and a Spoonful of Vinegar: Let it ſtew a little, put in a Gill of Gravy; when hot, diſh it.

Lobſters the Italian Way.

WHEN your Lobſters are boil'd, take the Meat out of the Tail and Claws, and cut it in Slices; put a little Butter in a Stew-pan, Parſley, Muſhrooms and Truffles cut ſmall, with a little Gravy, and a Glaſs of white Wine; ſeaſon it with Pepper, Salt, Nutmeg, ſweet Herbs, and Rockambole: Let it ſtew ſlowly, put the Meat of the Body and Juice of Lemon in it.

To dress Crabs.

TAKE the Meat out, and cleanse it from the Skins, put it into a Stew-pan, with two Gills of white Wine, some Crumbs of Bread, the Grate of a Lemon, Nutmeg, Pepper and Anchovy; put it on the Fire with a little Butter, stir it with the Yolk of an Egg, so dish it: You may put Claret, instead of white Wine, if you please.

To make Water Sokey.

TAKE some of the smallest Flounders you can get, cut the Fins close, put them in a Stew-pan, and as much Water as will cover them; put Salt and a Bunch of Parsley, boil them till they rise to the Top: Send them to the Table with the Liquor about them; put Parsley and Butter in a Cup.

To stew Trouts.

PUT your Trouts in a Stew-pan, with two or three Gills of white Wine, and a Quarter of a Pound of Butter, Pepper, Salt and Mace, minc'd Parsley, Thyme, and green Onions: Let them all stew a Quarter of an Hour, then mince the Yolks of two Eggs and put them Dish them and pour their own Liquor over them.

To souse Trouts.

PUT all Sorts of Spice, and a Faggot of sweet Herbs, in as much Water and Vinegar as will cover the Fish, boil them in it: When they are enough, let them lye in the Pickle till you are for eating them.

To fry Lobsters.

TAKE a boiled Lobster, and take out the Meat as whole as you can, slice it the long Ways, flour it and fry it in clarified Butter; or you may make a Batter of Cream, Eggs, Flour and Salt, dip them in it and fry them: Then beat some Butter up thick, with grated Nutmeg, Claret and Orange Juice. Lay the Lobsters in the Dish, and pour the Sauce on it.

To

To stew Crabs.

BOIL them, take the Meat out of the Bodies, save the great Claws, mash the Meat that is in the Body, and mix it with Claret, Vinegar, Salt, Nutmeg, and a Piece of Butter : Put them in a Stew-pan with chopped hard Eggs, let them stew a good while, then put them in the Shells. Put them in the Dish with the Claws broiled round them.

To boil a Piece of Sturgeon.

TAKE a Rand of Sturgeon, put a Mutchkin of Vinegar, two Chopins of Water, some Slices of Lemon-peel, Horse-radish, Bay Leaves, whole Pepper, Ginger, Cloves and Salt. The Liquor must boil before you put in the Fish : If it is to be eat hot, make the Sauce either of Oisters, Lobsters or Crabs ; if it is to be kept in Pickle to be eaten cold, don't put in Vinegar, but put in a good deal of Salt, and all Sorts of Spices.

To roast a Piece of Sturgeon.

LAY your Sturgeon in Salt and Water six Hours, then spit it, and baste it well for a Quarter of an Hour ; then drudge it with grated Bread, Nutmeg, Mace, Pepper, Salt, sweet Herbs, Lemon-peel cut small ; continue drudging and basting till it is enough. Make the Sauce of Gravy, Oister Liquor, Lemon-peel, sweet Herbs, Onions, Ketchup, Pepper, Salt, Mace, and some white Wine ; strain it off, and put in as much Butter as will thicken it : You may put in either Oisters, Prawns, Lobsters or Crabs.

To fry Sturgeon.

TAKE a Piece of fresh Sturgeon, and cut it in Slices Half an Inch thick ; slash it, and fry it in clarified Butter ; then take it up and clean the Pan, and put in Claret, Lemon-peel, Nutmeg, Pepper, Salt and Anchovy. Let all stew a while, then put in a Piece of Butter roll'd in Flour and Shalot.

To

To fry Sperlings.

DRY them, and rub them with an Egg, roll them in Crumbs of Bread, Lemon-peel, Parſley, Pepper, Salt, and fry them brown in clarified Butter. Send Parſley and Butter in a Cup.

To ſtew Sperlings.

PUT them in a Pan, with a little Gravy, white Wine, the Yolks of three or four Eggs minc'd ſmall, a good Piece of Butter, an Onion ſtuffed with Cloves, a little Pepper and Salt. Let them ſtew till done; put the Squeeze of a Lemon in it. Send it up hot.

To boil Mackarel.

BOIL them in Salt and Water, with a little Fennel: The Sauce is the Fennel chopped ſmall, with beat Butter, or ſcalded Gooſeberries, with Butter and Sugar.

To pickle Mackarel.

CUT them in Pieces, and ſeaſon them with Pepper, Salt, Mace and Cloves, rub them with it, and let them lye a while; then fry them in clarified Butter; then put them to drain; and when they are dry, put them in a Can, then boil Vinegar and Spiceries; and when it is cold pour it on them.

To broil Mackarel.

WHEN they are well clean'd, draw them at the Gills; wipe them and ſtuff them with Crumbs of Bread, the Liver, Parſley, Pepper, Salt, Nutmeg grated, Lemon-peel, Shalot, and wet it with an Egg, then brander them, and when done pour over them beat Butter.

To fry Maids.

SKIN them, and put them in Salt and Water, let them lye a while, then dry them with a Cloth; flour them, beat ſix Eggs, with a little Flour, Salt, Ginger, Nutmeg, Parſley ſhred ſmall, a little white Wine, beat

it

it it up pretty thick; have a Pan with Beef Drippings, or clarified Butter boiling hot; dip your Maids in the Batter, and fry them brown. Let the Sauce be Butter, Vinegar, the Livers of the Fiſh, and Nutmeg beaten together; put fried Parſley over them, and the Sauce in a Boat.

To boil Gurnets.

STUFF the Bellies with Bread Forc'd-meat, and boil them in Salt and Water; drain them well: The Sauce is beat Butter, Nutmeg, Lemon Juice, Shrimps, or Cockles, and a boiled Anchovy: When you broil them, you may give them the ſame Sauce, with a little Gravy in it.

To fry Whitings.

GUT them, and wipe them clean with a Cloth, and turn their Tails into their Mouths; make a Batter of Eggs, Flour, and a little Salt; dip them in it, and ſtrew on them Crumbs of Bread; then fry them a light brown. The Sauce is beat Butter and Anchovies, or Parſley and Butter.

To ſtew Scollops.

BOIL them very well in Salt and Water, take them out and ſtew them in a little of the Liquor, a little white Wine, Mace, Cloves, and a Piece of Butter rolled in Flour, a little Juice of Lemon and ſome Salt: You may do Cockles or Muſſels the ſame Way; but ſcald them in their own Liquor.

To make a Collar of Fiſh.

TAKE a large Eel, ſkin it, and pick off the Fleſh, and beat it in a Marble or wooden Mortar; ſeaſon it with beaten Mace, Nutmeg, Pepper and Salt, ſweet Herbs, Parſley, Lemon-peel and Shalots, all chopped ſmall; beat all well together, with an equal Quantity of Crumbs of Bread; then take

any

any flat Fifh that will roll, and lay it on the Dref-
fer. Take out all the Bones and Fins, and cover
your Fifh with the Forc'd-meat ; mix a Couple of raw
Eggs with it ; then roll it up tight, and open the Skin
of the Eel, and bind the Collar with it, fo that it may
be flat Top and Bottom. To ftand well in the Difh,
butter an Earthen Can, and fet it in it upright ; flour
it, and put a Piece of Butter on the Top, and round
the Edges. Let it be well baked, but take Care it is
not broke ; put two Gills of Water and a little Vinegar
in the Can ; take another Eel cut in Pieces, and put it
in a Sauce-pan, with a Bunch of fweet Herbs, Onion,
Truffles, Morels, and a few Mufhrooms ; cover it clofe,
feafon it with Cloves, Mace, Pepper and Salt : When
well ftewed, take out the Herbs and Onions, and put
in it a Bit of Butter work'd in Flour, a little Ketchup
and Lemon Juice. Make fome of the Forc'd-meat in
little Balls, and fry them a light brown ; when the Fifh
is enough lay it in the Difh, fkim all the Fat off it, and
pour the Gravy to your Sauce, let it all boil together
till it is pretty thick ; then pour it over the Roll, and
put in your Balls : Garnifh with Lemon and Pickles.

To ftew a Pike.

Lard with the Flefh of an Eel ; then put it in a
Stew-pan, with fome brown'd Butter and Flour, a little white Wine, Salt, Pepper, Nutmeg, an Onion ftuffed with Cloves, Lemon-peel, and fweet Herbs. Let
it ftew on a gentle Fire ; then put to it a Ragoo of
Mufhrooms, Oifters, and the Liquor wherein they are
ftewed. Difh your Fifh, pour over it the Ragoo, garnifh it with fried Oifters, the Rands of Fifh, Pickles, and
Slices of Lemon. When your Fifh is ftewing keep it
clofe covered, put a little Verjuice in with the Fifh.

F   C H A P.

CHAP. III.

To pot and make Hams, &c.

To pickle Tongues.

LET your Tongues be very well ſalted, and lye in
it two or three Days; then make a Pickle for
them: Put a Quarter of Salt-petre, a Quarter of a
Pound of Peter-ſalt, three Pounds of Bay Salt, and three
of white Salt, in ten Chopins of Water; let it boil two
Chopins away: See it be well ſkim'd; and when cold
put it on your Tongues, but dry them firſt in a Cloth.
This Pickle will ſerve either Pork, Geeſe, or Sheeps
Tongues. If you ſee it grows muddy, boil it again,
and put none of the Sediment in it. There muſt be a
Pound of coarſe brown Sugar in it.

To make Hams or Bacon.

SALT them on a Table, and lay a Weight on them
for two or three Days, then to every Ham or Flitch of
Bacon, take a Pound of white Salt, a Pound of Bay
Salt, two Ounces of Salt-petre, and two of Peter-ſalt,
a Quarter of a Pound of brown Sugar; mix them all
together, and warm them pretty hot; lay your Hams
in a Trough, and rub them very well, turn and rub
them every Day for three Weeks; then hang them up
to dry by a ſlow Fire, Wood, or Saw-duſt, is the beſt to
dry them with.

To boil Hams.

IF they are dry ſoke them in cold Water, and put
them in a Pot of cold Water with ſweet Hay about them.
A large Ham will take three Hours to boil it, a ſmall
one but two, and a middling one two and a Half. If
they are to be eaten hot, put Crumbs of Bread upon
them;

them; ftuff the Ham with Cloves if you like it, and put it before the Fire.

To make Mutton Hams.

CUT the hind Quarter of very large fat Mutton like a Ham, then rub it all over with Bay Salt and brown Sugar; let it lye a Day, then put it in the Pickle, made thus: Take a Gallon of Pump Water, two Pounds of Bay Salt, two of white Salt, fix Ounces of Salt-petre, and four of Peter-falt, one Pound of brown Sugar, one Ounce of Salt-prunella; put all in the Water, boil it well, and fkim it. When cold, put in your Hams, let them lye in it a Fortnight; then hang them up and fmoke them with Dale-duft or Shavings; they muft be dry before you make Ufe of them. You may pickle Bacon Hams the fame Way, or any Sort of Tongues. When you hang up your Mutton Hams, boil the Pickle and fkim it, and when cold you may put in Tongues, but falt them firft for three or four Days.

Another Way to make Mutton Hams.

CUT the Mutton Ham-ways, take an Ounce of Salt-petre, a Pound of Salt, a Pound of coarfe Sugar, two Penny-worth of Cochineal, mix them, and rub the Ham very well, lay it with the Skin Side down, and rub it every Day for fixteen Days, then hang it up to dry. It eats beft in broil'd Rafhers.

To make Veal Hams.

CUT a Leg of Veal like a Ham; take a Pound of white Salt, a Pound of Bay Salt, two Ounces of Saltpetre, mix them and rub the Ham with it, lay it with the Skin Side down for a Fortnight, rubbing it every Day with the Pickle; hang it up, it will be dry in fixteen Days. You may boil or roaft it.

To make Beef Hams.

TAKE a small Leg of Beef, cut it Ham-fashion ; an Ounce of Peter-salt and four Ounces of Bay Salt, a Pound of white Salt, a Pound of coarse Sugar; mix them, and rub the Ham ; lay it and all Hams in a Vessel at full Length that will hold the Brine ; turn and rub it every Day for a Month ; then hang it to dry, but not in too hot a Place.

To roast an Ox or Sheep's Heart.

TAKE all the Blood out of it, and stuff it with Forc'd-meat, made thus : Take a Quarter of a Pound of Beef Sewet, mince it small, two Handfuls of Crumbs of Bread, Pepper, Salt and Nutmeg, Lemon-peel, Parsley, Thyme, sweet Marjoram and Shalots, all shred small : Put in a chopped Anchovy, wet it with Eggs, and stuff the Heart with Cloves, or lard it if you please ; roll it in buttered Papers, and roast it well ; it takes a good deal of roasting ; roll some of the Stuffing in small Bowls, fry them, and put them in the Dish with the Heart ; take off the Papers, and put Gravy under it.

To roast a Haunch of Venison.

RUB it over with Butter, and put on it a buttered Paper, make a Paste of Flour, an Egg and Water, and put it on it, put the buttered Paper over it, tye it on with Pack-thread, and put it to a good Fire ; it takes three Hours roasting if but small, more if large ; take off the Paste and Paper, put Gravy under it, Claret Sauce in a Boat, and Currant Jelly on a Saucer: If you boil a Haunch of Venison, let it be well salted for seven or eight Days, then boil it in a large Pot of boiling Water, sending it up with Colly-flowers, Savoys or Cabbage.

To roast a Shoulder, or any Joint of Venison.

LARD it with Bacon, season it with Pepper, Salt, Nutmeg and Cloves, lay it four Hours in Steep of white Wine, Lemon Juice and sweet Herbs, then spit
it,

it, roaſt it at a gentle Fire, baſte it with its own Pickle; when roaſted, take what drips from it, and put to it Gravy, and a little Butter work'd in Flour, an Anchovy and Ketchup; boil it, and pour it under the Veniſon, ſo ſerve it up.

To ſtew Veniſon that has been roaſted or baked.
GET a little Gravy, ſome browned Butter and Flour, a Gill of Claret, a Bunch of ſweet Herbs, ſome Shalots, Ketchup, and an Anchovy, ſeaſon it with Pepper and Salt, boil it till it is ſmooth, then cut the Veniſon in thin Slices, and give it but one Scald; take out the Herbs, and ſqueeze in it the Juice of a Lemon, ſo ſerve it up hot.

To ſouſe Veniſon.
BOIL it in Water, Beer and Vinegar, ſkim it; then put in Thyme, Savoury and Bay Leaves, ſeaſon it with Pepper, Salt and Nutmeg.

To ſtew Veniſon.
CUT it in Slices, put it in a Stew-pan with Claret, Sugar, grated Bread, three or four Cloves, and a little Vinegar; let it ſtew for ſome Time, grate in Nutmeg, and ſerve it up; Veniſon may be haricot after the ſame Manner as Mutton is.

Veniſon in Blood.
THE Shoulder, Neck or Breaſt muſt be boned, and laid in Blood; ſeaſon it with Pepper, Salt, Winter Savoury, ſweet Marjoram and Thyme, all ſhred ſmall, with a little Beef Sewet chopped ſmall, and ſtirred on the Fire to be thick; then roll up the Veniſon with the ſet Blood and Herbs, and roaſt, or ſtove it gently in good Broth or Gravy, Claret and Shalots; ſo ſerve it up hot.

To dreſs Veniſon à la Royale in Blood.

SPIT your Veniſon, lay it down to the Fire till it is half roaſted, then take it off and ſtew it; make for it a Ragoo of Cucumbers, Sweet-breads and Aſparagus.

To recover Veniſon when it ſtinks.

TAKE as much Water in a Tub as will cover it, and put in a good deal of Salt, and let it ly three or four Hours; then take it out, and let it ly as long as before, in hot Water and Salt; take it out, and ſeaſon it with Pepper and Salt, but dry it firſt; put ſome freſh Sheeps Blood in the Diſh with it; it muſt be high ſeaſoned; don't uſe the Bones of the Veniſon for Gravy, but put good freſh Gravy in it, cover it with Paſte; it will eat beſt cold.

Veniſon in Avet.

CUT it into Pieces, the Bigneſs of your Hand, lard it with Bacon, ſeaſon it with Pepper and Salt, put it in a Stew-pan with Broth, white Wine, a Bunch of Herbs and Lemon-peel; the whole being ſtewed, thicken your Sauce with Butter and Flour, and put a little Vinegar in it: It is a firſt Courſe Diſh; ſerve it up hot.

A Civet of Veniſon.

BOIL the Breaſt or Neck, cut it into Cutlets, and when it is almoſt boiled, brown half a Pound of Butter, and a good Handful of Flour; then add half a Pound of Sugar, and as much Claret as will make it of a good Thickneſs, then put in the Veniſon, and give it three or four Boils, ſo ſerve it up; put the Juice of Lemon it it.

To keep Veniſon all the Year.

A Haunch of Veniſon being parboiled, ſeaſon it with two Nutmegs, a Spoonful of Pepper, and a good Quantity of Salt; put to it two Spoonfuls of Vinegar, make the Veniſon full of Holes, and put in your Spice and

Vinegar,

Vinegar, then put the Venison in a Pot, with the fat Side down, and cover it with two Pounds of Butter; then cover the Pot with coarse Paste, and bake it; when baked, take off the Paste, and lay a Trencher with a Weight on it, to keep it down till it is cold, then take off the Trencher, and lay the Butter flat all over the Venison, then cover it with Paper, and tye it down; send it to Table turned up Side down in a Dish.

To boil a Haunch of Venison.

SALT it for a Week, then boil it in boiling ter for two Hours and a Half, if large: Send it up with either Collyflowers, white Cabbages, or Savoys, and melted Butter: You may boil any Joint the same Way, but don't salt it so long, or boil it so much.

To broil Venison.

CUT your Venison into Slices about Half an Inch thick; season them with Pepper, Salt, and Crumbs of Bread; broil them over a brisk Fire. Serve them up with Gravy.

To make Venison Sokey.

BOIL the Venison, and make a Paste of the Crumbs of brown Bread, some Sugar, Pepper, Salt, Nutmeg and Orange-peel minc'd small, and as much white Wine as will wet it: Mix all with your Hand, and wrap the Venison in it; set it into the Oven for an Hour; then serve it up with white Wine boiled up with Sugar.

To roast a Fillet of Veal.

MINCE Beef Sewet very small, an Anchovy, Lemon-peel, Thyme, Parsley, sweet Marjoram, and an Onion; season it with Salt, Pepper, Nutmeg and Mace; add grated Bread to it: Mix all together with two Eggs, make Holes in the Veal, and stuff it with the Forc'd-meat; put a buttered Paper over it, that the

Stuffing

Stuffing does not come out. Spit it, and roast it well ; the Sauce is beat Butter, Gravy and Lemon : Garnish it with sliced Lemon, and red Beet Roots pickled.

To roast a Shoulder of Veal with farcing Herbs.

PARBOIL it a little, then mince some Thyme, Parsley, Winter Savoury and Shalot, very small, and mince sweet Herbs, chop four hard Eggs, a little Pepper, Salt and Nutmeg ; mix all this up with two raw Eggs, and stuff your Veal with it, but save some of it ; spit your Veal, roast it, put your Stuffing in the Dripping-pan, and, when the Meat is near roasted enough, put to it two Gills of Vinegar and a little Sugar. So serve it up.

To stew a Knuckle of Veal.

PUT it in the Stew-pot with two Chopins of Water, four Blades of Mace, a little whole Pepper, a Sprig of Thyme, an Onion stuffed with Cloves, a Crust of Bread ; cover it close, make it boil, then let it simmer for two Hours ; lay it in the Dish, and pour the Broth over it, take out the Thyme and the Onion ; or you may make the Sauce better, by putting in a little Ketchup, Walnut Pickle, Truffles, Morels and Mushrooms.

To broil a Shoulder of Veal.

HALF roast it, then slice off the most Part of it, and save the Gravy, put the sliced Meat in a Stew-pan, with a little Broth and its own Gravy, a little grated Bread, Oister Liquor, Vinegar, sliced Bacon, a Pound of Sausages out of their Skins made in Balls, and rolled in Yolks of Eggs, Mace, Nutmeg, Salt, Lemon-peel, and an Onion stuffed with Cloves. Let all stew half an Hour, then put in a Mutchkin of Oisters, and some sweet Herbs ; then take the Bone of the Veal and broil it, and dish it : Then put in the Liquor a Piece of Butter work'd in Flour ; let it boil, then pour it o-

over

ver your broil'd Meat. Garnish with fried Oisters, Barberries, and sliced Lemon.

To roast a Calf's Head.

GET a Calf's Head with the Skin on, and scald it, and boil it an Hour; when cold lard it with Lemon-peel; spit and roast it; when enough, make a Sauce of Gravy, Ketchup, Oisters, white Wine, Lemon, Forc'd-meat Balls, fried Sweet-breads, Mushrooms, Truffles and Morels; put in a Piece of Butter work'd in Flour; boil all together, and pour over the Head: You may do it skinned, if you please.

A Calf's Head Surprise.

YOU must bone it and not split it, clean it well, and fill up the vacant Place with Forc'd-meat, and make it in the same Form as before: You may put in the Middle a Ragoo, and cover it with Forc'd meat. Rub it with Eggs, and strew over it Crumbs of Bread and sweet Herbs, Lemon-peel shred small; season it with Pepper, Salt and Nutmeg; bake it, and put a savoury Sauce under it. Blanch the Tongue, and let it hang out of the Mouth.

To boil a Calf's Head.

BOIL and bone it, then have in Readiness the Palate boil'd tender, Yolks of hard Eggs, Oisters scalded, and Forc'd-meat; season it with Pepper, Salt and Nutmeg: Stuff all in the Head, tie it in a Cloth, boil it three Hours, put Gravy under it, garnish it with Bacon.

Beef à la Daube.

GET a Buttock of Beef, lard it, and force it with Forc'd-meat, then pass it off brown; put in some Broth and a Faggot of sweet Herbs, season it with Pepper, Salt, Cloves, Mace; stove it four Hours very tender, and make a Ragoo of Morels, Truffles, Mushrooms, Artichoke Bottoms, Sweet-breads and Palates, white

G   Wine

Wine and Lemon Juice. Garnish with Petty-Patees and Pickles.

To make Escarlot Beef.

TAKE a Brisket of Beef, half a Pound of coarse Sugar, two Ounces of Bay Salt, one Ounce of Saltpetre, a Pound of common Salt; mix all together, and rub the Beef, put it in an Earthen Pan, and turn it every Day: Let it lie a Fortnight in the Pickle, then boil it with Savoys, or a Pease Pudding. It eats very well cold.

Beef la Vinaigre.

GET a Slice of Beef three Inches thick, most lean, from the Buttock, stew it with a little Water, and a Gill of white Wine; season it with Pepper, Salt, Cloves, a Faggot of sweet Herbs, and a Bay Leaf: Let it boil till it is very tender; then set it a cooling; and when cold serve it up, with Slices of Lemon and a little Vinegar.

To roast a Tongue and Udder.

BOIL the Tongue till it will blanch, put it in cold Water, it will blanch the better, then lard it with Fat of Bacon an Inch long, and stuff the Udder with Cloves, then spit and roast them, baste them with Butter. Serve them up with Gravy, but send in a Boat Claret boiled thick as a Syrup, with Sugar and Currant Jelly, or a savoury Sauce.

Ox Tongues à la mode.

BOIL and blanch and lard it, then brown it off, and stove it one Hour in good Gravy and Broth; season it with Pepper, Salt, Cloves, and a Faggot of sweet Herbs; put in Morels, Truffles, Mushrooms, Sweetbreads, and Artichoke Bottoms; skim off the Fat, and serve them either hot or cold.

To collar Beef.

TAKE a broad Runner of Beef, bone it, rub it with white Salt and Salt-petre, turn it and rub it every
Day

Day for eight Days; then dry it in a Cloth, and ſeaſon it with Pepper, Cloves, and *Jamaica* Pepper; roll it very hard, and put it in a Cloth, bind it with broad Net-ting, and put it in a Pot of boiling Water; let it boil three Hours, then take it up and hang it by one End, and when it is almoſt cold take it out of the Cloth: It is to be eaten cold; you may ſend it to Table either whole or in Slices. You may collar a Flank the ſame Way, but take off the Skin.

To ſtew a Rump of Beef.

CUT off the large Bone, that it may lye flat in the Stew-pan, ſcore the Inſide, and ſeaſon it with Pepper, Salt, Cloves and Mace; ſhread a little Thyme, Parſley, Winter Savoury, and ſweet Marjoram; put Seaſoning between every Score if you like it; lard it with Ba-con, and a Slice of Bacon laid in every Score: Put it in your Stew-pot with a Pint of Water, a little Rockam-bole or Shalots; let it ſtew on a gentle Fire for two Hours, then turn it, and make a Ragoo of Palates and Eyes, Forc'd-meat Balls, and Kernels, with ſome of the Liquor it is ſtewed in; thicken it with brown'd Butter and Flour: Put in your Ragoo a Half Mutchkin of white Wine, and the Juice of a Lemon, the Grate of a Nutmeg, and Muſhrooms if you have them. You may make a Ragoo for it if you pleaſe the ſame Way, of Carots, Turnips, Artichoke Bottoms, Truffles, Morels, Muſhrooms and Oiſters: You may ſtew any Piece of Beef the ſame Way. Boil your Roots before you put them in your Ragoo.

To make Dutch *Beef.*

TAKE ſix Pound of a Buttock of Beef, without Bones, rub it all over with five Ounces of coarſe Su-gar; let it lye two Days, then wipe it, and take a Mutchkin of white Salt, two Ounces of Salt-petre, and three of Peter-ſalt; dry all before the Fire, and rub it well into the Beef; then put it in a brown glazed Pan
that

that will hold the Beef, and turn it, and rub it every Day for three Weeks : Then put it in a Canvas Bag, and hang it up in any Place where it will dry gradually ; turn it often that the Brine does not settle. When dry boil it, and you may either flice or fcrape it when it goes to Table.

Beef Steaks with Oifter Sauce.

CUT your Steaks off any tender Part of the Beef, flat them with your Chopping-knife, and put them on a hot clean Brander, on a clear quick Fire, turning them often, that the Gravy does not run out, have your Sauce ready, make it thus : Scald your Oifters, and wafh them clean in their own Liquor, then ftrain the Liquor into a Sauce-pan, put to it a Piece of Butter work'd in Flour, two or three Shalots, pounded Pepper, Cloves and Nutmeg, falt it to your Tafte ; put a Glafs of white Wine, and the Rind and Juice of a Lemon in it : So pour it on your Afhet of Steaks boiling hot. Garnifh them with Pickles.

To make hung Beef.

TAKE a Surloin of fat Beef, falt it well with white and Bay Salt, Salt-petre, and brown Sugar ; let it lye in it for a Fortnight, turning and rubbing it every two Days ; then hang it to dry ; it eats well either in Rafhers, or with Fowls and Greens, but it muft not be cut till it is thorough dry.

To boil a Rump of Beef the French Way.

BOIL it for Half an Hour, take it up in a deep Difh, cut Gafhes in the Side to let out the Gravy, then put Pepper and Salt in every Gafh ; then fill the Difh with Claret, and fome Blades of Mace, fet it on a Chaffing Difh of Coals, and cover it clofs, and let it ftew an Hour and a Half : Turn it often, take off all the Fat, put in a Handful of Capers, five Onions, and fix hard Lettices, flice them both, put in a Spoonful of Verjuice ;

juice; boil all till the Meat is tender. So ferve it up on Sippets.

To ftew a Rump of Beef.

BOIL it till it is half enough; take it up and peel off the Skin; then take Pepper, Salt, Mace and Nutmeg, Parfley, fweet Marjoram, Savoury and Thyme fhred, ftuff them in large Holes thro' the Fat, and lay all the reft of the Seafoning over the Top, and lay it all over with Eggs to bind it; put the Gravy that comes out, with a Mutchkin of Claret, and a Gill of Vinegar, in a deep Pan with the Liquor, you may fill it to the Top. Cover it, and bake it four Hours; then put it in a Difh, and pour the Liquor over it.

To grillard a Breaft of Mutton.

HALF boil a Breaft of Mutton, fcore it in Dice, then rub it over with an Egg; take Crumbs of Bread, Pepper, Salt, Thyme, fweeet Marjoram, Chives and Parfley; mix all together, and lay it on it, then broil it gently for Sauce; take Butter, Gravy, Capers, Shalot and Cucumbers, all fhred fmall; garnifh it with pickled Onions, red Cabbage and Kidney Beans.

To make Mutton Cutlets.

CUT a Neck of Mutton in fingle Bones, flat them with the Chopping-knife, feafon them with Pepper and Salt, rub them with Eggs, and lay all over them Forc'd-meat; make it thus: Chop a little of the lean Mutton, with twice as much Sewet, as much Crumbs of Bread as Mutton, Pepper, Salt, the Grate of a Lemon, Parfley, Thyme and Shalot; chop all very fmall, and mix them up; wet them with Eggs, roll your Cutlets in buttered Papers, and broil them on a clear Fire: They will take a Quarter of an Hour: When done, take them out of the Papers; the Sauces muft be Butter and Gravy, Lemon and Ketchup: You may do Veal the fame Way, but it takes longer broiling; garnifh them
with

with Pickles; if Veal, with Lemon, Mushrooms, and
Beet Roots.

To roaſt a Collar of Mutton.

BONE a Breaſt of Mutton, and rub it with Eggs;
lay all over it Forc'd-meat, made as above, roll it up
very tight, and bind it cloſs : You may tye it on a Spit,
or do it in the Oven ; make a Haſh to put under it;
cut your Mutton in thin Bits, brown a little Butter and
Flour, put in a little Gravy, put a Bunch of ſweet Herbs,
the Rind of Lemon, and two Onions ſtuffed with
Cloves, Pepper and Salt, boil it well; then put in your
Haſh with Muſhrooms, Cucumbers, and Kidney Beans,
mince it, but not ſmall: Don't let your Mutton boil,
but give it a Scald or two; it muſt be roaſted before
you cut it; put it on the Diſh, and the Collar o-
ver it; take off the Binding, and throw out the Onions
and Herbs : Put Lemon Juice in the Haſh. Garniſh
with Pickles.

To roaſt a Leg of Mutton with Oiſters.

TAKE ſome Crumbs of Bread, a little Beef Sewet,
ſome hard Eggs, an Onion, three Anchovies, Thyme,
and Winter Savoury, twelve Oiſters, Lemon-peel and
Parſley, mince them ſmall ; ſeaſon it with Pepper, Salt
and Nutmeg; mix all theſe together, and wet them
with raw Eggs, ſtuff the Mutton under the Skin in the
thickeſt Place, and half roaſt it ; cut off ſome of the
Under-ſide of the fleſhy End in little Bits, put them in
a Sauce-pan, with a Mutchkin of Oiſters and their Liquor, ſeaſon them with Mace and Salt ; put in a good
Piece of Butter in Flour ; and when the Mutton is done,
diſh it, and pour the Sauce round it.

A Shoulder of Mutton in Epigramme.

TAKE a Shoulder of Mutton, half roaſt it, and
take off the Skin as neatly as you can, the Thickneſs
of a Crown, leaving the Shank-bone to it ; then cut
the

the Meat in thin Slices, the Bignefs of a Shilling; put it into good Gravy with a Piece of Butter, fome grated Bread, Pepper, Salt and Nutmeg, an Onion, Anchovy, and Pickles fhred; rub the Skin over with an Egg, and ftrew it with Crumbs of Bread, Pepper, Salt, Chives and fweet Herbs, fhred fmall; brander it, but don't let the Hafh boil much; difh the Hafh, and put on it the broiled Bone and Skin; you muft not cut them afunder.

Carbonaded Mutton.

CUT a Joint of Mutton in Steaks, and try them; then ftew them in good Broth, with Crumbs of Bread, a Bunch of fweet Herbs, Mufhrooms, Salt, Pepper and an Onion ftuffed with Cloves; take out the Herbs and Onion before you fend it up.

To boil Sheeps Tongues with Oifters.

BOIL fix Sheeps Tongues in Water and Salt till they are tendr; peel off the Skin, cut them in thin Slices, put them in a Stew Pan with a Chopin of Oifters, a little Claret, Cloves and Mace; fet them a ftewing, then put in fome Butter, and the Yolks of three Eggs well beaten, fhake them well; don't put in the Eggs till you are going to difh them. You muft not let the Eggs boil in them, but be fcalding hot.

To roaft a Calf's Head with Oifters.

CUT the Head as for boiling, take out the Brains and the Tongue, parboil them, blanch the Tongue, and minch them with a little Sage, Beef-fewet and Oifters, with Yolks of Eggs and Crumbs of Bread, Pepper, Salt, Nutmeg, grated Lemon-peel; parboil and dry the Head, fill the Skull with thefe Ingredients, then ftuff it with Oifters, and faften it to the Spit; as it roafts preferve the Gravy, put to it a Glafs of white Wine, Salt, Nutmeg, Lemon-peel and Shalot, a Piece of Butter work'd in Flour, fome Oifters, and a little Lemon-juice, beat it up thick. When the Head is done, difh it, and pour the Sauce about it.

To drefs Calves Feet.

BOIL them tender, flit them in the Middle, put them in a Stew-pan with a Gill of Grvay, a Piece of Butter, a little Onion, Parfley chopped fmall, Pepper and Salt, a Spoonful of Vinegar ; ftew them all together, fo difh them. You may make them fweet, and put Currants and white Wine in them ; thicken them with the Yolks of two Eggs.

Cakes of Beef to be fried or brandered.

CHOP fome of the tendereft Part of the Beef very fmall, and pound it as much as for Saufages, mix Half the Quantity of Beef-fewet with it ; feafon it with Pepper and Salt, you may put Onions and Parfley in them, wet them with an Egg, make them in Cakes, and fry them in their own Gravy, or brander them on Papers.

To force the Infide of a Surloin of Beef.

LIFT up the Fat carefully, cut out the Meat to the Bone, and chop it fmall ; cut a Pound of Sewet fine, and as many Crumbs of Bread, a very little Parfley, Lemon-peel, and two Shalots ; feafon it with Pepper, Salt and Nutmeg, mix all together with a Glafs of Claret and raw Eggs ; then put it in the fame Place, and fkewer the Fat over it. Paper it, and don't take off the Paper before you difh it. You may put Gravy or Claret to it. Spit the Meat before you put in the Forc'd-meat.

A Neat's Tongue the Polifh *Way*.

BLANCH off the Skin and boil it, cut it in two, but not quite off ; ftick it with Slices of preferved Lemon, and Bits of Cinnamon ; then put a Bit of Sugar, a Glafs of white Wine, and a little Gravy : Then let the Tongue ftew a while, and difh it with the Sauce about it,

To

To fry a Neat's Tongue.

BOIL and blanch it, then cut it in thin Slices, feafon it with Nutmeg, Cinnamon and Sugar, dip them in the Yolks of Eggs, put fome Butter and a little Vinegar in a Pan, and when it is boiling hot, drop in the Tongue and Eggs by Spoonfuls ; when they are done difh them. The Sauce is beat Butter, white Wine and Sugar.

To ftew a Neat's Tongue whole.

PUT a raw frefh Tongue in a Stew-pan with good Broth, white Wine, Pepper, Salt, Cloves, Mace and Capers, with Slices of Carots and Turnips : Set this over a gentle Fire, and let them ftew two Hours, then take up the Tongue and blanch it, and put fome Marrow to it, and let it have a Boil or two, and difh it on Sippets, and pour all over it.

To bake Ox-cheeks.

LET them lye in Water all Night, then bone them and ftuff them with Cloves ; feafon them with Pepper, Salt and Mace; put them in a Pan, one Cheek laid clofe upon the other : Put Bay Leaves on them and a Chopin of Claret, cover the Pan clofs and bake them well. When they are baked pour off the Fat, and mix it with melted Butter, and pour over the Cheeks. They are to be eaten cold with Muftard and Sugar ; the Gravy is to be all poured from it before you put the Butter on.

To roaft a Leg of Mutton with Cockles.

STUFF it all over with Cockles and roaft it. Put Gravy under it.

To pot Beef.

TAKE a Buttock of Beef, and cut off fome thin Slices, and ftrew on it a little Salt-petre ; let it lye four days in it, turning it every Day ; then put it in a Can with fweet Butter, or fweet Sewet fhred fmall : Cover it with a coarfe Pafte made of Meal, and bake it

H   in

in a hot Oven for three Hours ; then take it out, and take all the Greaſe and Gravy from it ; when it is cold ſtring it and pound it fine ; then ſeaſon it with Pepper, Salt, Cloves, and Nutmeg, then draw ſome ſweet Butter to Oil, and ſkim it, and pour it from the Bottom ; to every two Pound of your pounded Meat put a Pound of your oiled Butter, and work it up well together, put it in ſmall white Patees ; and, when cold, melt ſome Butter, and pour it on them. You may pot Veniſon the ſame Way.

To make Beef Ollops.

CUT thin Slices of Beef where it is tender, and beat it well with your Rolling-pin ; then ſeaſon it with Pepper, Salt, Cloves, Mace and ſweet Herbs, and Lemon-peel very fine ; ſeaſon it with Spice as above : Lay a Lair of this all over your Ollops, and roll them up tight ; put them in a Can with a little Butter, cover them cloſs and bake them ; when they are done, take them out in Slices, and put them on a Diſh, pour on them ſome of their own Gravy, with a little white Wine and the Juice of a Lemon : Don't make it ſour, you may thicken it with a little Butter and Flour, grate Nutmeg in it.

To make Veal Collops.

TAKE a hind Quarter of Veal, and cut the thick Part in very thin Slices, beat them with a Rolling-pin, ſeaſon them with pounded Mace, Cloves, Pepper, and the Grate of a Lemon, then fry them a light brown in ſweet Butter ; when they are fried, get ſome good brown Gravy, and thicken it with a little Butter and Flour, boil it with an Anchovy, and a whole Onion, a little Ketchup, and the Juice of half a Lemon : when boil'd put in your Collops, and give them one Boil ; if they are not ſeaſon'd enough, put in more of that you ſeaſon'd your Collops with ; put Forc'd-meat and an

Anchovy,

Anchovy, and a little Salt. You may put Muſhrooms in them and Oiſters, but ſcald them firſt.

To make Forc'd-meat Balls.

CHOP ſome of the tendereſt Part of Veal or Mutton, very fine, with an equal Quantity of Beef or Mutton Sewet ; ſeaſon it with Pepper, Salt, Nutmeg, Cloves, and the Grate of a Lemon, and a little ſweet Herbs ; wet it with two Eggs, and work it together with your Hand, make it in ſmall Balls, and fry it in ſweet Butter : Flour your Hands when you roll them.

Another Sort of Forc'd-meat Balls.

CRUMB a Penny Loaf, and add to it eight Ounces of Butter, or Beef Sewet, minc'd very fine, Lemon-peel, Parſley, and a Bit of Onion ſhred fine ; ſeaſon it with Pepper, Salt, Nutmeg, wet it with two Eggs, roll it in your Hands to a Paſte, then make it in ſmall Balls the Bigneſs of a Nutmeg ; fry them in Butter.

Another Sort of Forc'd-meat Balls.

CHOP an equal Quantity of any tender Meat, with Beef or Mutton-ſewet, and the ſame Quantity of Crumbs of Bread, with Lemon-peel, Parſley and Onion ſhred ſmall ; ſeaſon it with Pepper, Salt, Nutmeg and Cloves : Wet it with Eggs, and work it up together, then roll it in ſmall Balls. Fry them in Butter.

To make Veal Fricandos.

CUT a Neck of Veal in Chops, letting two Bones be together, put them in a Stew-pan with a little Water, Lemon-peel, Onions, Pepper, Salt, Mace and Anchovy, and a little ſweet Herbs tied in a Bunch, let it ſtew on a ſlow Fire till the Head is boil'd ; then take out your Herbs, Lemon-peel and Onions, and thicken it with Butter work'd in Flour, put a little white Wine and the Juice of a Lemon in it, and Muſhrooms if you
have

have them, and some boil'd Artichoke Bottoms cut in Dice.

To force a Leg of Mutton or Lamb.

CUT all the Meat out, but don't break the Skin, to every Pound of Meat put Half a Pound of Beef or Mutton Sewet, chop them very fine, shread sweet Herbs, Lemon-peel and Shalots, mix them with it; season it with Pepper, Salt, Cloves and Nutmeg, wet it with two Eggs, mix all together and fill the Skin; spit it, and roll about it a well buttered Paper: Tye it closs that the Stuffing does not come out, it will take a good while to roast it. Put Gravy in the Dish with it, and a Ragoo of Palates and Sweet-breads: Fry the Loin, and lay it round it.

To make a Mutton or Lamb Hash.

HALF roast either a Shoulder or Jiggit of Mutton or Lamb, cut it in thin Slices; save the Gravy; put it in your Pan with a little Butter work'd in Flour, some Pickles, Pepper, Salt, Ketchup, Onions, and the Rind of a Lemon cut small; if it is too thick, put in a little Water: Two or three Boils does it.

To make minc'd Collops.

TAKE any Part of the Beef that is tender, and mince it small, to every Pound of it put a Quarter of a Pound of Sewet minc'd very fine, put it in a Toss-pan, with a little Gravy or Water, and some Onions shred small; season it with Pepper, Salt and Cloves: Let it stew on a slow Fire till it is tender, then work a very small Bit of Butter in Flour, and give it a Boil in it; so serve it up. You may cut Pickles in it if you please.

To make Beef Collops.

CUT your Collops broad, and very thin, flat them with your Chopping-Knife, flour them, and fry them a light brown: Make your Sauce of Gravy, a little Butter work'd in Flour, and a little Ketchup; season it
with

with Pepper, Salt, Mace and Onions: When boil'd put in your Collops, and Pickles with them. You do either Lamb or Mutton the fame Way. Don't boil your Meat in the Sauce, but pour it over them. You may brander them, and pour the fame Sauce with Oifters on them.

Entry of Sheeps Trotters forced.

SCALD the Trotters, and let them ftew in a little Water well feafoned; take them up when the Bones will come out, ftretch them on a Table, put Forc'd-meat in them, and roll them up one by one; place them in a Difh, and moiften them with a little Butter; ftrew on them Crumbs of Bread, Pepper, Salt and fweet Herbs; put them in the Oven; when brown, difh them, and put a Ragoo Sauce on them.

Veal Olives.

TAKE ten or twelve thin Veal Collops, rub them over with an Egg; then lay on them Forc'd-meat, and roll them up, roaft or bake them: When done, pour over them a Ragoo of Sweet-breads. Garnifh the Difh with Oranges.

Another Way.

TAKE the Flefh of a Fillet of Veal, and half the Quantity of Beef Sewet chopped very fmall; add to it Mufhrooms, Oifters, and two Anchovies, chop them all fmall; feafon them with a little Thyme, fweet Marjoram, Parfley, Lemon-peel, all fhred fmall; Pepper, Salt, Nutmeg and Mace; then take the Veal Caul, and lay it all over with the Forc'd-meat: You may roll it in two or three Collars; roaft or bake it; when done, cut it in Slices, and ferve it up with ftrong Gravy.

To stuff a Rump or Round of Beef.

CHOP two Handfuls of Parsley very small, and one of Beef Shewet shred small; mix them and Pepper and Salt together, make Holes with a Knife in the Beef, and stuff them full of it: The Beef is to ly salt four Days before it is stuffed; boil it tender: You may eat it either hot or cold.

White Scots Collops.

CUT the Veal into thin Slices, beat them with the Rolling-pin: You may lard them if you please; season them with Pepper, Salt, Cloves, Mace, Lemon-peel, and grated Bread, dipping them first in Eggs; stew the Knuckle well, with a Bunch of sweet Herbs, two Anchovies, Cloves, Mace, Pepper and Salt; strain it, and when you are going to send it up, thicken it with a Bit of Butter work'd in Flour; give it two or three Boils, then put into it the Yolks of three Eggs well beaten, a Glass of white Wine, and the Juice of a Lemon, and give it a good Heat on the Fire, but don't let it boil, stirring it all the while. Your Collops being fried, but not brown, lay them in the Dish, and pour your Sauce over them. Garnish it with Mushrooms and Oisters; don't make it too sour.

To stew a Knuckle of Veal.

LAY at the Bottom of your Pot four long wooden Skewers, wash the Veal, and lay it in the Pot with three Blades of Mace, some whole Pepper, a Sprig of Thyme, a small Onion, a Crust of Bread, and two Quarts of Water; cover it closs, and let it come to the Boil, then let it only simmer for two Hours; then take it up, and strain the Broth over it; put young Pease or Asparagus in it.

Lamb with Rice.

HALF roast a fore Quarter of Lamb, put a Pound of Rice into two Quarts of good Broth, three Blades
of

of Mace, Salt and Nutmeg; let it ſtew an Hour; take it off, and put in the Yolks of four Eggs, and a Pound of Butter; then put in the Lamb in Joints in a Diſh, with the Rice over it, waſh it with Eggs, and bake it half an Hour: You may do Hens or Chickens the ſame Way, but leave them whole.

To make a Calf's Head Haſh.

H A L F boil your Head, and cut the one Half in thin Slices; put it in your Pan with Gravy, a Bunch of ſweet Herbs, the Rind of a Lemon, a whole Onion, and an Anchovy; ſeaſon it with Pepper, Salt, Mace and Nutmeg. When it is almoſt boiled, thicken it with Butter work'd in Flour; put in a little ſweet Cream: Score the other Half, and ſtrew on it Crumbs of Bread, ſhred Parſley, Lemon-peel, Pepper, Salt and Nutmeg; put it in the Dripping pan to brown, baſte it with Butter; when done put it in your Diſh, and before you pour your Haſh about it, put in a little white Wine, ſome Lemon Juice and Muſhrooms, if you have them, and Oiſters; you may make it brown without Cream.

To make a Lamb's Head Haſh.

B L A N C H and clean your Head very well, half boil it, cut the Haricals in thin Slices, and take a little of the Water it is boiled in, and put your Haſh in it, with an Onion ſtuffed with Cloves, the Rind of a Lemon, Pepper and Salt, a little Ketchup; thicken it with Butter work'd in Flour, take out the Brains, and mix them with Crumbs of Bread, grated Lemon-peel, Nutmeg, Pepper, Salt, and an Egg; then put them in the Head again, and lay it in the Dripping-pan till it is well roaſted, then put it in your Diſh, and pour your Haſh round it. Garniſh all your Haſhes with Lemon, and put a little of the Juice in them.

Another

Another Way to drefs a Lamb's Head.

HALF boil the Head, cut it through the Scull into Halves, take out the Brains, mince the Haricals fmall,
and the Brains amongft them, put them in the Stew-
pan with a little Gravy, or fome of the Water that they
were boiled in, with a little Butter work'd in Flour,
the Grate of a Lemon, Onion and Parfley minced fmall,
a little Ketchup, the Squeeze of a Lemon, Pepper, Salt
and Nutmeg; boil all together, put the Head in a Dripping-pan, rub it over with an Egg, and throw on it
Crumbs of Bread, fweet Herbs fhred fmall, Pepper,
Salt and Nutmeg; bafte it with Butter. When it is
done enough, put it on the Difh with the Hafh about
it, fry the Liver in thin Slices, and put it about
your Difh.

To ftew a Lamb's Head.

PUT the Lamb's Head in your Sauce-pan, with a
little good Broth, made of a Neck of Beef; put all
the Haricals in but the Liver; when they are enough,
put in a good deal of Spinage, a little Parfley, and an
Onion; feafon it with Pepper, and Salt, and let it ftew
on a flow Fire: You may put in it half a Pound of
Prunes, and thicken it with Crumbs of Bread, if you
pleafe.

To drefs any Sort of Liver.

CUT the Liver in thin Pieces, and rub it all over
with Eggs; take Crumbs of Bread, fweet Herbs, Onions, and Lemon-peel fhred fmall, and ftrew it on it,
feafon it with Pepper and Salt: You may either fry or
broil it; make your Sauce of a little Gravy, thickened
with Butter work'd in Flour, the Juice of a Lemon, a
little Ketchup, and grated Nutmeg.

To roaft a Ham or Gammon of Bacon.

TAKE off the Skin, and lay it to fteep in luke warm
Water; then lay it in a Pan, pour on it a Mutchkin
of Canary, and let it fteep in it twelve Hours; then
spit

fpit it and paper it over the fat Side; pour the Canary it was foaked in, into the Driping-pan, and bafte it with it all the while it is roafting; when it is roafted enough, pull off the Paper and drudge it well with Crumbs of Bread, and Parfley fhred fine, brown it well and fet it to cool. Serve it with green Parfley.

To roaft Pork without the Skin.

TAKE any Joint of Pork not falted, and lay it to the Fire till the Skin may be taken off; then take it up and take off the Skin; then falt it and roaft it, make Sauce for it of Claret, Crumbs of Bread and a little Water; boil all together, put to it fome Salt, a Piece of Butter, Lemon-juice, or Vinegar; when the Pork is roafted flour it; then difh it, and pour the Sauce to it.

To roaft a Breaft of Pork.

TAKE a Fore-quarter of Pork and cut off the Knuckle, divide the Neck from the Breaft, take out all the Bones, rub it well with Salt, fhred Thyme and Sage fmall; mix with it Nutmeg, Cloves and Mace; ftrew them all over the Meat, then roll it up tight with the Flefh inward; tie it faft together, fpit it long-ways and roaft it; put Gravy and Muftard under it.

To broil Pork Steaks.

CUT a Loin or Neck of Pork in thin Steaks, feafon them with Salt and Sage fhred fmall; lay them on the Brander, then feafon the other Side; let the Sauce be beat Butter, Vinegar and Muftard.

To drefs a Pig the French Way.

SPIT your Pig, lay it down to the Fire, and let it roaft till it is thoroughly warm; then take it off the Spit and divide it into twenty Pieces; fet them to ftew in white Wine, and ftrong Broth, feafoned with Nutmeg, Pepper and Salt, two Onions, and two Anchovies cut fmall, and a little Butter and Vinegar; ftew

I   them

them all, and when enough diſh it in the Liquor it
was ſtewed in, with ſliced Orange or Lemon.

A Hog's Head Cheeſe Faſhion.

BOIL it till the Bones come out, then ſeaſon it
with Pepper, Salt and Cloves; while it is hot put the
thin Side of one half, and the thick of the other together; put a Cloth over and under it in a ſmall Broth-
diſh, and lay a Weight on it as broad as the Head is, till
it is cold; then take it out of the Cloth; you may ſend
it whole to the Table, or in Slices. It is to be eaten
with Muſtard and Vinegar, and Onion, if you pleaſe.

Pork Brawn.

GET a Fore-quarter of the beſt and firmeſt Pork
you can get, cut off the Shank and bone it, ſalt it with
a quarter of an Ounce of Salt-petre, and half an Ounce
of Petre-ſalt, two Penny worth of Cocheneal; pound
them and mix them with a little Salt and brown Sugar;
then lay it on a Table with a Weight upon it for four
Days; then wipe it dry and roll it up hard, and bind
it with broad Tape; put it in boiling Water, and let it
boil four Hours, ſtill keeping the Pot full of Water;
if it is large, it will take five Hours boiling.

In Imitation of Brawn.

BOIL a Set of Nolts Feet very tender, then take
a Piece of Pork, boil it near enough; then put the
Fleſh of the Feet in the Middle of the Pork, let both
be boiled with Salt; roll it up tight, and put Tapes about
it; boil it till it is tender; when cold put it in Souſe.

A Pig in Jelly.

CUT it in Quarters, and lay it in a Stew-pan with
two Calves Feet, and the Pig's Feet; put in a Pint of
Rheniſh Wine, the Juice of four Lemons, and ſome of
the Rind, and one *Engliſh* Quart of Water; ſeaſon it
with Nutmeg, Salt and Mace; ſtove it gently for two
Hours;

Hours; let it ſtand till cold, then clear the Jelly; and when it is almoſt cold put it on the Pig; you may cut the Pig into any Shape you pleaſe, and pour the Jelly over it.

To dreſs a Loin of Pork with Onions.

PUT a Loin of Pork to roaſt, and put twenty ſmall Onions in the Dripping-pan under the Pork; let the Fat drop on them, when the Pork is nigh enough put the Onions into the Sauce-pan: Let them ſimmer o-ver the Fire a Quarter of an Hour, ſhaking them well, then pour out all the Fat; ſhake in a little Flour, a Spoonful of Vinegar, and two Tea Spoonfuls of Mu-ſtard, give them a Boil. Lay the Pork in the Diſh, and the Onions in a Sauce Boat.

To roaſt a Quarter of young Pig, Lamb Faſhion.

CUT the Pig in Quarters, and take off the Skin, ſcore it in the Middle with a little Blood, roaſt it a light brown, it will eat like Lamb, with Spearmint, Su-gar and Vinegar. The other Part of the Pig you may do in Jelly thus: Bone it, and boil it in a ſmall Quantity of Water, with two Penny-worth of Iſinglaſs, whole Pepper, Cloves, Mace, Lemon-peel and Salt: When it is boil'd as tender that you may thruſt a Straw in it, take it out and cut it in Dice, dry it on a Cloth, put a Gill of white Wine, the Juice of a Lemon, and the Whites of two Eggs beaten in the Liquor the Pig was boil'd in, and run it thro' a Jelly Bag. Pleaſe put your Pig that you cut in Dice in a Bowl; and when the Jelly is almoſt cold, pour it over them.

A Pig Rolliand.

BONE it, leaving the Head whole, and rub it over with Eggs; ſeaſon it with Pepper, Salt and Nutmeg, and lay over it ſome Forc'd-meat: Then roll it up, and ei-ther roaſt, bake, or ſtove it. You may cut it in four Pieces, and ſend the Head in the Middle: Make the

Sauce

Sauce of the Brains and Gravy, Butter, Vinegar, and chopped Sage if you like it.

To make Bologna Saufages.

TAKE a Pound of Bacon, fat and lean together, a Pound of Beef, a Pound of Veal, a Pound of Pork, and a Pound of Beef Sewet, chop them very fine, fweet Herbs and Sage fhred very fmall, and Pepper; and, to feafon it pretty high, get a large Gut and fill it, boil the Water, and prick the Gut for fear of burfting. Boil it foftly an Hour, then lay it on clean Straw to dry; it will keep good a Year in a dry Place.

To fry Saufages with Apples or Potatoes.

TAKE a Pound of Saufages and fix Apples or Potatoes, cut them as thick as a Crown, fry them with Saufages a light brown, difh them up hot; ftew'd Cabbage, and fried Saufages, or Peafe Pudding and Saufages eat very well.

Oifter Saufages.

TAKE a Pound of the Lean of a Leg of Mutton, and two Pound of Beef Sewet, fhred very fine, three half Mutchkins of Oifters, fhread them likewife, mix thefe with fome of the Oifter Liquor, Pepper, Salt, Cloves, Mace and three raw Eggs; and make them up as you ufe them, and fry them in Butter.

Oxford Saufages.

CHOP the Lean of a Leg of Veal or Mutton, with four Pound of Beef Sewet, or Butter; feafon it with Pepper, Salt, Cloves and Mace; pound them well, with five or fix Eggs, and as you ufe them roll them out long-ways with Flour; when you fry them boil the Butter, and then put in the Saufages; fry them a light brown, this will ferve for Forc'd-meat Balls.

A

A Souſe for Brawn.

BOIL Wheat Brawn and Salt very well, then ſtrain it; and, when cold, put in the Brawn: There muſt be a good deal of Salt; new boil it every Fortnight.

To make Sauſages.

TAKE the tendereſt Part of a Leg of Pork, and chop it very ſmall; to every Pound of Fleſh put a Pound of Hog's Fat, or Beef Sewet; when both is finely chopp'd pound them together in a Mortar; ſeaſon them with Salt, Black and *Jamaica* Pepper; they muſt be high ſeaſoned: Let them lye a Day before you put them in the Skins. Let your Skins be very clean, and lye a while in Salt and Water. Yeu may put chopped Sage in them. You may make Mutton the ſame Way; but put no Sage in them.

Pigs Petty-toes.

WHEN the Pig is opened, get the Draught and Feet clean, and boil them; then get a little Gravy, and a Bit of Butter and Flour, an Onion, and two or three Leaves of Sage minc'd ſmall: Cut the Feet in two, and mince the Draught very ſmall; ſeaſon it with Pepper and Salt, boil them together, and ſerve it up; it muſt be a young Pig's Draught.

To roaſt a Pig's Haſlet.

CUT it aſunder, and waſh it well; ſtuff the Heart with Crumbs of Bread, ſhred Sage, Onion, Parſley and ſweet Marjoram, Pepper, Salt and *Jamaica* Pepper; work all this up with a little Butter: Spit them, and ſtrew Crumbs of Bread, and ſome of the ſame Seaſoning all over it, but firſt rub it with an Egg to make it ſtick: Roll the Caul, or a butter'd Paper over it, and tye it faſt; but when you think it done take off the Paper: It takes two Hours to roaſt it. Serve it up with Gravy and Butter, and a little Sage, with a Drop of Vinegar in it.

To

To make a Ragoo of Tripes.

WHEN boiled, cut them in Bits, put them in a Stew-pan with a very little Water, and season them with Pepper, Salt, and a Blade of Mace, with shred Parsley and Onions; when tenderly stewed, put to them a little Cream and Butter, work'd in Flour; serve them up with Sippets under them: You may do Cow Heels the same Way, but instead of Cream, put Mustard.

To dress a large Pig's Feet and Ears.

BOIL them tender in Salt and Water, then cut your Ears in thin Slices, and your Feet in Quarters: When boiled, fry them, and for their Sauce, get melted Butter, Onions, Parsley, Vinegar and Mustard; boil your Parsley and Onions in your Butter, chopping them first.

To make a Ragoo of Mushrooms.

WASH and dry them, put them in a closs covered Sauce-pan, with a little Pepper, Salt, and a Blade of Mace: Put three Spoonfuls of Water in them, put them on a slow Fire. They take a great while stewing; when tender, chicken them with a little Butter work'd in Flour; and before you send them to the Table, put two Spoonfuls of white Wine in them, and half an one of Vinegar or Lemon.

To make a Ragoo of Kidneys.

TAKE them, and cut them in thin Slices, flour them, and fry them in Butter: When enough, pour in a little Gravy or Water, season them with Pepper, Salt, and shred Onion and Parsley, with a little Vinegar: You may put in a little Ketchup. Give them but three Boils after you season them.

To ragoo a Breast of Veal.

STUFF it with Forc'd-meat between the Flesh and the Bones, and lard it with Bacon if you like it,
then

then half roaſt it, and put it in a Stew-pan with Gravy, and ſtove it till it is enough; then put in Forc'd-meat Balls, Muſhrooms, Truffles, Morels and Oiſters; ſeaſon it with Pepper, Salt, Mace and Nutmeg; the Truffles and Morels muſt be waſhed and half boiled before you put them in; thicken it with brown'd Butter and Flour, put in a Glaſs of white Wine and ſome Lemon Juice.

A Ragoo of Lamb's Stones and Sweet-breads.

BLANCH them in boiling Water, then wipe them dry, and fry them a light brown; then put them in a Stew-pan with ſome good Gravy, Pepper, Salt, and an Onion, ſtuffed with Cloves, Muſhrooms and Truffles; let them ſimmer over a gentle Fire; then put in a Piece of Butter rolled in Flour, a little white Wine and Lemon Juice, and boil them, keeping them ſtirring all the Time to mix the Butter. You may cut them in Slices, and parboil them with blanched Cocks Combs, and not fry them, but toſs them with the ſame Ingredients as before; or you may dip them in Batter, made of a little Ale, Flour, and two Eggs; then fry them, and diſh them with nothing but fried Parſley over them, beat Butter, and Juice of Orange in a Cup.

To ragoo a Neck of Veal.

CUT it in Steaks, ſeaſon it with Pepper, Salt, Cloves and Mace; lard them with Bacon, dip them in Eggs, make up a Sheet of Cap Paper ſquare, and pin the four Corners an Inch high, butter it, ſet it on the Gridiron on a ſlow Fire, put in the Meat, let it do leiſurely, keeping it turning and baſting; when it is enough, have ready Gravy, Muſhrooms, Pickles, Forc'd-meat Balls, and fried Oiſters; ſeaſon it pretty high, lay the Veal in the Diſh, and pour the Sauce over it: Put into it white Wine and Lemon Juice.

To ragoo Veniſon.

LARD a Piece of Veniſon with Bacon, well ſeaſon-ed with Pepper and Salt, fry it a light brown, then ſtew it two Hours in Broth or boiling Water, and ſome Claret; ſeaſon it with Pepper, Salt, Nutmeg and Le-mon-peel, thicken it with Butter work'd in Flour, put a little Lemon Juice and Capers in it.

A Ragoo of Livers.

GET the Livers of Fowls, Turkeys or Geeſe, take off the Gall, blanch them; then put them in a Stew-pan, with as much Gravy as will cover them, a Bit of Butter rolled in Flour, Pepper, Salt, Oiſters and Ketchup: Let them ſtew twelve Minutes if large, but ſix if ſmall. You may put in Crumbs of Bread, and an Onion ſhred ſmall.

To ragoo a green Gooſe.

CUT the Gooſe in two, put it in a Stew-pan with ſome Butter, ſliced Onions, Lemon, Pepper, Cloves and Salt: You may put in a Bunch of ſweet Herbs, put it on a ſlow Fire, ſtir and turn it often, then make a Ragoo of green Peaſe, a little Butter, and ſome good Gravy, Pepper, Salt and Nutmeg; ſhake in a little Flour; diſh your Gooſe, and pour the Peaſe on it.

A Ragoo for a Duck à la Braiſe.

HALF roaſt the Duck, and carbonade it, then make a Ragoo of Sweet-breads, fat Fowls Livers, Cocks Combs, Muſhrooms, if in Seaſon, Aſparagus Tops, Ar-tichoke Bottoms and Truffles, all blanched and half boiled; then ſtew them in Gravy, ſeaſoned with Pepper, Salt, Cloves, and ſhred Shalots: Put the Duck in the Middle of the Diſh, and pour the Ragoo over it.

To ragoo Pigeons.

LARD your Pigeons, cut ſome of them in two, ſeaſon them with Salt, Pepper, Cloves and Mace; then
brown

brown fome Butter and Flour, and put in your Pigeons, and brown them; then put in as much Gravy as will cover them, with a Faggot of fweet Herbs, and let them ftew on a flow Fire; when they are enough ftewed, take out the Herbs, and put in Shalots, Anchovies, Oifters and Mufhrooms. You may put about them, when they are difhed, roafted Larks, or any fmall Birds.

A Ragoo of a Calf's Head.

BOIL it, and cut it in long fmall Pieces, an Inch long, and the Breadth of your Finger; put them in a Stew-pan with a little Gravy, Truffles, Morels, Oifters, Artichoke Bottoms in Slices, Juice of Lemon, Pepper, Salt and Mace; thicken it with Butter and Flour, boil it, and put white Wine in it.

To make a Ragoo of Onions.

GIVE them a Scald, then drain them, and put Gravy, Pepper and Salt to them: Let them fimmer on a flow Fire a good while, then put to them a Piece of Butter rolled in Flour. They may be eaten with any roafted or boiled Meat.

A Ragoo of ftuffed Cucumbers.

TAKE as many Cucumbers as will fill your Difh, pare them, and fcoop out the Seeds, blanch them with boiling Water, then put them in cold Water, ftuff them with Veal, Beef, and Sewet fhred very fmall; feafon it with Pepper, Salt, Onions, Lemon-peel and Spice. Thicken it with Butter and Flour.

To fry Tripe Ragoo.

CUT them into fmall Pieces, dip them in the Yolks of Eggs, and ftrew on them Crumbs of Bread; fry them of a brown Colour, drain them from the Fat, and fend them up hot with Butter and Muftard in a Sauce Boat.

K

To

To roast Tripe.

CUT them in square Pieces, make a Ragoo of Forc'd-meat, Crumbs of Bread, Butter, Pepper, Salt and Nutmeg, and the Yolks of two Eggs ; spread it on the Tripe, roll them up tight, and tye your Rolls on the Spit, flour and baste it. Serve them with melted Butter and sliced Orange.

Tripes the Polish *Way*.

CUT the Tripes in Pieces, and strew them with Crumbs, Parsley, green Onions, Pepper and Salt ; then put into the Stew-pan a Lump of Butter, and when it is brown, put in the Tripes. Let them stew till they are of a good Colour; the Sauce is Butter and Lemon.

To boil Tripes.

CUT them in Pieces, and boil them in Salt and Water till they are tender : You may either send them in their own Broth, with Onions and Pepper in it, or boil Onions and chop them ; then put them in beat Butter, and send it in a Boat ; some Leeks, Parsley and Onions with them.

To make a Ragoo of Palates and Eyes.

WHEN they are cut out of the Ox or Cow's Head, take the Black out of the Eyes; then blanch them in scalding Water, and blanch and skin the Palates; boil them in Salt and Water, when boiled cut your Palates in thin Slices, and your Eyes in round ones, but let them both be very thin ; put them both in your Stew-pan with some good Gravy, an Onion stuffed with Cloves, a Bunch of sweet Herbs, Pepper and Salt; stew them well, then take out your Herbs and put in a little Ketchup, brown some Butter and Flour, then pour all in, keeping it stirring all the Time ; put a little Lemon Juice or Vinegar in it before you serve it up, and Forc'd-meat Balls, Oisters, and white Wine.

To

To make a Ragoo of Sheeps Tongues and Sweet-breads, or Kernels.

BOIL your Tongues and blanch them; cut them in very thin Slices, and your Kernels in Dice; stew them in Gravy with boiled Artichoke Bottoms cut in Quarters; then season them with Salt, Pepper, Cloves, and Anchovies; brown your Butter and Flour, put them in it, keeping them stirring all the Time; put Lemon Juice, or a very little Vinegar, in it: You may put Truffles and Morels in it, if you please.

To make a Ragoo of Truffles and Morels.

BOIL them in Water, when boiled strain the Water they are boiled in, and pick and clean them; put them and their own Liquor in a Stew-pan, with Butter, and Flour, Pepper, Salt, Cloves, Anchovies, a whole Onion, and a little Gravy; when they are stewed well, put a little white Wine and the Juice of a Lemon in it: Serve them up garnished with Forc'd-meat Balls and sliced Lemon.

To make Brain Cakes.

BOIL and blanch the Calf's Brains, chop some of them, and mix them with Crumbs of Bread, Spice, Salt, the Grate of a Lemon, sweet Herbs shred small, and an Egg; then cut in Pieces what you leave, and rub them with an Egg; strew Flour on them; fry them all in a Pan of boiling Liquor; put in the chopped Brains in Spoonfuls, the other in Lumps; garnish your Heads with these.

To make Veal Cutlets.

CUT a neck of Veal in single Bones, and rub them over with Eggs; strew on them grated Bread, Salt, Pepper, Nutmeg, shred Parsley, Shalots, and Lemon-peel; mix them with the Crumbs of Bread; brander them on buttered Papers, or you may do them in the Oven on Tin Plates: For your Sauce, get a little Gravy, vy, a Bit of Butter worked in Flour, a little white Wine; feafon it with Nutmeg and Salt; put in it a chopped Anchovy, and fome Mufhrooms, if you have them; garnifh your Difh with Pickles and fliced Lemon; put a little Lemon Juice in your Sauce. You may do Mutton or Lamb the fame Way.

To mince Fowl, Veal, or Lamb.

WHEN your Fowl or Flefh is half roafted, mince it fmall; put it in your Stew-pan with a little white Gravy, a Piece of Butter worked in Flour, a Blade of Mace, a little Pepper and Salt, a whole Onion, the Rind of a Lemon, and a little of the Juice, a minced Anchovy, fome Mufhrooms likeways. Give it but one or two Boils, for fear of making the Meat hard; garnifh it with fliced Lemon: Take out the Onion and Lemon-peel before you fend it to the Table.

To fry Veal Sweet-breads.

HAVING larded them with Bacon, run a Skewer through them, or a Spit, and roaft them till they are brown; then lay them in a Difh, and put Gravy under them.

To farce Veal Sweet-breads.

SCALD the Sweet-breads, and lard them with Bacon, make a Hole in them, and ftuff it with good Forc'd-meat, don't make the Hole quite through, then bake them in a Pan; make a Ragoo of Mufhrooms, Truffles, Artichoke Bottoms, and Cocks-combs, and Forc'd-meat Balls, and a little good Gravy thicken'd with the Yolks of Eggs: Difh the Sweet-breads, and put a little Juice of Orange, Salt, Mace, and Nutmeg, in the Ragoo; then pour it about them: You may at another Time blanch fome Sweet-breads, and cut them in Slices; flour them and fry them, and put beat Butter with Gravy, Nutmeg and Orange about them.

Rolled

Rolled Fricandoes of Veal.

CUT Slices of a Leg of Veal, beat them, lard them, lay them on the Table, the larded Side downwards : Cover them the Thickness of a Crown, with Forc'd-meat made of Veal, Beef Sewet or Marrow ; season it with Pepper, Salt, Nutmeg and Lemon-peel, and a chopped Anchovy : Put Eggs to bind them, roll them up, and you may do them in the Oven, or fry them in a Pan of boiling Fat. You may either put a Ragoo of Sweet-breads and Palates under them, or Gravy, and the Juice of a Lemon. Be sure to drain the Fat well from them.

To roast a Calf's Liver.

LARD your Liver with Bacon fastened on the Spit, roast it at a gentle Fire ; baste it well, and serve it up with beat Butter, Gravy, and a little Vinegar. A Calf's Liver brander'd gets the same Sauce.

To broil any Sort of Midriffs.

TAKE the largest and freshest you can get, clean and scald them well, stuff them with Forc'd-meat, or with Onion, Sage, Pepper and Salt ; then sew them up, and lay them to broil on a moderate Fire ; serve them up with Gravy, with or without Claret.

CHAP. IV.

To make Pyes and Pasties, &c.

To make a Venison Pasty.

BONE and season your Venison, and let it lye all Night in Seasoning, boil the Bones that come out of it into good Gravy, put it into the Pasty-pan, with good Puff Paste about it ; it takes a great while to bake it.

When

When it comes out of the Oven shake it; and if there is not Gravy enough in it, put in more; if it is to be eaten hot, not else, Pepper and Salt is the Seasoning.

To make a Mutton Pasty as good as Venison.

BONE your Fore-quarter of Mutton, and put it in Steep in Claret and its own Blood, a Mutchkin of each, let it lye all Night, season it with Pepper and Salt; put it in your Dish with all that it is steep'd in about it: Cover it with Puff Paste, bake it two Hours in a hot Oven. When it comes out of the Oven, shake the Dish; and if it wants Gravy put it in. You may put Blood and Claret in a Venison Pasty, if you please.

To make a Pigeon Pye.

CUT off the Pinions and Feet, draw them, and chop the Liver and Gissart; mix it with Crumbs of Bread, chopped Parsley, Lemon-peel and Onion work'd up with a Piece of Butter, Pepper and Salt; Season your Pye with Pepper and Salt; put the Stuffing in their Bellies, lay them in the Dish on their Breasts, and put a little Butter on them; put the Pinions in the Dish with them. Cover the Pye with Puff Paste, so bake it in a quick Oven. You may eat it either hot or cold; you may make it without Stuffing if you please.

To make a Lamb Pye.

CUT your Lamb in middling Pieces, season it with Pepper, Salt and Cloves: Put it in your Dish with hard Yolks of Eggs and Artichoke Bottoms, and a little Gravy or Water. Cover it with Puff Paste: You may put in Raisins and Prunes if you please.

To make a Veal Florentine.

CUT your Veal in small Pieces, season it with Pepper, Salt, Cloves and Mace: Put them in your Dish with Currants and Raisins, a little Bit of Butter, and the Squeeze of a Lemon, and a Gill of Water. Cover your

your Diſh with Puff Paſte; and when it comes out of the Oven, have a Caudle of a Gill of Gravy, a Gill of white Wine, a little Nutmeg, thickened with the Yolks of two Eggs, put a litle Sugar in it, and pour it in your Pye. This Caudle will ſerve for any ſweet Pye. Shake the Diſh after it is in it.

To make a Chicken Pye.

SCALD your Chickens, and cut them in Quarters, waſh them very clean; ſeaſon them with Pepper, Salt, Cloves and Mace; put them in your Diſh with Forc'd-meat Balls, Yolks of hard Eggs, and Artichoke Bottoms. You may make it without this if you pleaſe; put a little Butter and Gravy. You may put Fruit in it, if you like it ſweet, and make a Caudle for it as above. You may leave the Chickens whole if you pleaſe.

To make a Calf's Foot Pye.

BOIL your Feet and mince them with a little Beef or Mutton Sewet, and ſome Apples ſhred ſmall, a little Cinnamon and Mace pounded, ſome Currants well waſhed and picked; put them all in a Diſh with Puff Paſte over them, three Quarters of an Hour bakes them: Then have a Caudle of Sherry, Nutmeg and Sugar, thickened with Eggs; the Oven muſt be no hotter than will bake the Paſte. You may make a Chadren Pye the ſame Way. Put a Gill of Brandy in it.

To make an Eel Pye.

CUT off the Head and Fins, and cut them two Inches long; ſeaſon them with black and *Jamaica* Pepper, Cloves and Salt. Put them in your Diſh, with ſome Butter and Crumbs of Bread, a little white Wine and Lemon Juice, and Gravy or Water, Half a Mutchkin of either. Cover it with Puff Paſte.

To

To make a Goose Pye.

BONE and season it with Pepper and Salt: If your Goose be very fat, bone a Turky, or a Pair of Fowls, and put in with it. You may either raise it or put it in a Dish: It is to be eat cold. It takes a great while to bake it.

To make a Trout Pye.

CUT off the Fins and Heads, season them with black and *Jamaica* Pepper, Mace and Salt, put some Butter in the Bottom of your Dish, then your Trouts; put Gravy and a little Claret in it: Cover it with Puff Paste. When the Paste is baked they are e-nough. They are good hot or cold. You may bake Carp or Pike the same Way.

To make a Mutton Steak Pye.

CUT a Neck of Mutton in single Bones; season it with black and *Jamaica* Pepper, and Salt, lay them in your Dish with Artichoke Bottoms if you have them, put Gravy or Water in the Dish, and a little chopped Shalot. You may make a Beef Steak Pye the same Way. Put some Oisters in it if you please, and hard Yolks of Eggs.

To make a Lobster or Shrimp Pye.

BOIL your Lobsters and Shrimps, take off the Shells, cut the Lobsters in large Pieces, the Shrimps whole. Put Butter in the Bottom of your Dish; sea-son them with Pepper, Mace, Salt and Nutmeg. Put a little Gravy, Oister Liquor, white Wine, and the Juice of a Lemon in it. You may put both in the Pye if you please. Put Puff Paste on it. A very little bakes it.

To make an Oister Pye.

GET the largest Oisters you can, wash them clean in their own Liquor, and give them a Blanch;

get

get alſo half a Dozen Sweet-breads, and cut them in
Pieces, put Gravy and Butter in the Diſh; then lay a Lair
of each, till your Pye is full, and a Lair of Forc'd-meat
Balls ; ſeaſon it with Pepper, Salt and Cloves ; put a
little Oiſter Liquor in it, and ſome Lemon Juice. When
baked put in a Caudle of Sherry, the Grate of a Nutmeg, thickened with the Yolks of two Eggs. You may
put the Yolks of hard Eggs in it if you like them, and
Artichoke Bottoms, or Truffles and Morels.

To make a Skirret Pye.

BOIL and peel your Skirrets, put them in the
Diſh, with Butter on the Bottom of it, and a few Crumbs
of Bread ; cover them almoſt with Cream, Nutmeg and
Mace pounded; ſweeten it with Sugar, cover it with
Puff Paſte : When it comes out of the Oven, pour in
a Caudel made of white Wine, Sugar, and the Grate of
a Nutmeg, thickened with the Yolks of two Eggs.

To make minc'd Pies.

BOIL a large Ox Tongue, blanch it, and chop it
ſmall, put double the Quantity of Beef Sewet as you
have of Tongue, and the double of Fruit, Currants
waſhed and picked clean, the Raiſins ſton'd and minc'd,
your Sewet minc'd very fine, and half a Dozen Apples minc'd; ſeaſon it with Cloves, Mace, Nutmeg,
Lemon-peel, Cinnamon, and a little Sugar and Salt :
Put half a Mutchkin of Brandy in it : When you put
it in your Pan, put Puff Paſte over and under it : You
may put candied Citron, Lemon, and Orange-peel,
if you pleaſe.

To make an Apple Pye.

PARE and quarter your Apples, take out the
Cores, put Sugar, beat Cinnamon, and the Grate of
a Lemon in it, and the Bigneſs of an Egg of Butter :
if you pleaſe you may put Marmalade of Orange, or
Quince in it ; Cover it with Puff Paſte. A Pear Pye

L   is

is made the same Way, but put the Juice of a Lemon in it; and if your Apples are dry, put Lemon Juice in it: When either is cold, you may pour Cream over them, if you please.

To make a Beef Steak Pye.

CUT a very tender fat Piece of Beef in thin Slices, beat it with the Rolling-pin, season it with Pepper, Salt, and Cloves, strew it with a little chopped Shalot, fill your Dish, and cover it with Puff Paste: when it is baked, put in a little Gravy: You may put Oisters in the Pye, if you please, and if you do, put in with your Gravy a Glass of white Wine. Make a Mutton chopp'd Pye the same Way: You may put in it Forc'd-meat, Truffles, Morels, and Artichoke Bottoms, but put them between the Lairs of the Steaks.

To make a Goose-berry Pye.

IF your Goose-berries are very young, put them in a Stew-pan, and stove them with Sugar; when cold, put them in your Dish, and nick the Paste that covers them. When the Paste is baked, they are enough: You may send them to the Table as they are, or cream them. If you cream them, cut off the Lid, and pour it on them: If it is thin, boil it, and thicken it with the Yolks of two Eggs, and sweeten it to your Taste, but take Care it is not curdled: When it is cold, pour it on, cut the Lid in Pieces, and stick it round the Pye.

To make a Hare Pye.

CUT your Hare in Pieces, break the Bones, and season it to your Taste with Pepper, Salt, Cloves, and Mace; lay it in your Dish with Slices of Butter and Lemon-juice: Cover it with Puff Paste.

To make a Gibblet Pye.

WHEN your Gibblets are well scalded and blanched, break the Bones, and season them with Pepper, Salt, Cloves,

Cloves, and Mace ; put them to ſtew in as much Water as will cover them ; ſet them on a ſlow Fire, and when they are tender ſet them to cool : If you can get the Blood, make a Pudding in the Skin of the Neck thus : Strain the Blood, and put in it a little Sewet ſhred ſmall, ſome Crumbs of Bread, a Gill of Cream, Pepper, Salt, Nutmeg, a little ſweet Herbs ſhred ſmall, and an Onion ; lay the Pudding in the Middle of the Diſh, and the Gibblets round it; pour the Broth they were boiled in over them ; let them be well ſeaſoned : Cover the Diſh with Puff Paſte.

To make a Lark Pye, or any ſmall Birds.

T A K E the Larks and ſeaſon them with Pepper, Salt, and Mace; ſtuff them with Forc'd-meat, and lay them in the Diſh with Puff Paſte about the Diſh, the Yolks of hard Eggs, Artichoke Bottoms, and a Lair of Forc'd-meat ; put ſome Butter over them, and cover it with Puff Paſte : When baked make a Caudle of Gravy, a Glaſs of white Wine, a little Bit of Butter worked in Flour, and the Grate of a Nutmeg ; boil it and keep it ſtirring till the Rawneſs is off the Flour ; then pour it in the Pye ; then ſhake the Pye, and ſend it up hot : You may make it without Forc'd-meat, or Artichoke Bottoms the ſame Way.

To make a Muir-fowl or Partridge Pye.

S E A S O N them with Pepper, Salt, Cloves, and Mace, very well; take Cabbage Lettice that is whole, and blanch them ; lay one between every Fowl ; chop a little Shalot, and ſtrew it on the Lettice, with a little of the Seaſoning, as before : Cover the Diſh with Puff Paſte, cut it in the prettieſt Faſhion you can : When it is baked make a Sauce of two Gills of Claret, a little Gravy, an Anchovy, and a little Nutmeg ; pour it in the Pye and ſhake it, ſo ſend it up hot.

A

A Partridge Pye.

TAKE your Partridges and feafon them with Pepper, Salt, Cloves, and Mace; then take fix Cabbage Lettice; boil them four Minutes, fqueeze the Water well from them; put Puff Pafte in the Difh, and lay in the Partridges, with a Lettice between every one, and Saufages: Firft fry them a little, and put in a Glafs of white Wine, and a Piece of Butter; cover it with a thick Pafte; bake it two Hours. For the Sauce, have Gravy well feafoned; put it in the Top of the Pye, with a Funnel, and fhake the Pye: You may put in Claret in ftead of white Wine, if you pleafe.

To make a Pye of Mutton and Potatoes.

TAKE a Breaft of Mutton, and cut it in Steaks; feafon it with Pepper and Salt; lay a Lair of Mutton and a Lair of Potatoes, fcraped and fliced, then a Lair of fliced Onions, fo go on till you fill the Difh; feafon them between every Lair; cover it with Puff Pafte two Hours; bake it; put a Piece of fweet Butter in it, and Gravy, when it comes out of the Oven.

To make a Pye of Kernels and Artichokes.

BLANCH the Kernels, and boil the Artichoke Bottoms; boil Eggs hard, take out the Yolks; put Butter in the Bottom of the Difh, then the Kernels; then a Lair of Artichoke Bottoms, and a Lair of the Yolks of Eggs: So fill the Difh in Lairs; feafon them with Pepper, Salt, Cloves, Mace, and Lemon-peel; put Butter over them; then cover it with Puff Pafte; have ready a Ragoo of Truffles, Morels, Gravy, with a little brown'd Butter and Flour, a Glafs of white Wine, an Onion ftuffed with Cloves, and the Rind of a Lemon; boil them, then cut off the Top of the Pye, and pour your Ragoo on it; put on the Top again, and fend it up hot.

To make an *Apple Pye with Potatoes.*

PEEL and flice the Apples, half boil the Potatoes, pare and flice them in Lairs in the Diſh with Sugar, Cinnamon, grated Lemon-peel, and a Piece of Butter. You may put Currants, Raiſins, and candied Orange ; cover the Pye and bake it. Send it up hot.

To make an *Apple Pye with Cheſnuts and Almonds.*

Pare and quarter the Apples, ſcald the Cheſnuts, and take off the Skin, blanch the Almonds ; lay them in Lairs in the Diſh : Put in candied Orange and Lemonpeel, and fine Sugar ; put in a Bit of Butter : When the Apples are full ripe, put in the Juice of a Lemon. Cover it with Puff Paſte : It is to be eaten either hot or cold. If cold, cream it.

To make a *white Fricaſey of Lamb.*

CUT a Neck and Breaſt of Lamb in middling ſmall Pieces, put them in hot Water to blanch, then put them in cold Water ; when they are blanch'd put them in a cloſs cover'd Stew-pan, with a Mutchkin of Water, a Bunch of ſweet Herbs, a whole Onion ſtuffed with Cloves, the Rind of a Lemon, and a Blade of Mace : Lt them ſtew on a gentle Fire till the Meat is enough ; then put in a good Piece of Butter work'd in Flour, and a Gill of thick Cream, keep it ſtirring all the while it is on the Fire. After you put in the Butter, when the Rawneſs is off the Flour, put in a Glaſs of Sherry, and the Squeeze of a Lemon. Don't make it too ſour, or put it on the Fire after ; ſalt it to your Taſte : Take out the Onion and Herbs, ſo ſerve it up. Garniſh it with Lemons and Muſhrooms.

To make a *white Fricaſey of Muſhrooms.*

WASH the little white Muſhrooms in Milk and Water, put them down to boil in a little Water and a Blade of Mace, a little white Pepper, with a whole Shalot. When they are tender, put to them a little
Cream,

Cream, and a Bit of Butter worked in Flour. When you put them down to boil, put but a very little Water in it, and let them be very cloſs covered : Juſt as you are ſending them up, put a little white Wine and a very little Lemon Juice, keeping it ſtirring all the Time.

To fricaſey Tripes or Cow-heels.

LET them lye in Souſe till they are a little ſour, then take them out and dry them with a Cloth ; make a Batter of Eggs and Flour and dip them in it, put them in your Pan to fry when the Liquor is boiling hot. The Sauce for them is Butter and Muſtard.

To make a white Fricaſey of Chickens.

CUT your Chickens in Quarters, then cut every Quarter in two, put them in a Pan with Water to co-ver them, and give them a Boil or two; then put them in cold Water, take off the Skin and blanch them ; put them in a cloſs covered Pan with Muſh-rooms, and Truffles with them, a Piece of Butter, a little Flour, a little Salt, a Blade of Mace, a whole O-nion ſtuffed with Cloves, a whole Anchovy, and the Rind of a Lemon ; ſhake the Pan till the Flour mixes, put them on a flow Fire. When they are boil'd enough put in a Gill of thick ſweet Cream, and juſt as you are going to ſend it up put in a little white Wine, and a very little Juice of Lemons. You may beat the Yolks of two Eggs, and mix them with the Sauce to thicken it, but take great Care not to curdle them. You may make it without Muſhrooms, or Truffles, if you pleaſe.

To make a Fricaſey of Rabbets.

CUT them in Quarters and blanch them as above, then boil them ; when they are enough throw off the Water, and put to them ſome white Gravy, Anchovy, an Onion ſtuffed with Cloves, Pepper, Salt, Mace, and the Rind of a Lemon, a good Piece of Butter work'd in Flour, and a Bunch of ſweet Herbs. Let them boil

a

a good while, then put in a little good Cream, and juſt as you are going to diſh it, put in a little Sherry, and a very little Lemon Juice.

To make a brown Fricaſey of Chickens or Rabbets.

BROWN your Butter and Flour, then put in Gravy, ſhake it that it does not go to Lumps ; put in your Meat with Pepper, Cloves, and *Jamaica* Pepper, an Onion and Lemon-peel, put a little Ketchup and the Juice of a Lemon ; ſalt it to your Taſte. Garniſh them with Lemon.

To fricaſey Kernels and Oiſters.

BLANCH the Kernels, cut them in Dice, and ſcald the Oiſters, pick and waſh them clean in their own Liquor, then put them both in a Stew-pan, with a little white Gravy, and ſome of the Oiſter Liquor, ſtrained very clear ; an Onion ſtuffed with Cloves, Mace and Lemon-peel, with a Piece of Butter rolled in Flour, and a Gill of Cream : Give them eight or ten Boils, then ſhake in a little white Wine and Lemon Juice, but don't put it on the Fire. After the Wine and Juice goes in, take out the Lemon-peel and Onion, then ſerve it up.

A white Fricaſey of Cows Palates.

BOIL, blanch and ſkin them, then cut them in Shaves the croſs Way, as broad as your Finger, put them in a Stew-pan with Muſhrooms, Truffles, white Gravy, three whole Shalots, white Pepper, two Anchovies, Salt and Mace, a Piece of Butter, a little Flour, and a Gill of Cream ; put them on a ſlow Fire, and when they are very tender, take them off, and put in a Glaſs of white Wine, and Lemon Juice : Don't put them on the Fire after. Put Sippets in the Diſh under them.

A

A white Fricasey of Lambs Stones, Kernels, and Cocks Combs.

BLANCH and boil the Cocks Combs till they are tender, blanch the Kernels, nick the Skin of the Lambs Stones, and turn them out of the Skins ; then blanch them, and put them all in a Pan with Veal Gravy, whole white Pepper, Mace, Salt, and a whole Onion ; stew them on a slow Fire, then put in a little thick Cream, the Grate of a Lemon, and a Bit of sweet Butter ; take it up, and mix it with the Yolks of two Eggs well beaten ; then put it on the Fire till it is scalding hot ; then put in a little white Wine, and send it away.

A white Fricasey of Oisters.

SCALD them, and wash them in their own Liquor, then put them in a Pan with some white Gravy, and some of their own Liquor, Cream, white Pepper, Mace and Salt, a good Piece of Butter rolled in Flour, a whole Onion, and the Rind of a Lemon : Give them a Boil or two, then dish them on Sippets: You may make a white Fricasey of Cockles or Scollops the same Way.

To fry Chickens, Lamb, or Veal.

CUT the Chickens in Quarters, and your Lamb or Veal in small Joints, put them to stew in as much Water as will cover them ; set them on a slow Fire, in a closs covered Pan : When they are almost enough, put in a good Handful of Parsley, and a few green Onions ; then, a little before you take them up, put in four or five Eggs, with pounded Pepper, Salt and Mace, then dish them up.

A white Fricasey of Skirrets or Parsnips.

BOIL, blanch and skin them, then put them in a Pan, with as much Milk as will cover them, with a good Piece of Butter, white Pepper, Mace pounded, and two whole Onions : Boil them on a slow Fire, then

then thicken them with the Yolks of two or three Eggs. The Parſnips and Skirrets muſt be cut an Inch long. Don't let them boil after you put in the Eggs: You may do Potatoes the ſame Way: Take out the Onions, and ſerve them up.

To ſtew Chickens with Peaſe and Lettices.

TAKE two Chopins of young Peaſe, and three Cabbage Lettices; ſlice the Lettice, and put the Peaſe in a Sauce-pan, with a Mutchkin of good white Gravy, two Chickens truſſed for boiling; rub the Chickens with a Bit of Butter, and put a Piece of Butter in with the Peaſe; put in a Faggot of ſweet Herbs, if you like it; ſeaſon it with Pepper and Salt; put your Chickens in the Middle of your Diſh, and pour the Peaſe over them: You may ſtove Lamb or Ducks the ſame Way.

Boiled Ducks and Onions.

BOIL your Ducks very white, then boil twelve Onions very tender, ſhifting the Water to take off the Taſte; chop them, and draw eight Ounces of Butter, with two Gills of Cream; when it boils, ſtir in the Onions, and a little Salt, lay your Ducks in the Diſh, and pour your Onions over them. Rabbets are done the ſame Way.

To boil a Turkey or Fowls with Sellery.

BOIL your Turkey or Fowls in a Pot of boiling Water, rub Butter and Flour on the Breaſts, and tye them up in a Cloth. You may ſtuff where their Crops were, thus: Two Handfuls of Crumbs of Bread, one of Sewet ſhred ſmall, Lemon peel, Parſley, Thyme, ſweet Marjoram, and a little Onion, all ſhred ſmall; ſeaſon it with Pepper, Salt and Nutmeg; wet it with an Egg, and work it together, ſo ſtuff them full: Cut the Sellery about half an Inch long, waſh it clean, and boil it tender; ſtrain it, and put it in as much white Gravy as you want Sauce, with a

M   good

good Piece of Butter work'd in Flour; feafon it with an Onion, ftuffed with Cloves, Pepper, Salt, Mace, Lemon-peel and Nutmeg; boil it well, then take out the Onion and Lemon-peel, and put in a little white Wine and the Juice of half a Lemon : Don't make it too four ; you may boil Fowls or Turkies, with Oifter Sauce to the Meat.

Or this Sauce for Hens or Chickens.

BOIL the Liver, and two Eggs hard, chop them fmall, mince Parfley and Lemon-peel; then put them all into beat Butter, with Gravy in it, and a little Lemon Juice.

To roaft a Pig.

WIPE it very dry, and put in the Belly a Cruft of Bread, few it up, and fpit it, drudge it very well with Flour, let it have a very good quick Fire, and let it be very faft turned : When you think it is done, wipe off the Flour, and rub it with a Bit of Butter ; it will take an Hour and a Quarter to roaft : If large, cut off the Head, and put the Jaws and Ears round the Difh ; take out the Brains, and chop them fmall; put them in a little melted Butter and Gravy, Pepper, Salt, a little Sage chopped very fmall, and an Egg boiled and chopped fmall ; pour it about the Pig; you may cut it down the Back, or fend it whole, but take out the Bread before you fend it to Table.

To make a white Fricafey Sauce for boiled Fowls, Chickens or Turkeys.

GET white Broth, boil in it the Rind of a Lemon, an Onion ftuffed with Cloves, Mace, whole Pepper and Salt : When it is boiled a while, put in a Gill of Cream and the Yolks of two Eggs beat well together : Keep it ftirring one Way on the Fire : Put a Piece of Butter in it, and juft as it is going to Table, put the Juice of a Lemon and a little white Wine in

it:

it: Don't make it four: Take out the Onion and Lemon-peel.

To make a *Mutton Haricot.*

TAKE a Neck or Loin of Mutton, cut them in Steaks, fry them a light brown, but not too much: Put to them some good Broth, a Faggot of sweet Herbs, some diced Carots and Turnips fried, and three small Cabbage Lettices; stew all well together, with six small Onions, if you like them; season it with Pepper, Salt and Cloves; skim off all the Fat, and dish it up; there is not to be too much Broth in the Dish.

To roast *Chickens in Paste.*

TRUSS them as for boiling, stuff them with Forc'd-meat, and make as much Puff Paste as will cover them, then wrap it about the Chickens, with buttered Papers over it, tied at each End: It will take an Hour to roast them: You may put a Ragoo of Truffles and Morels, or Gravy and Mushrooms under them, but take off the Papers. You may do Ducks the same Way.

Chickens and Sellery.

BOIL them white, and make the Sauce thus: Boil the white Ends of Sellery, cut it in Pieces an Inch long, strain it, and put it into beat Butter, with Mushroom and Oister Liquor: Then pour it boiling hot over your Chickens.

Chickens farced with Oisters.

LARD them, then mince Parsley, Truffles, Onions, Mushrooms and Oisters; season it with Pepper, Salt and Mace; put to it the Yolk of an Egg, and a Piece of Butter; put all this in the Chickens Bellies, then tye both Ends of them, and roast them; put a Ragoo of Oisters about them: You may do Howtoudies, or any white Fowl, the same Way.

Chickens

Chickens with Gravy forc'd.

TAKE Sweet-breads, Mushrooms, Anchovies, Marrow or Butter, Lemon-peel and Chives, all cut small; mix them with Crumbs of Bread, Pepper, Salt and Nutmeg; wet them with an Egg, then raise up the Skin of the Breasts of your Fowls, stuff it, and stitch it up again, and lard them: You may fill their Bellies with Oisters, and roast them: Put Gravy under them in the Dish: You may do Pheasants, Turkies, or what Fowl you please, the same Way.

Chickens Royal.

LARD them, and put good Forc'd-meat in their Bellies, and half roast them; then stove them in good Gravy; make a Ragoo of Mushrooms, Morels, Truffles and Cocks Combs; lay the Chickens in the Dish, and pour the Ragoo over them. You may do Pigeons the same Way.

Chickens with Tongues, Colly-flowers and Greens.

BOIL your Chickens in Water and Salt, and your Sheep or Hogs Tongues in another Pot: Skim them, then put the Colly-flowers in the Middle, and a Tongue between every Chicken, and the Greens round them; put melted Butter over them.

To boil Chickens and Asparagus.

BOIL the Chickens white, with Forc'd-meat in their Bellies, cut the Asparagus an Inch long, boil them in Water, then dissolve a little Butter and Salt in Water, with minc'd Parsley; then put in the Asparagus, and boil it better; thicken the Sauce with more Butter, Cream, and a little Flour; season it with white Wine, Nutmeg and Lemon Juice. You may do Sauce for a Fowl the same Way.

To roaſt young Turkies.

PUT in their Bellies Forc'd-meat, made of their Livers, ſcalded Oiſters, green Onions, Parſley, mince them all, Crumbs of Bread, Salt, Nutmeg, and grated Lemon-peel ; mix them all with a Piece of Butter, and a raw Egg : You may either lard them, or roll them in Shaves of Bacon, then paper and roaſt them ; put Gravy in the Diſh with them, and Breadſauce in a Sauce-boat made thus : Boil ſome Bread and Water, with a little white Gravy, an Onion ſtuffed with Cloves, a Blade of Mace, and a little Salt ; boil it ſmooth ; put in it a good Lump of Butter, then give it a Boil ; take out the Onion before you ſend it to Table. You may roaſt Chickens the ſame Way.

Ducklings à la Mode.

CUT them in Quarters ; you may lard the Legs, and brown them off ; then ſtove them in half a Mutchkin of Claret, the ſame of Gravy, two Shalots, one Anchovy, Pepper and Salt ; ſtove them tender, ſkim off the Fat, ſqueeze in a Lemon, ſo ſerve it up hot.

Stov'd Ducks the Dutch *Way.*

TRUSS two Ducks, and lard one ; ſeaſon with Pepper and Salt, and fill the Bellies with ſmall Onions ; lay in the Bottom of the Stew-pan half a Pound of Butter ; then put in the Ducks, and cover them with ſliced Onions : Stove this two Hours gently, keeping it covered all the while ; when the Ducks are tender, diſh them, ſhaking a little Vinegar in them.

To dreſs a Wild-duck with Lemon Juice.

HALF roaſt the Duck, and carve it ; on the Breaſt put Salt, Pepper, and the Juice of a Lemon in every Inciſion ; lay it on the Breaſt in a Stew-pan, with a very little Gravy ; then turn it and diſh it hot in its own Gravy, a Glaſs of Claret, and two Shalots ſhred ſmall.

To

To ftew Ducks, wild or tame.

HALF roaft them, then put them in a Stew-pan with two Gills of Claret, and four of Gravy, Pepper, Salt, Shalots, or Rockambole; cover them clofe: You may ftuff the Ducks with Forc'd-meat, and make a Ragoo of Sheeps Tongues, Truffles, and Morels. Serve them up hot with the Breaft up, and the Sauce that they were ftewed in about them, with all the Ingredients.

To drefs Ducks with Oifters.

T A K E Ducks, wild or tame, trufs them; make a Ragoo of Sweet-breads, Oifters, Mufhrooms, Truffles, Chives, Parfley, Crumbs of Bread, Lemon-peel, Pepper, Salt, and Eggs; ftuff the Ducks with it, and ftew them in a clofs covered Pan, with Gravy, Claret, browned Butter and Flour, Pepper, Salt, Shalot, or Onions; put Oifters fried in Butter about them in the Difh, with the Liquor they are ftewed in. You do Teal or Widgeon the fame Way.

To roaft a green Goofe.

S T U F F it with Bread Forc'd-meat; roaft it crifp, and let the Sauce be a little Spinage Juice, fcalded Goosberries, a Bit of Butter, Flour, Sugar, or Gravy, and green Onions fhred fmall. You may give young Ducks the fame Sauce.

To drefs a Goofe with Onions or Cabbage.

S A L T it for a Week, then boil it an Hour; make the Sauce of boil'd Onions, chopped fmall, mixed with melted Butter; or, you may boil Cabbage, and chop and ftew them in Butter, Pepper, and Salt; difh the Goofe, and put the Onions or Cabbage about it, with fried Saufages.

To foufe a Goofe.

B O N E your Goofe, cut the Flefh fquare; lay it a fteeping in white Wine, Salt, Pepper, Cloves, and
Mace;

Mace, for twelve Hours ; then take it out, and lay Pieces of Anchovies over it; and Ham minced small; then roll it up hard, and boil it in boiling Water, and the Wine it was steeped in, with Salt, Pepper, and Mace ; boil it pretty well, then put it in a Can, and when you are going to serve it up, cut it in two, and lay over it green Parsley.

To dry a Goose.

G E T a fat Goose, and salt it well with a Handful of common Salt, a quarter of an Ounce of Salt-petre, a quarter of a Pound of coarse Sugar ; mix all together, and rub the Goose very well ; let it lye in this Pickle a Fortnight, turning and rubbing it every Day; then roll it in Brawn, then hang it to dry for a Week; it will keep three Months in a dry Place : It eats well cold, or hot, but boil it well in a large Pot full of Water : If eaten hot, send Cabbage, or Greens, about it.

To boil a Goose.

P U T it in a Pot with Water, or Broth ; let it boil, and skim it clean; put in a little Salt, three sliced Onions, a few Cloves, Mace, Raisins, Currants, and Crumbs of Bread ; stew it on a slow Fire, dish it on Sippets ; put a little white Wine in it, and put Slices of Lemon, and Barberries over it.

To boil the Gibblets.

B L A N C H them, then boil them in Water, Salt, and Mace ; serve them up on Sippets, with melted Butter, and scalded Grapes.

To roast a Goose.

S T U F F it with boiled Potatoes, and Onions, chopped small, seasoned with Pepper and Salt ; or, you may stuff it with Apples, or roast it without any Stuffing; but season it high, and roast it an Hour and
a Quarter

a Quarter. Put Gravy in the Difh, and Apple Sauce in a Bowl.

To roaft Partridges.

A S they are roafting, bafte them well and drudge them; put Gravy in the Difh under them, and make a Sauce thus : Boil fome thin Slices of fine ftale Bread in as much Water as will make it thick and fmooth, with whole Pepper, Mace, and an Onion ftuffed with Cloves : When it is fmooth, put in a good Piece of Butter; ftir it and give it a Boil or two, put in a little Salt, fo fend it in a Sauce-boat with your Partridges. You may lard them, if you pleafe.

To drefs Partridges à la Braife.

T R U S S their Legs into their Bodies ; give them a Scald, then lard them ; feafon with Pepper, Salt, Cloves, and Mace, fweet Herbs, Chives, and Parfley, all fhred ; take a Stew-pan with a Cover, lay Slices of Bacon in it, then thin Slices of Beef over them, with Slices of Carots and Onions, Parfley, fweet Herbs, Pepper, Cloves, and Mace ; then lay in the Partridges on their Breafts, and lay over them Slices of Beef, then Slices of Bacon ; cover the Stew-pan, and let them ftew with Fire over and under them ; make a Ragoo of Cocks Combs, Livers of fat Fowls, Sweet-breads, Truffles, Mufhrooms, Artichoke Bottoms, and Afparagus Tops, according to the Seafon ; when your Partridges are ftewed enough, take them up, drain them and difh them with the Ragoo about them ; or, you may fend them up with a Ragoo of Cucumbers, made thus : Pare and flice them, and fome Shalots ; put them between two Plates, with a little Pepper and Salt, for two Minutes ; then drain off the Liquor that comes from them ; then put them in a clofs covered Pan with a Piece of Butter, and let them ftew on a flow Fire till they are foft ; then fhake in a little Flour and Gravy, keeping them ftiring
all

all the while. Put in a chopped Anchovy, and a Spoonful of Ketchup.

Partridges with Oifters.

THEY muft be very frefh, draw them; mince their Livers, and fome fcalded Oifters, the Yolks of hard Eggs, Parfley, fweet Herbs, and Shalots, fhred fmall; Pepper, Salt, and Cloves; work them in a Piece of Butter, and ftuff your Partridges with it; roll them up in Slices of Bacon, and Paper, fpit them; then get fome more Oifters, blanch and pick them; put them in fome of their own Liquor, a little good Gravy, a Bit of Butter roll'd in Flour, a Glafs of white Wine, the Juice of half a Lemon with the Peel; Shalots cut fmall, pounded Mace, Pepper, and Salt; boil it, and difh your Partridges, and pour it round them.

To hafh Partridges.

HALF roaft your Partridges, cut them in Quarters, and joint the Breaft and Rump afunder; put them in a Stew-pan, with fome good Gravy, the Rind of a Lemon, an Onion ftuffed with Cloves, Pepper, Salt, Mace, Truffles, and Morels; a Piece of Butter roll'd in Flour, a Glafs of white Wine, and fome Lemon Juice; let them all ftew on the Fire a Quarter of an Hour, then difh them.

To roaft Pheafants.

BLANCH and lard them with Bacon, then roll them in buttered Papers; roaft them at a flow Fire: When almoft done, take off the Papers to let them have a Colour, and difh them with good Gravy; fend the fame Bread-fauce as for Partridges, in a Sauceboat with them. You may fend either Oifters or Sellery Sauce with them.

To boil Pheafants, Partridges, Chickens, or Quails.

PUT them in a Stew-pan with as much Water as will cover them, with Mace, Nutmeg, Cloves, a Piece

N   of

of Butter, and fome Crumbs of Bread; Lemon-peel,
Onions, and white Wine; let them all ftew on a flow
Fire till enough; then take out the Lemon-peel and
Onion; turn your Fowl very often; put in the Yolks
of hard Eggs, chopped very fine with a little more
Butter; give it a Boil, then difh them all up. Put
in the Juice of a Lemon.

A Pupton of Pigeons

TAKE favoury Forc'd-meat rolled out like Pafte,
in a butter'd Difh; lay Pigeons over it, then Sweet-
breads and Mufhrooms, then another Roll of Forc'd-
meat; cover it and bake it: When enough, turn it on
another Difh, and your Gravy over it. Send it up hot.

Pigeons boiled with Rice.

STUFF their Bellies with chopped Parfley, Pepper and Salt rolled in a Bit of Butter; put them into
a Chopin of Broth, with a little beat Mace, a Bunch
of fweet Herbs, and an Onion; cover them clofs, and
let them ftew for a Quarter of an Hour; then take
out the Onion and fweet Herbs, and take a good Piece
of Butter rolled in Flour, put it in and keep it ftirring
till the Butter is diffolved; then have ready half a
Pound of Rice boiled tender, put it to the Pigeons,
with Salt and Nutmeg, give them a Scald; then put
the Pigeons in the Difh, and pour the Rice over them.

To ftew Pigeons.

STUFF them with Forc'd-meat, then half roaft
them; then put them in a Stew-pan, with a Chopin
of Gravy, a little white Wine, or Claret, Pepper, Cloves,
Salt, Mace, Lemon-peel, pickled Mufhrooms, and Oifters fcalded and picked, with fome of their Liquor and
a fcored Onion; let them ftew till they are done; thicken the Sauce with Butter and Flour; take out the
Onion, and fend it up hot. You may do Ducks the fame
Way.

To fry Pigeons.

BLANCH them and cut them in two, beat them flat, and put them in a Stew-pan, with Onions, Parsley, Pepper, Salt, Cloves, a Piece of Butter, a Ladleful of Broth, or the Liquor they were in; let all these stew a little while, take them out and dip them in Batter made of Eggs and Flour, then fry them; dish them, and pour over them the Liquor they were stewed in, but strain it first: Put the Juice of a Lemon in it.

To broil Pigeons.

YOU may either broil them whole, or slit them down the Back; salt and pepper them; lay them on the Brander, broil them gently, and turn them often; make the Sauce of Butter, their Livers boiled and chopped with Parsley and Shalot: You may put a little red Wine in it and Lemon Juice. If you do them whole, put Forc'd-meat in them.

To boil Pigeons.

PUT them in warm Water to blanch, then boil them in Salt and Water fifteen Minutes; boil a Piece of Bacon, and take off the Skin; then put Crumbs of Bread on it, and lay it before the Fire; boil Spinage, Greens, or Colly-flowers; put the Bacon in the Dish, then the Pigeons, and the Garden things about it. You may dress any tame Fowl the same Way: Don't put Salts in the Collyflowers when you boil them.

To do Pigeons à la Daube.

STUFF their Bellies with Forc'd-meat made thus: Take a Pound of Veal, and a Pound of Beef Sewet; beat it in a Mortar, and season it with Pepper, Salt, and Nutmeg; put as much Crumbs of Bread as Sewet; brown them in clarified Butter, then shake in a little Flour, and put in it some good Gravy, and Onion stuffed with Cloves, Pepper, Salt, Mace, and Lemon-peel;

peel ; let them ſtew a while : Put a Ragoo of any
Sort about them, or the Liquor they are ſtewed in.

Pigeons ſtoved with Cabbage Lettice.

S T U F them as before ; ſeaſon them with Pepper, Salt, and Cloves ; brown them with Butter, then
put them to ſtove with Cabbage Lettice cut in Quarters,
and two green Onions, a little Gravy, a Glaſs of Wine,
and ſome Lemon Juice ; let them all ſtew on a ſlow
Fire, then diſh them. Put Forc'd-meat Balls and Lemon about them.

Pigeons diſguiſed.

S E A S O N them with Pepper and Salt ; make Puff
Paſte, and roll each Pidgeon in Paſte ; tye them in a
Cloth ; boil them in a good Deal of Water for an Hour ;
untye them carefully that they don't break ; diſh them
and pour Gravy about them. So ſerve them up hot.

A ſtewed Pheaſant.

S T E W it in white Gravy, and when it is almoſt
enough, put in it Salt, Pepper and Mace, then take
boiled Artichoke Bottoms, Cheſnuts roaſted and ſkin-
ned, and put them in with a good Piece of Butter
rolled in Flour, a Glaſs of white Wine and Lemon
Juice : Let them ſtew a while, then diſh your Pheaſant and Sauce ; put Forc'd-meat Balls or Sauſages a-
bout it : A good Fowl will do as well, but truſs it
with the Head on like a Pheaſant.

To roaſt Growſe, or what is called Moor-fowl.

T W O makes a Diſh ; lard one of them, then ſpit
and roaſt them well ; for the Sauce, take good brown
Gravy, Crumbs of Bread browned in a Pan, with a
very little Bit of Butter, a Gill of Claret, a ſhred Shalot,
Pepper and Salt.

To roaſt Snipes or Woodcocks.

DON'T draw them, ſlit them a-croſs, toaſt ſome Bread, and lay it in a Plate under them, that the Trale may drop in it : When roaſted well, lay them on the toaſted Bread, and pour beat Butter with Gravy over them : Send them up hot.

To ſtew Larks, or any other ſmall Birds.

TOSS them in a Stew-pan with ſome Butter, an Onion ſtuck with Cloves, ſome Muſhrooms, and the Livers of the Birds, with a little Gravy : Let them ſtew on a ſlow Fire ; then beat two Eggs, with ſome ſhred Parſley ; mix it by Degrees with the Sauce ; put in ſome Salt and the Grate of a Lemon. Juſt as it is going to be diſhed, put in a little Lemon Juice.

To roaſt Larks.

PUT them on a Skewer, tye them to the Spit, baſte them and drudge them with Crumbs of Bread and Salt ; then have Crumbs of Bread, and lay it in the Diſh with them.

To roaſt Curlews.

WHEN they are gutted, thruſt them like a Woodcock, ſeaſon them with Pepper and Salt : You may put Forc'd-meat in them, roaſt them well, baſte and drudge them, put Gravy, Claret and Orange Juice in the Diſh under them.

To roaſt Quails.

STUFF their Bellies with Crumbs of Bread, chopped Parſley, Shalot, Oiſters, and ſweet Marjoram ; put a Piece of Butter in it, and a raw Egg, all work'd up together ; then ſpit and roaſt them : When done, put Gravy, Anchovy, and the Juice of a Lemon in the Diſh under them.

To

To roaſt Plovers.

PUT into their Bellies, Pepper, Salt, chopped Anchovies and Shalots : Don't roaſt them too much, and put good Gravy under them in the Diſh.

To ſtew Plovers.

SEASON them with Pepper, Salt and Cloves, put them in a Stew-pan with Gravy and Shalots ; put them on a ſlow Fire ; when they are half done, ſkim off all the Fat, and ſtrain it, then put into it two Gills of Claret, and an Onion ſtuffed with Cloves ; then ſtove them till they are done ; diſh them, and pour the Sauce over them. You may do wild Ducks, Teals or Widgeons the ſame Way. Take out the Onion.

A jugged Hare.

CUT it in Pieces, lard the Quarters with Bacon, put it in a Can that has a very narrow Mouth, with whole Pepper, Cloves and Mace : Cover the Can cloſs, that the Steam cannot come out ; then put it in a Pot of Water, and let it boil in it three Hours, ſtill filling the Pot with Water up to the Can's Neck, but not as high as it can get into it. You may put Onions and a Faggot of ſweet Herbs in it, if you pleaſe ; then put it in the Diſh, ſalt it to your Taſte, and take out the Herbs and Onions.

To roaſt a Hare.

LARD the Hare, and put a Stuffing in the Belly, with Crumbs of Bread, the Heart, Beef Sewet and the Liver chopped ſmall, Parſley, Onion and ſweet Herbs ſhred fine ; ſeaſon it with Pepper, Salt, Nutmeg, and the Grate of a Lemon ; wet it with an Egg, then ſew it up and ſpit it, and baſte it with Cream till all the Blood is ſok'd out : Let it dry, then flour and ſalt it, and baſte it with Butter : For Sauce, you may give it beat Butter, Gravy and Claret Sauce in a Boat.

To

To roaſt a Hare another Way.

LARD the Hare, take grated Bread, Eggs, Currants, Nutmeg, Cinnamon, Sugar, and a little Cream : Make all theſe in a Pudding, ſtirring it in a Pan on the Fire for ſix Minutes ; then put it in the Hare's Belly, ſew it up, ſpit it, roaſt it, and baſte it with Butter. You may give it Claret Sauce and beat Butter.

To roaſt a Hare with the Skin on.

TAKE out the Bowels, wipe the Inſide with a Cloth, put a Pudding in it, of either ſavoury or ſweet, as be-fore ; ſew the Belly up, then looſen all the Skin, and rub Butter all over the Fleſh ; then ſew up the Skin, and roaſt it, baſting it with boiling Water and Salt, till it is half roaſted, then let it dry ; and when it ſmokes, pull it off by Pieces, then baſte it with Butter, and drudge it with Flour or grated Bread. The Sauce is beat Butter, or Gravy and Claret.

To haſh a Hare.

HALF roaſt it, then cut it in Quarters, put it in a Stew-pan, with Pepper, Salt, Cloves, Lemon-peel, whole Onions, a Bunch of ſweet Herbs, and a little Gravy and Claret. You may thicken it a little with brown'd Butter and Flour : Take out the Lemon-peel, ſweet Herbs and Onions.

To mince a Hare.

WHEN there is any Hare left that has been roaſted, mince it ſmall, put it in a Stew-pan, with two Gills of good Gravy, a little Parſley, Lemon-peel, Onions and ſcalded Oiſters, all ſhred ſmall, a Piece of Butter rol-led in Flour, Pepper, Salt and Mace, a Glaſs of white Wine, and a little Lemon Juice : Give it two or three Boils, keeping it ſtirring all the Time, then ſend it up hot ; or you may half roaſt it, and then haſh it the ſame Way.

To

To boil Rabbets.

LET them steep in warm Water a Quarter of an Hour, then put them in a Pot of boiling Water and Salt. Three Quarters of an Hour boils them. For the Sauce, you may boil Onions, chop them, and mix them with a Gill of Cream and a good Piece of Butter; pour it over them boiling hot, and put Salt in it; or you may boil the Livers, chop them with Parsley and Pickles, mix them with a Gill of Gravy, a good Piece of Butter rolled in Flour, and a little white Wine seasoned with Pepper, Salt, Mace and Nutmeg. You may lard them with Bacon if you like it.

Boiled Rabbets with Sausages.

STEW the Rabbets in as much Water as will cover them, with Pepper, Salt, Cloves, Onions and sweet Herbs. When half done, take out the Rabbets, and strain the Broth, then blanch some Lettice and Spinage, and put them and the Rabbets in the Broth, with a Piece of Butter rolled in Flour, some Mushrooms or Truffles, if you have them: Fry Sausages, and when you dish the Rabbets and Sauce, put the Sausages about them. When you roast Rabbets, beat Butter, their own Liver, and Parsley minced small, is the Sauce.

To stew Rabbets the French Way.

CUT them in Quarters, lard them with Bacon, then stew them in strong Gravy, with a little white Wine, Pepper, Salt and Mace, browned Butter and Flour, and the Juice of a Lemon. Send them hot to Table.

To collar Salmon.

TAKE a Side of Salmon, cut a Piece of the Tail, rub the other Piece with Eggs, make a Forc'd-meat of the Tail, chop it small, with a Handful of Oisters that is parboiled, the Yolks of six Eggs boiled hard, and two Anchovies; chop them all small; season it with Pepper, Salt, Mace, Nutmeg, and some grated Bread; work
them

them up with two raw Eggs, and lay it all over the Salmon, but firſt ſeaſon it with all the Spices as above. Roll it up in a Collar, and bind it with broad Tape, and boil it in boiling Water, Salt and Vinegar, for two Hours on a ſlow Fire, then take it out and let it cool, and ſkim all the Fat off the Water it was boiled in ; take off the Bindings of the Collar, and when both is cold, put it in the Water it was boiled in.

To collar Pork.

TAKE a Piece of Pork and bone it, ſtrew it with Salt, Pepper, Cloves, Mace, Parſley, Sage, Thyme and ſweet Marjoram, all ſhred ſmall; then cut Slices off a Leg of Veal, and ſeaſon them as above. Lay them in the Pork, rub them and the Inſide of the Pork with raw Eggs, then roll it up in a Collar very hard, bind it with broad Tapes, and put it in a large Pot of boiling Water. It will take three Hours boiling, then take it out of the Pot, and when it is cold, you may make Uſe of it, and keep it in the ſame Souſe you do Brawn.

To collar a Pig.

CUT off the Head and Feet, and ſlit it down the Belly, take out all the Intrails, bone it, and lay it in Water to ſoke out the Blood, then dry it with a Cloth, ſeaſon it with chopped Sage and Parſley, white Pepper, Salt and Mace, roll it up very hard, and roll a Cloth about it; tye both Ends, put it in a Pot of boiling Water, with a little Salt in it. It will, if large, take an Hour and a Half to boil it: When you take it out of the Pot, hang it up by one End till it is almoſt cold: You may ſend it to Table either whole or in Slices.

To collar a Fore-quarter of Lamb, or a Breaſt of Veal.

BONE them, and ſeaſon them with chopped Parſley and ſweet Herbs, black and *Jamaica* Pepper, Cloves and Salt ; roll them up hard, and bind them with a Cloth tied at both Ends, put them in boiling

O   Water.

Water. The Lamb will take an Hour and three Quarters, but the Veal will take but an Hour and a Half:
Hang them by one End, till almoſt cold, then take
them out of the Cloth.

To collar Cow Heels.

WHEN the Hair is well cleaned off the Feet,
boil them till the Bones come out, then ſeaſon them
with black and *Jamaica* Pepper, and Salt, roll them
up tight, and boil them half an Hour more in their own
Broth; hang them up till almoſt cold, then take them
out of the Cloth.

To collar a Calf's Head.

CUT your Head in two, and waſh and ſoke it in
warm Water, put it to boil, and when the Bones come
out, ſeaſon it with Salt, Cloves, Pepper and Mace; then
ſhread ſweet Marjoram, Thyme and Parſley, and ſtrew
them on it; put the thin Part of one Side to the thick
Part of the other, roll it up, and boil it for an Hour in
its own Broth, then take it out, and hang it up till almoſt cold, then take it out of the Cloth.

To make a very good Collar of a Hog's Head.

WHEN it is clean waſhed, put it down to boil, and
a Set of Cow Heels down with it; when boiled, take
out all the Bones, and ſeaſon them with black and *Jamaica* Pepper, and Salt; cut out the black of the Eye,
put your Feet in the Middle, and roll it up very tight
in a Cloth, boil it in its own Broth an Hour, hang it
up by one End, and when almoſt cold, take it out of
the Cloth. You may collar a Cow's Head the ſame
Way, leaving out the Feet.

To collar Eels.

GET large Eels, cut off the Head and Fins, bone
them, ſeaſon them with black and *Jamaica* Pepper,
Cloves and Salt; roll them up very hard, and put them
down

down to boil in Water, Salt and Vinegar, with a few Bay Leaves : Boil them fo tender, that you may thruft a Straw in them ; take them out, and boil the Liquor better, with whole Spice in it. Let it cool, and fkim off all the Fat ; then put in your Eels in your cold Liquor.

To pot a Cow's Head.

LET it blanch in Water all Night, then put it to boil, and when it is enough, all the Bones will come out ; take out the Black out of the Eyes, and cut it in thin Bits ; feafon them with Pepper, Salt, Cloves, and Mace ; lay all the Bits in any Thing that will bear the Fire : You may have it in what Shape you pleafe, according to what you bake it in : Mind to put a Bit of Fat and Lean always together in different Pieces, one on the other ; clarify a Chopin of the Broth it was boiled in, and when your Bits are all laid in your Can, pour it over them : You may put a Gill of white Wine and a Gill of Vinegar in it ; cover the Can clofe, and bake it two Hours : When it comes out of the Oven, put a light Weight on it, and when cold take it out : You may fend it to Table either whole or in Slices. It is to be eaten with Muftard and Vinegar cold.

To pot Pigeons.

CUT off the Feet and Wings ; feafon them with Salt and Pepper ; chop the Liver and Gizzard very fmall, mix a good Handful of Crumbs of Bread with them, a little Parfley, Onion, and Lemon-peel fhred fmall ; a good Piece of Butter ; wet it with an Egg ; work it up together, and put it in the Pigeons Bellies ; then put them in a Can with a good Piece of Butter ; cover it clofe, and put it in the Oven : It is better than doing them on the Fire. You may do them without ftuffing, if you pleafe : But you muft put Butter in their Bellies if you take them out of the Veffel that they were baked in, and put them in fmall Pots, they
will

will keep a long while ; but you muſt drain all the Gravy from them, and put clarified Butter over them.

To make Liver Puddings.

HALF boil a Hog's Draught, mince it very ſmall ; to every Pound of it put a Pound of the Hog's Lard cut ſmall, or a Pound of Beef Sewet ; you muſt put a Pound of Crumbs of Bread in it; ſeaſon it with Pepper, Salt, and Clove Pepper : You may put Currants in them, if you pleaſe ; wet it with a very little Water ; fill and boil them as you do the Blood Puddings : If you put Currants in them, put a little Sugar too.

The proper Sauces for wild Fowl.

DUCKS, Veal, and Plover muſt be roaſted very well ; the Sauce is Gravy, Crumbs of Bread, Sha-lots, and a little Claret ; ſeaſon it with Pepper and Salt. Partridges and Moor-fowl muſt be very well roaſted. Their Sauce is a little Bread boil'd in Water, a Blade of Mace, an Onion ſtuff'd with Cloves, a good Piece of But-ter, and a little Salt : You may put a little white Wine and Ketchup in it. Woodcocks and Snipes are roaſted well, with their Guts in them ; put toaſted Bread, and beat Butter under them : Under other Fowls put Gravy ; and put about any ſmall Birds fried Crumbs only. The proper Sauce for roaſted Veniſon is Claret boiled very thick, with Sugar or Currant Jelly.

To pot Woodcocks, or Snipes.

DON'T take out the Trale ; ſeaſon them with Salt and Clove Pepper ; put them in a Can with a good deal of ſweet Butter ; cover it cloſe, and bake them ; when baked, take them out of the Can, and let all the Butter drain from them ; put them in ſmall Pots, clarify the Butter they were in, add more to it, and pour it on them : Don't let any of the Gravy be in it. They muſt be covered with Butter.

To

To pot a Hare.

ROAST or bake the Hare, and when cold, pull all the Flesh from the Bones; pound it and season it with Pepper, Salt, Cloves, and Mace; put in an equal Quantity of sweet Butter as you have of Hare; clarify the Butter, and mix it with the Hare, then put it in small Pots; and when cold, pour clarified Butter on it: You may send it to Table in these Pots. You may pot Moor-fowl or Partridges the same Way.

To pot a Calf's Head.

BOIL it and two Calves Feet in as much Water as will cover them, with Pepper, Salt, Cloves, and Lemon-peel; boil it till the bones come out, then strew on it a little Salt; boil the Broth it was boiled in till it is in a very stiff Jelly; cut the Head in thin Slices, the Breadth of a Crown; skin the Tongue and Palates, and slice them; cut the Eyes in round Rings; place them all regular in a Bowl that will bear the Oven; then take the Broth, and put in it whole Pepper, Cloves, Mace, and Lemon-peel, and the Juice of a Lemon, or a little Vinegar; clarify it with the Whites of two Eggs, and let it run through a Jelly-bag; then pour it over the Head, and put it in the Oven for half an Hour. The Oven must not be hot.

To pot Beef.

TAKE the Lean off a Buttock of Beef; cut some thin Pieces, and rub it with Salt-petre; let it lye in it three Days, then dry it with a Cloth; put it in a flat Can, with Butter over and under it, cover the Can closs with coarse Paste; put it in the Oven for four Hours, then take it out and drain all the Butter and Gravy from the Beef; and when it is cold, and very clean of all the Fat, string it and pound it very fine; rub it thro' a coarse Search, then season it with white Pepper, Cloves, Mace, and Salt; to every Pound of the Beef, after it is put through the Search, put a Pound of of clarified Butter, ſkim it clean, and pour it from the Bottom, that none of the Milk or Sediment go in it; then mix it with the Beef, and put it in ſmall white Tart-pans; and when it is cold, pour clarified Butter over it. You may pot Veniſon the ſame Way.

To pot Tongues.

PICKLE them red, as you do to dry, then boil them tender, and peel them; rub them with Pepper, Cloves, and Mace; then turn them round on their Side in Pots that will hold but one; cover them with Butter; bake them when they come out of the Oven, pour off all the Gravy, and put the Butter that was over them and more clarified Butter over them. They will keep a great while.

To pot Veniſon.

TAKE a Piece of Veniſon, Fat and Lean together, lay it in a Diſh, and put Pieces of Butter over it; tye over the Diſh ſome coarſe Paper or brown Dough; put it in the Oven, and bake it very well, then take it out of the Gravy, and when it is cold and well drain-ed, pound it, both Fat and Lean, but firſt ſkin and bone it; ſeaſon it with Salt, Pepper, Cloves, Nutmeg and Mace, all pounded fine; then clarify the Butter that it was baked in, with as much added to it as will moiſten it, and put it in ſmall potting Pots: You muſt be ſure to take out all the Strings, and let it be beat to a Paſte. Cover the Pots with clarified But-ter.

To pot Beef or Veniſon in Slices.

TAKE lean Beef, and cut it in Slices, beat them with the Roller, and lard them; ſeaſon them with Pep-per, Salt, Cloves and Mace; put them in a Diſh, and bake them with Butter over them; cover them cloſs. You may put Onions and ſweet Herbs to them, if you pleaſe. They are to be eaten either hot or cold.

To

To pot Salmon the Newcastle *Way.*

TAKE the Salmon, and scale and wipe it very clean, but don't wash it; salt it well, then let it ly till the Salt is melted and drained from it, then season it with Pepper, Cloves and Mace : Put it in a Pot with Butter over it, cover it closs, and bake it : When baked, pour all the Gravy from it ; and when it is cold, put clarified Butter over it. You may do Carp, Tench, Trouts, and several Kinds of Fish, the same Way.

To pot a Pike.

SCALE it, and cut off the Head, split it, take out the Bones, wipe it clean, and salt the Inside with Bay, Salt and Pepper ; roll it up round, and put it in a Pot with Butter over it ; cover it closs, bake it an Hour, then pour all the Liquor from it, and lay it to drain on a a Cloth, then put it in a potting Pot, and pour clarified Butter on it.

To make Marrow Pasties.

CUT half a Pound of Marrow in Bits, shread six Apples, and the Yolks of three hard Eggs, a Pound of Currants, pick them clean, plump them before the Fire, and mix all together ; season it with the Grate of a Lemon, pounded Cinnamon, Mace, Nutmeg, a very little Sugar and Salt : Put them in Puff Paste. You may either bake or fry them.

To dress a Veal or Lamb's Ear, properly called Kidneys.

SLIT the Kidneys, Fat and all, rub it with an Egg, strew on it Crumbs of Bread, Parsley, Thyme, Onion, Pepper and Salt ; fry it in a Pan. You may mince it if you please, and season it with Sugar, Nutmeg, and a little Salt ; wash a few Currants in warm Water, and plump them before the Fire : Mix all together with the Grate of a Lemon, roll a little Puff Paste, and fry them in it. You may make them without Sugar or

Currants

Currants, if you pleafe; and if you put an Egg in them, you may do them on Toafts before the Fire.

To make Blood Puddings.

WHEN the Beaft is killing, ftir the Blood with your Hand, and break the Lumps : Put Salt in it; while hot, ftrain it, boil a Chopin of Groats in Milk, and put them in when they both are cold. To every Pint of this, put a Pound of chopped Sewet, fhred fweet Herbs and Onions; feafon it to your Tafte with Pepper and Salt, clean the Skins very well, fill three Parts of them, tye them, have a Pot of boiling Water, and put them in : Let them not boil at firft, but take them out and prick them a little to let out the Wind : When they are almoft cold, put them in again. Do this three or four Times, till they are a little hard, then they won't burft in the boiling; ftir them in the Skins when you are putting them firft down.

To make a Yorkfhire Pudding.

BEAT eight Eggs, and beat in them a Pound of Flour, putting a Mutchkin of Milk in by Degrees in it; fhread half a Pound of Beef Sewet very fine, and mix in it; feafon it with Salt and Ginger; three Hours boils it. You may bake a Pudding made the fame Way.

To make a Plumb Pudding.

BEAT eight Eggs and half a Pound of Flour, two Gills of Milk, and half a Pound of Raifins fhred, half a Pound of Currants wafhed and picked clean, half a Pound of Beef Sewet fhred fmall, and mix all together; feafon it with Nutmeg, Ginger, Salt, and a Glafs of Brandy. Two Hours boils it.

To make Almond Puddings in Lemon or Orange Skins.

BOIL your Skins, firft cut a Hole on the Top, and take out all the Infide, boil them tender in Water, then boil them in Syrup; blanch a Quarter of a
Pound

Pound of fweet Almonds, and four bitter ones, pound
them fine, mix them with a Gill of Cream, two Eggs,
and two Spunge Bifcuits; crumb them fmall; feafon
it with Sugar to your Tafte, put them in a Sauce-pan,
and ftir them one Way on the Fire, till the Rawnefs is
off the Eggs: Take care it does not curdle; then fill
your Skins, and put the Bit that you cut out in its Place
again. This is enough for an Afhet. Send them hot
to the Table.

To make a Peafe Pudding.

TAKE a Pound of fplit Peafe, and tye them in a
Cloth, giving them Room to fwell. Let them boil an
Hour, then take them up, and blend them with a Spoon,
put in them a good Piece of Butter, a little Salt and Pepper. Put them again in the Pot, let them boil half
an Hour, and put beat Butter about them.

To make an Almond Pudding.

BLANCH and pound half a Pound of fweet Almonds, and fix bitter ones, very fine, keeping them
wetting as they are pounding with Brandy or Ratafia;
beat the Yolks of twelve Eggs to a Cream, and pound
and fift half a Pound of Sugar, and mix it with your
Eggs by Degrees, keeping them whifking all the Time;
then your Almonds, then put in fix Ounces of oiled
Butter; put it in the Oven as foon as you can, with Puff
Pafte about the Difh. You may make half the Quantity
of any of thefe Puddings, if you pleafe to try them,
but put them in a very fmall Afhet. They are all ap-
proved Receipts.

To make a Citron Pudding.

POUND five Ounces of Citron very fine, with fix
Ounces of fine Sugar: Beat the Yolks of nine Eggs to
a Cream, and whifk them together, with a Spoonful
of the Juice of Spinach, and a little Brandy. Juft as
it is going in the Oven, put into it fix Ounces of

P   oiled

oiled Butter. Half an Hour bakes it. Keep it beating till it goes in the Oven.

To make a Rice Pudding.

WASH your Rice very well, and boil half a Pound in a Chopin of new Milk, till it is almoſt dry; then ſtir ſix Ounces of Butter in it, and let it cool a little; beat five Eggs, but three of the Whites, mix all together with a Gill of Cream, the Grate of an Orange or Lemon, a Quarter of a Pound of powdered Sugar, and a little Brandy. You may put Currants or Raiſins in it, if you pleaſe. Put Paſte about the Diſh, put a little beat Cinnamon and Nutmeg in it.

Another Way to make a Rice Pudding.

BOIL a Chopin of Milk, and thicken it with four large Spoonfuls of the Flour of Rice, blend the Rice in a little cold Cream or Milk, then ſtir it in your Milk on the Fire, with grated Lemon-peel and Nutmeg; ſweeten it to your Taſte, and when boiled pretty thick, take it off, and ſtir in it five Ounces of Butter; ſet it to cool, beat ſix Eggs, but three Whites, and when it is cold, mix them together, and put Paſte about the Diſh. You may make an Oat-meal Pudding the ſame Way: Put a little beat Cinnamon in them, and Nutmeg.

To make a Potatoe Pudding.

BOIL the large white Potatoes, peal and pound half a Pound of them very well, beat twelve Eggs, four Whites, very thick, and whiſk in them half a Pound of fine powdered Sugar, then your Potatoes, grated Nutmeg, and a large Glaſs of Brandy: Put half a Pound of oiled Butter in it. Juſt as it is going into the Oven, put Puff Paſte about the Diſh. It takes three Quarters of an Hour to bake it. You may make a Carot Pudding the ſame Way.

To

To make a Sagoe Pudding.

WASH and pick your Sagoe, put it to boil in a Chopin of Water: There muſt be half a Pound of Sagoe; boil it with the Rind of a Lemon, and a Stick of Cinnamon; when boiled pretty ſtiff, put in two Gills of white Wine, and a grated Nutmeg: Take it up, and when cold, put to it ſix Eggs, but three Whites, well beaten; ſweeten it to your Taſte, and put it in the Oven, not too hot: When the Paſte is baked, it is enough. You may make a Millet Pudding the ſame Way; but there muſt be eight Eggs, and half the Whites in it.

To make an Apple Pudding.

BAKE or roaſt ſix or ſeven large Apples, ſkin and core them, then rub them through a Search with the Back of a Spoon, beat a Quarter of a Pound of Biſcuit, and mix with it; then beat eight Eggs, but three Whites, and beat them all up very well together, with beat Cinnamon, the Grate of a Lemon, and a little Orange-flower Water; ſweeten it to your Taſte, and juſt as you are going to put it in the Oven, put into it four Ounces of clarified Butter. Put Puff Paſte about it: A little bakes it.

To make a Gooſe-berry Pudding.

SCALD two Chopins of Gooſe-berries, and rub them through a Search with the Back of a Spoon: Pound ſix Ounces of Spunge Biſcuits, and mix with them eight Eggs, but half the Whites, and half a Pound of fine powdered Sugar; then put in the reſt with Orange-flower Water. A very little bakes it.

To make a Tanſy Pudding.

BEAT ten Eggs, with eight Ounces of fine Sugar, then put in half a Mutchkin of Spinage Juice, a Mutchkin of Cream, a little Brandy and Nutmeg, eight Ounces of Spunge Biſcuit, or white Bread grated fine, a little Juice of Tanſy to your Taſte; the Tanſy muſt be pounded and ſhred; a Quarter of a Pound of blanched and
pounded

pouuded Almonds; mix all thefe well together in a
Stew-pan, with three Ounces of Butter; fet it on the
Fire, ftirring it till it is hard, then put it in your Difh,
and bake it. Strew Sugar and fliced Orange on it. You
may make a Tanfy withou. Almonds the fame Way.

To make a Marrow Pudding.

L A Y thin Slices of Bread on your Difh, then lay
on your Marrow in Lumps, then ftrew on Currants,
fo fill your Difh or Pudding-pan with Lairs; put a
little beat Cinnamon, Nutmeg and Mace between the
Lairs; beat eight Eggs, but two Whites, and a Chopin
of Milk fweetened to your Tafte; cover it. You may
bake it without a Cover, if you pleafe.

To make an Oat-meal Pudding.

B O I L a Quart of Water, feafon it with Sugar, Salt,
Brandy and Nutmeg; thicken it with Oat-meal, till
you can hardly ftir the Spoon in it; add to it half a
Pound of Currants, butter your Pan very thick. Pour
it in, and half an Hour bakes it.

To make a Four-hour Pudding.

S T O N E and mince a Pound of Raifins; wafh
and pick a Pound of Currants; mince a Pound of Beef
Sewet very fine; beat eight Eggs with four Spoonfuls
of Flour, a Gill of Brandy, a little Bit of Cinnamon, and
Nutmeg; ftir them all together, butter your Bag, and
tye it up very clofs; leave no Room, for it will not
fwell: You muft boil it four Hours. The Sauce is
Butter and Wine.

To make a Bread Pudding.

C U T all the foft of a Penny Loaf; boil a Mutchkin of Milk with a Stick of Cinnamon, and the Rind of
a Lemon, and pour it on your Bread; your Bread muft
be cut in thin Slices; cover it up clofs for half an
Hour; beat fix Eggs, a little Sugar, a Glafs of Brandy
and

and Nutmeg; mix all with your Bread : You may put in Currants, and a little Beef Sewet, if you pleafe; butter your Bag, and tye it up very clofs; an Hour and an half boils it ; an Hour, if there is not Sewet and Currants in it.

To make a Flour Pudding.

BEAT eight Eggs, and mix in it three Spoonfuls of Flour, the Grate of a Lemon, Nutmeg, Sugar, a Glafs of Brandy, a little Salt, and a Mutchkin of Milk; butter and flour your Cloth; tye it up clofs, it takes three Quarters of an Hour to boil ; let it, and all Puddings that are boiled, be put in boiling Water, and the Boil never given over till you fend them up : Melted Butter and Wine is the beft Sauce for thefe Puddings. Keep them ftirring in the Pot as they are boiling.

A boiled Rice Pudding.

TAKE half a Pound of Rice, tye it loofe in a Cloth, and boil it half an Hour ; then add to it a good Piece of Butter, a little Cinnamon, Sugar, Salt, and the Grate of a Lemon; ftir all together, and tye it up very clofs ; then boil it for an Hour. White Wine and Butter is the Sauce.

To make a Sewet Pudding.

SHREAD a Pound of Sewet very fine, a Pound of Flour, a Pound of Currants, fix Eggs, a little Ginger, Nutmeg, Sugar, and Brandy; mix all together. Boil it three Hours.

To make an Oat-meal Pudding.

GET a Mutchkin of coarfe Oat-meal, a Pound of Sewet fhred fmall, half a Pound of Currants, feafon it with Sugar, Salt, Nutmeg, Mace, and the Grate of a Lemon; beat four Eggs and add to it ; put it in your Cloth, and leave Room for it to fwell. Two Hours will boil it.

To make a Cuſtard Pudding.

BOIL a Mutchkin of Cream, with a Stick of Cinnamon, and the Rind of a Lemon and Orange ; Sweeten it to your Taſte ; beat the Yolks of eight Eggs, and mix your Cream in them by Degrees ; butter a white Stone Bowl, and put it in it ; then butter a thick Piece of Cloth, and tye it on the Bottom of the Bowl ; turn the Top down in boiling Water half an Hour ; boil it, and tye it very faſt.

An Orange Cuſtards, or Pudding.

RUB the Out ſide of four *Seville* Oranges with Salt, then pare them ; lay the Peel in Water till the Bitterneſs is off them ; then pound them very fine, and put in the Yolks of ten Eggs, and a Chopin of Cream ; mix them well, and ſweeten them to your Taſte ; put half a Pound of clarified Butter in it, if you bake it for a Pudding, and Puff Paſte about the Diſh ; but if for Cuſtards, put no Butter in, but put it in Cups. They both are to be baken.

To make a Lemon Pudding.

GRATE the Rind of three clear Lemons ; put it to ſteep in Brandy ; then grate two *Naples*, or Spunge Biſcuits, and mix with it ; beat the Yolks of ten Eggs and two of the Whites, and pound eight Ounces of Sugar very fine, and with the Eggs put in the Biſcuits, the Rind of the Lemon, and Brandy, keeping it beating all the while ; put Puff Paſte about the Diſh, and juſt as you are going to put it in the Diſh, beat in half a Pound of clarified Butter. The Butter muſt be almoſt cold.

A Carot Pudding.

BOIL as many good Carots as will be half a Pound ; cut them and pound them fine with half a Pound of fine Sugar ; then beat ten Eggs and three Whites, and mix them with the Carots ; grate an Orange in it, and juſt as you are going to put it into the

Oven,

Oven, put into it half a Pound of clarified Butter. All the Butter that is put in baked Puddings muſt be cla-rified, and the Skim and Bottom taken from it.

A Yellow Pudding.

GRATE the Crumbs of a fine Two-penny Loaf, and put it in a Pudding Diſh, and pour on it three Mutchkins of Milk, or Cream, five or ſix Eggs, a Pound of Beef Sewet, half a Pound of Raiſins, and a Pound of Currants, ſome Saffron ſteeped in Roſe Water, and ſtrained into it ; ſweeten it to your Taſte, and bake it. Pour the Milk on the Bread boiling hot.

To make a Barley Pudding.

PUT to a Quart of Cream, or Milk, the Yolks of ſix Eggs, and three Whites ; beat them well ; ſeaſon it with Nutmeg, Salt, a little Orange-flower Water, and the Grate of an Orange and Lemon ; then put in ſix Handfuls of Pearl Barley, but boil it a little in Milk firſt ; put in it twelve Ounces of melted But-ter ; mix all together, with ſix Ounces of Sugar ; but-ter a Diſh, and pour it in. It takes a good while to bake it.

To make a boiled Apple Pudding.

MAKE a good Puff Paſte, roll it out half an Inch thick ; pare the Apples, and ſcore them ; fill the Paſte and cloſe it up ; tye it in a Cloth, and boil it two Hours, if a large one three, then turn it out into the Diſh ; cut a Piece out of the Top of the Paſte, and put But-ter and Sugar in it to your Taſte ; then lay on the Piece again. A Pear, Damſons, or any Sort of Plumbs, Apricock, Cherries, Raſpberries, Currants, Gooſe-ber-ries, or Mulberry Puddings may be made the ſame Way. Send beat Butter, a little white Wine, and Su-gar in a Bowl.

To make an Orange Pudding.

BOIL the Skins of three Oranges very tender; pound them very fine in a Marble or wooden Mortar; pound half a Pound of fine Sugar, and beat the Yolks of twelve Eggs to a Cream; mix your Sugar in them, then your Orange, beat them very well together; have eight Ounces of Butter melted to Oil, skim and bottom it; let it be as cold that it will but just pour before you put it in, and don't put it in till you are putting the Pudding in the Oven; put Puff Paste about the Dish, wipe it up before you put it in the Dish; half an Hour bakes it. You must oil, skim and bottom all your Butter for baked Puddings, and let it be almost cold before you put it in.

To make a Lemon Pudding.

GRATE the Rind of four Lemons, and put it in a Glass of Brandy; beat the Yolks of ten Eggs till they are very thick, and pound and sift half a Pound of Sugar, and beat it up well with your Eggs, then put in the Lemon Rind, and just as it is going into the Oven, put in eight Ounces of Butter, as above; put Puff Paste about the Dish of all baked Puddings. Half an Hour bakes it. Boil two Lemon Skins, and pound and mix them with this.

To make a Pudding of whole Rice.

PUT half a Pound of cold Butter on the Bottom of your Pudding-pan; strew over it six Ounces of Rice, then half a Pound of Raisins, or Currants, a grated Nutmeg; put over it two Chopins of new Milk: You may colour it with Saffron, it both eats and looks the better; grate the Rind of a Lemon, or Orange in it; don't stir it, but put it in a very hot Oven: It takes two Hours to bake it; sweeten it to your Taste; always stone the Raisins, wash, dry and pick the Currants, and wash and dry your Rice.

To

To make Clary Cake.

BEAT six Eggs very well with Salt and Nutmeg; shread a Handful of Clary, and mix with them ; fry them, or put it in a Dish in the Dripping-pan when Meat is roasting, and it will bake. You may make one the same Way with Chives and Parsley.

To make Pancakes.

BEAT six Eggs, and thicken them well with Flour, a little Ginger and Nutmeg, a little Salt, Sugar, and a Glass of Brandy ; put to them a Mutchkin of Milk; fry them in Butter, either thick or thin, as you like.

To make Custard Pancakes.

BEAT eight Eggs ; mix in them with four Spoonfuls of Flour, a Glass of Brandy, a little Ginger and Nutmeg, Sugar, and the Grate of a Lemon ; put to them a Mutchkin of Cream, and a little melted Butter; they will not turn in the Pan, but you must hold the upper Side to the Fire till crisp.

To make Pancakes.

BEAT four Eggs, a little Ginger, Nutmeg, and Salt ; make them thick with Flour, then put in a Mutchkin of Two-penny ; fry them crisp, and then you may put in Sugar, if you please.

To make Apple Dumplins.

MAKE Puff Paste not too rich, and pare and scoop out the Cores of as many large Apples as will fill your Dish at the black End ; then put in the Place where you scoop out the Core, Currant Jelly or Marmalade of Oranges ; roll out your Paste thin, and roll up the Apples in it separately ; tye them up in Pieces of Cloth, and put them in a Pot of boiling Water : An Hour and a half boils them. Melted Butter, white Wine, and Sugar, is the proper Sauce.

Q

To make fried Pan Puddings.

T O a Mutchkin of Milk put three Quarters of a Pound of Flour, ſix Ounces of Beef Sewet ſhred as fine as Flour, ſix Ounces of Currants waſhed and plumped, a little Salt, Nutmeg, a Glaſs of Brandy, and three or four Eggs ; mix all well together ; fry them in a Pan of Fat, and make them a little larger than Fritters.

Pancakes.

T A K E five Eggs, beat them very well with ſix Spoonfuls of Flour, the Grate of a Lemon, a little Ginger and Salt, and a Mutchkin of Milk ; fry them very criſp, and then ſtrew Sugar on them, and ſend them in very hot.

To make French Fritters.

T A K E two Gills of Water, an Ounce of Butter, a little Cinnamon, Sugar and Brandy, and grated Lemon-peel ; ſet it over the Fire, and boil the Water ; ſtir in the Flour as faſt as you can, till in a Paſte ; work it till it is like Paſte for ten Minutes; put it in a Bowl, work it with the Yolks of ſix Eggs and one White, till it is in a light Paſte ; drop them in a Pan of boiling Fat, with a Spoon or a Knife ; fry them a light brown, diſh them, and throw Sugar on them.

To make Apple Fritters.

B E A T four Eggs, make them pretty thick with Flour; put two Gills of Milk, a little Salt, Sugar, and Nutmeg into it ; it muſt be as thick that it will ſtick to the Apples ; pare and cut them in thin Slices, and take out the Cores, but don't break the Slices ; put them in the Batter, and have a good deal of boiling Beef-dripping, and drop them in one by one till your Pan is full ; fry them a light brown ; then take them out, and put in more till they are all done ; ſtrew on them Sugar when you diſh them : Any Kitchen-fee

fee that is sweet and clean will fry them. All Fritters are fried the same Way.

To make Potatoe Fritters.

BOIL and pound six Potatoes ; mix them with five Eggs well beaten, a Gill of Cream, a little Sugar, Nutmeg, the Grate of an Orange, two Ounces of oiled Butter, and a little Brandy ; beat all well together, drop them in a Pan almost full of boiling Fat, and fry them a light brown. Strew Sugar on them when dished.

To make Currant Fritters.

BEAT four Eggs with six Spoonfuls of Flour, and a little Salt, Sugar, Nutmeg, Ginger, and the Grate of a Lemon ; then put in it half a Mutchkin of Cream, a Dram, and a Quarter of a Pound of Currants washed, picked and dried ; drop them by Spoonfuls in a Pan almost full of boiling Fat. Fry them a light brown.

To make Barm Dumplins.

MAKE a light Dough, as for Bread, with Barm, Flour, an Egg and Water ; then boil a Panful of Water, and put the Dough in it, making it into little round Balls as big as an Egg ; then flat them with your Hand, and put them in the boiling Water : Ten Minutes boils them : Take care they don't fall to the Bottom. Send them to the Table with beat Butter in a Cup. Put Salt in them.

To make Hard Dumplins.

MIX Flour and Water, an Egg, and a little Salt, like a Paste ; roll them as before, then boil them in boiling Water for half an Hour : They are best boiled with Beef. Send Butter in a Cup with them.

Another Way to make Apple Dumplins.

PARE and core your Apples, and cut them in small Pieces ; then pare and core a Quince, and grate it among the Apples ; then make a good Puff Paste ; roll

it

it in small Pieces, and put in the Apples and Quinces; fasten them up and tye them in different Places in a a Cloth, and boil them; and when they are enough, take them out of the Cloth; cut a Bit out of the Top, and put in them Sugar and Butter, then dish them, and put the Tops on them again.

A Florendine of Oranges, or Apples.

CUT half a Dozen *Seville* Oranges into Slices, and save the Juice; take out the Pulp, and lay them in Water twelve Hours; then boil them in Water till they are tender, keeping the Pan full of Water all the Time; then boil all the Juice, with a Pound of Sugar, and the Oranges cut in thin Slices; then boil ten Pipins in Water and Sugar; put them in the Dish, and half the Oranges among them; cover it with a Lid of carved Puff Paste. A Florendine of Currants is made the same Way.

An Almond Florendine.

BLANCH and beat very fine a Pound of Almonds with Orange-flower Water; beat eight Eggs, but half of the Whites; mix them with two Gills of Cream, and half a Gill of Brandy, half a Pound of clarified Butter, a Pound of Currants well washed and picked; season it with Sugar, Cinnamon, and Nutmeg, all pounded fine; mix them all very well; put them in a Dish with Puff Paste under and over them: You may put candied Lemon, and Citron in thin Slices in it, if you please. A little while bakes it.

To make a plain Tansy.

TAKE a fine stale Penny Loaf, and cut the Crumb in thin Shaves; put it in a Bowl, then boil a Mutchkin of Cream, and when boiled, pour it over the Bread, then cover the Bowl with a Plate, and let it ly a Quarter of an Hour; then mix it with eight Eggs well beaten, two Gills of the Juice of Spinage, two Spoonfuls of the Juice of Tansy, and sweeten it with Sugar, Nutmeg,

and

and a little Brandy ; rub your Pan with Butter, and put it in it ; then keep it ſtirring on the Fire till it is pretty thick ; then put it in a buttered Diſh ; you may either bake it, or do it in the Dripping-Pan under roaſted Meat.

To boil a Tanſy.

C U T the Bread, as in the other Tanſy, and pour a Mutchkin of boiling Milk on it, cover it up, then beat eight Eggs with a little of the Grate of a Lemon or Orange, Nutmeg and Sugar ; put to it ſome Juice of Spinage, and a little Tanſy Juice ; ſtir all well together, then tye it up in a Cloth, and boil it an Hour and an Half ; when you diſh it ſtick it with candied Orange, and cut a *Seville* Orange in Quarters round it ; ſend beat Butter, white Wine and Sugar in a Cup with it to the Table.

A Pipin Tanſy.

P A R E and cut as many Pipins as will cover the Bottom of a Diſh, then take half a Penny Loaf, crumb it fine, pour on it a Mutchkin of Cream, and eight Eggs well beaten ; ſeaſon it with Sugar, Nutmeg and Ginger ; put in a Gill of Spinage Juice, and a Spoonful of Tanſy Juice ; beat all together, then put in your Slices of Apples, butter your Frying-pan, and put in the Tanſy ; when the Pan is hot, you muſt fry it on both Sides, or you may bake it in the Oven ; ſend beat Butter, Orange and Sugar to Table with it.

To make a White Pot.

T A K E two Chopins of Milk, mix with it nine Eggs well beaten, a little Roſe Water, grated Lemon-peel, Nutmeg, and Sugar ; cut the Crumb of a Penny Loaf in thin Slices, and lay them in a Pudding-pan, then pour the Milk over them. You muſt put a little Butter on the Top. Put it in a ſlow Oven. Half an Hour bakes it.

Another

Another Sort of White Pot.

LAY a Lair of Marrow on the Bottom of the Diſh you intend to bake it in, then lay all over it Slices of fine Bread cut very thin ; ſtrew over the Bread ſton'd Raiſins, putting grated Lemon-peel, Nutmeg and Ginger between them ; then take a Chopin of Cream, and ſeven or eight Eggs well beaten, with Sugar, and a little Nutmeg ; mix them with the Cream, and pour it over them ſoftly, till the Diſh is full : Let it ſtand a while before you put it in the Oven : Lay Slices of Bread, and Bits of Butter on the Top of all. You may make it with Currants, if you pleaſe.

A Rice White Pot.

BOIL a Chopin of Cream or Milk, then put in two Ounces of pick'd Rice, Sugar, Ginger, Cinnamon and Mace beaten ; ſet it by to cool, beat ſix Yolks of Eggs, and two Whites, and mix them with the Cream ; then put in four Ounces of pick'd and waſhed Currants, and a little Salt. You may bake it with or without Paſte, boil the Rice a little, or put the Powder of Rice in it, inſtead of whole Rice.

Pancakes Royal.

MIX two Gills of Cream with two Gills of Sack, then beat up twelve Eggs, with Sugar, Cinnamon, Nutmeg and Ginger ; mix them with as much Flour as will let them turn, then put in the Cream, and fry them with clarified Butter. The Pan muſt be always hot before you fry Pancakes.

Common Pancakes.

TAKE a Chopin of Milk, eight Spoonfuls of Flour, grated Nutmeg and Ginger ; beat all together with a Glaſs of Brandy ; let it ſtand a while, then fry them, and ſend them in hot with Sugar and Oranges.

Iriſh

Irish *Pancakes.*

BOIL a Mutchkin of Cream, with the Rind of an Orange, and some Cinnamon; then set it to cool: Beat eight Eggs, and but four of the Whites, with Sugar, Nutmeg, a little Salt, and two Gills of Flour; then beat three Ounces of sweet Butter, and mix the Cream and Eggs together, with a Glass of Brandy: Put a very little Bit of Butter in the Frying-pan, and when it is hot, put in two Gills of the Batter: They will not turn, but you must hold them before the Fire, to brown the upper Side.

To make Rice Pancakes.

BOIL a Chopin of Cream, thicken it with three Spoonfuls of the Flour of Rice, stir in half a Pound of Butter, and a grated Nutmeg; put it to cool, then beat eight Eggs and mix with the Cream; put in a little Salt, and sweeten it to your Taste; mix them well, and fry them in Butter; serve them up hot; if they don't fry well, put in a Spoonful of Flour.

Oat-meal Pancakes.

BOIL a Chopin of Milk, and blend in it a Mutchkin of the Flour of Oat-meal, thus: Keep a little Milk, and mix the Meal by Degrees in it, then stir in the boiling Milk; when it is pretty thick, put it to cool, then beat up six Eggs with Sugar, Nutmeg, the Grate of a Lemon, and a little Salt: Stir all together, and fry them in Butter, putting in a Spoonful of the Batter at a Time. Serve them up hot, with beat Butter, Orange and Sugar.

Chopped Apples in small Pancakes.

TAKE a Mutchkin of Milk, sweeten it to your Taste, then beat six Eggs, with Nutmeg, and the Grate of Lemon-peel; mix them with five or six Spoonfuls of Flour; then put in the Milk by Degrees, a Glass of Brandy, a little Salt, and Ginger; beat them up well,
then

then put in chopped Apples. It muſt be pretty thick with them, then fry them in ſmall Pancakes.

To make criſp Pancakes.

TAKE four Eggs with Ginger and Salt, mix in them ſix or ſeven Spoonfuls of Flour, and a Mutch-kin of Two-penny. You may put Lemon-peel and Nutmeg in them ; fry them very thin in Butter : When you fry them firſt, if there is not enough of Flour, put in a little more.

To make a Clary Amulet.

BEAT eight or ten Eggs, with a little Pepper, Salt and Nutmeg ; then put into it two Gills of Cream, and a Handful of Clary chopped very fine . Mix them well together, put ſome Butter or Beef-drippings in your Frying-pan, and when it is boiling hot, pour in your Amulet ; fry it on both Sides, and ſend it up hot. You may make one of Parſley and Chives the ſame Way.

To poach Eggs and Spinage.

BOIL the Spinage in Water and Salt ; chop them very ſmall, then ſqueeze them between two Trenchers, and mix them with a good Piece of ſweet Butter ; ſalt them to your Taſte, then poach ſix or ſeven Eggs in boiling Water and Salt, letting the Water boil before you break in the Eggs ; place the Spinage in an Aſhet, then lay the Eggs over them ; take them up with an Egg-ſpoon, and don't break them ; poach Eggs for Gra-vy the ſame Way ; pour the Gravy ſcalding hot in the Diſh, and lay your poached Eggs in it.

Eggs with Cabbage Lettice.

SCALD ſome Cabbage Lettice in Water ; ſqueeze them well, then ſlice them and toſs them up in But-ter, with a little Gravy ; ſeaſon it with Pepper and Salt, then let them ſtew for half an Hour on a ſlow Fire, being cloſs covered ; then poach Eggs, and lay over them ;

them when they are diſhed: You may put Sauſages
in the Diſh round them.

To butter Eggs.

TAKE eight Eggs; put them in a Stew-pan after
they are well beaten with a little Salt and Nutmeg;
put to them a Quarter of a Pound of ſweet Butter,
and a Spoonful of ſweet Cream, keep them ſtirring all
the Time they are on the Fire from the Bottom of
the Pan, then put them on toaſted Bread when they
are thick.

Fried Bacon and Eggs.

CUT thin Slices of Bacon and fry them a light
brown; then take them up and clean the Pan; cover
them; put a little Butter in the Pan, when it is clariſied, break into it your Eggs; when they are a light
brown, hold the Pan before the Fire to harden the
other Side, for they muſt not be turned: Put the Bacon
in the Diſh, and the Eggs over them.

To make an Amulet.

GET what Quantity of Eggs you think will fill
the Diſh; ſeaſon them with Pepper and Salt; ten
Eggs will fill a ſmall Diſh; ſhread Parſley and Chives,
and beat them and the Eggs with a Gill of Cream very
well; then fry them in a Pan of good clariſied Butter
or Beef-dripping on both Sides: You may put in
Gravy inſtead of Cream: You may put cut Slices of
Oranges over it in the Diſh.

Eggs and the Juice of Sorrel.

POACH your Eggs in Water, and have ſome Sorrel pounded; put the Juice of it in a Diſh with ſome
Butter, two or three raw Eggs, and Salt and Nutmeg;
make all in a Sauce, and pour it on your poached Eggs.
So ſerve them up.

R   *A*

A pretty Dish of Whites of Eggs.

TAKE the Whites of twelve Eggs, beat them up
with four Spoonfuls of Rose Water, a little grated Lemon-peel, Nutmeg and Sugar ; mix them well, and
boil them in four small Bladders ; tye them in the
Shape of an Egg, and boil them hard, they will take half
an Hour ; lay them in the Dish, when they are cold mix
two Gills of Cream with half a Gill of Malaga, a little
Orange-juice and Sugar ; then take out the Eggs, and
pour the Cream over them in the Dish.

Eggs poached in Cream.

FILL a Dish almost full of Cream ; put it on the
Fire, and when the Cream boils, break as many Eggs
in it as the Dish will hold ; season it with Pepper, Salt,
and Nutmeg ; cover them with another Dish, but take
care they are not too hard.   Then serve them up.

Oisters or Cockles fried with Eggs.

WASH them well in their own Liquor ; give them
a Scald, let them cool ; then beat ten or twelve Eggs,
and mix them with Crumbs of Bread, Pepper, Nutmeg, and Salt ; put in a Gill of Cream ; beat them
well, then put in your Oisters or Cockles ; have the
Pan with clarified Butter, then drop them in ; turn
them, and fry them a light brown : When one Panful
is done, put more, so do till they are done.   You may
send Butter and Lemon-juice in a Cup, or Gravy. They
are very pretty to garnish any Dish of Fish.

To make Puff Paste.

TO two Pound of Flour, you must have a Pound
of Butter ; rub in the Flour two Ounces of the Butter, and put in it two Eggs ; then wet it cold, wet as
much as will make a stiff Paste ; work it very smooth,
then roll out the Paste, and stick it all over with Butter ;
shake Flour on it, then roll it like a Collar, double it up
at both Ends, that they meet in the Middle : Roll it
out

out the same Way, and put it up as before, till all
the Butter is in it.

Paste for any raised Pies.

TO half a Peck of Flour, take two Pound of Butter;
boil it in a Chopin of Water, make a Hole in the Flour,
and pour in the Butter and Water; don't let the Sediment at the Bottom go in: Skim it clean, then work it
up to a Paste, and before it is quite cold, raise it up
into any Shape you please, either small or great Pies;
if the Paste is not wet enough, boil Water, and put in
it. Do the same in all standing Paste.

Another Sort of Paste.

TAKE half a Peck of Flour, and boil a Pound of
Butter, and half a Pound of render'd Mutton Sewet in
a Chopin of Water; wet it with it, and work it well
while it is hot; raise it into any Shape for Pasties or Pies
you please; it stands better with the Sewet mixed with
Butter, than all Butter, but let it be very sweet.

A Paste of Drippings.

TAKE a Pound and a half of Drippings, boil it in
Water, and strain it; then let it cool, and take off the
Fat; scrape it, and boil it so for four or five Times,
then work it well up into three Pounds of Flour, and
wet it with cold Water till it is a Paste. It will be a
very good Pye Crust; or if you wet the Flour with it
and boiling Water, it will make raised Pies, but you
must raise it while it is very hot.

Cold Water Paste for Pasties.

LAY down half a Peck of Flour, wet it with two
Eggs and cold Water, work it in a Paste, then roll it out,
and put over it a Pound and a Quarter of Butter, and
flour it; then roll it like a Collar, and roll it again:
Do that five or six Times, till you see the Butter is well
mixed

mixed with the Paste, then you may cover any Sort of Pies with it.

Paste for Tarts.

TAKE a Pound of Flour, and rub it in a Quarter of a Pound of Butter, and a little fine Sugar ; wet it with an Egg, and as much Water as will make it into Paste ; then roll it into what Form you please for Tarts or Puddings.

To make Apple Tarts.

PARE two Oranges thin, and boil them in Water till they are tender ; then shread them small, and pare twenty Pipins, quarter and core them, and put to them as much Water as will cover them ; then put them on the Fire, and turn them softly, then put in half a Pound of Sugar, and the Orange-peel that was shred, and the Juice of the Orange, and let them boil till they are pretty thick ; when they are cold, put them in your Crusts, with open Paste over them ; glaze them with the White of an Egg, and grated Sugar, then bake them a light brown.

Goose-berry Tarts.

PUT Paste in the Patties, and give the Goose-berries a Scald ; when they are cold, put them in the Patties, with Sugar under and over them ; cover them with nicked Paste, and glaze them as before. Bake them in a slow Oven.

Prune Tarts.

STEW a Pound of Prunes, with a little Sugar and Water ; stone some of them, and put in some of them without stoning ; put Puff Paste under them and over them, with a little of the Liquor they were stewed in, so bake them. Glaze all Tarts as in the first Receipt of Tarts. You may stew the Prunes in Claret, if you please.

Chesnut

Chefnut Tarts.

ROAST the Chefnuts, peel them, and put Pafte in the Patties; then put in your Chefnuts, and between every two Chefnuts, put a Bit of Marrow rolled in Eggs, and fome Orange and Lemon-peel cut fmall; then make a Cuftard, and put it over them; bake them a little, then fend them up hot or cold.

To make Sweet-meat Tarts.

PUT Puff Pafte in the Bottom of the Patties, then put into them any Sort of preferv'd Fruit, then cut Pafte in any Shape you pleafe, or crofs bar them ; then glaze them, and put them in a flow Oven for a Quarter of an Hour. When the Pafte is done, they are enough.

To keep Goofe-berries for Tarts.

TAKE the Goofe-berries before they are full grown, but come to their Tafte ; pick them off the Stems, then put them in Bottles that are very clean and dry, cork them very clofs, put them in a flow Oven, and when they turn white they are enough ; then rofin the Corks, and keep them in Sand : When you are going to ufe them, boil them in a Syrup, and when they are cold put them in Puff Pafte, and cut Holes in the Top ; bake them in a flow Oven. You may keep red and black Currants the fame Way.

Peach Tarts.

TAKE half ripe Peaches and pare them, and flice them in two, and take out the Stones, put fome fine powdered Sugar in the Bottom of a Stew-pan, place your Peaches in it, put them over the Fire, and ftir them often, then put Pafte in the Patty-pans ; and when the Peaches are cold put them in the Patties with the Syrup they were boiled in, cover them with rich Pafte, and bake them in a flow Oven ; put the Kernels of the Peaches in the Tarts. You may do Apricocks the fame Way.

To

Raspberry Tarts.

PUT Paste in the Patties, then lay in the Raspberries, strew over them some fine Sugar; cover and bake them in a slow Oven : When they are cold you may put Cream on them. You may make Tarts the same Way of all Sorts of Fruit, but put a carved Paste Lid on them.

To make Orange Tarts.

BOIL the Skins of two bitter Oranges in four or five Waters, till all the Bitterness is off them, and the Skin is so tender that you may thrust a Straw in them ; then drain them, and pound them and six Ounces of fine Sugar into a Paste, with some of the Juice of the Oranges, and some Pipins shred small ; mix it all together, and put it into your Patty-pans with Paste under them, and cross Bars over them ; put them in the Oven, half an Hour bakes them. You may make Lemon Tarts the same Way.

To make Orange Cheese-cakes.

BOIL the Skins of three Oranges in five or six Waters till the Bitterness is off them, then pound them very fine, with half a Pound of fine Sugar ; beat the Yolks of eight Eggs and two Whites, till they are very thick and white ; then mix the Oranges with them, and eight Ounces of oiled Butter : Put Paste in the Patty-pans, and half fill them ; half an Hour bakes them in a slow Oven. Lemon Cheese-cakes are made the same Way ; but you need not shift the Water they are boiled in, and put the Grate of an Orange or Lemon in them : Put a little Brandy in both.

To make Cheese-cakes.

TAKE two Chopins of Cream, or good Milk, and the Yolks of three Eggs, and four of the Whites, beat them very well ; mix them with the Milk, and set it on the Fire, when it boils take it off and drain the Whey gently from it ; put to the Curd grated Nutmeg,

beat

beat Cinnamon, and three Spoonfuls of Rofe-water, as much Malaga, fome fine Sugar, four Ounces of But- ter, a Quarter of pounded Bifcuits, and a Quarter of Currants, pick and wafh them; but before you put them in, blend all the reft very well together, then mix them in. You may bake them in any Shape or Cruft you pleafe.

To make Potatoe Cheefe-cakes.

BOIL and peel the Potatoes, and pound fix Ounces of them, then beat five Eggs, but three of the Whites, and mix the Potatoes with them, and four Ounces of Sugar, grated Lemon and Orange-peel, Nutmeg, and a Glafs of Brandy; then, a little before you put them in the Patties, put in four Ounces of oil'd Butter almoft cold. Put Puff Pafte in the Patties under them.

To make Egg Cheefe-cakes.

BEAT two Eggs well, and thicken them with Flour, then beat three Eggs, and mix them with a Mutchkin of Cream and fix Ounces of Butter, put it on the Fire, and keep it ftirring one Way; when it is almoft boiling put in the two Eggs and Flour, keep it ftirring, and when it is boiled pretty thick, take it off the Fire, and feafon it with Sugar, Salt, grated Lemon-peel, and Nutmeg; when they are cold put in half a Pound of Currants wafh'd, pick'd and dried; put Pafte in your Patties, and bake them half an Hour.

To make Almond Cheefe-cakes.

TAKE half a Pound of Almonds, blanch and pound them, keeping them wetting with Brandy, or Rofe- water; beat five Eggs, but one White, mix them and your Almonds with fix Ounces of fine Sugar, the Grate of two Oranges or Lemon-peel, fix Ounces of Butter oil'd, fkim and bottom it; then juft as they are going into the Oven put in the Butter, beat all well together, put Puff Pafte in the Patties, put a little Brandy in them, then

then put them in the Oven. Half an Hour bakes them.

To make Almond Custards.

BOIL a Mutchkin of Cream with Cinnamon, and Orange or Lemon-peel in it; beat the Yolks of seven Eggs, and mix them with a little of the Cream before you boil it; then mix all together, with a Quarter of a Pound of Almonds blanched and pounded, and a little Orange-flower Water; sweeten them to your Taste; put them on the Fire again, and keep it stirring one Way till it is almost boiling; then take it up, and put it in Cups; take out the Cinnamon and Peel: You may put the Cups in the Oven to colour them, or you may send them to Table as they are. Grate Nutmeg on them.

To make Custards of Rice.

BOIL a Mutchkin of Milk with two Ounces of fresh Butter in it; keep out a little of the Milk, and stir in it two Spoonfuls of the Powder of Rice, and two Eggs well beaten; then mix them with the boiled Milk; put in a Spoonful of Orange-flower or Rose-water; sweeten it to your Taste; put it on the Fire, and keep it stirring till it is pretty thick; boil the Rice in the Milk before you put in the Eggs, and don't let it boil after the Eggs go in, but let it be scalding hot.

To make Custards.

BEAT six Eggs very well, leave out four of the Whites; mix them with a Mutchkin of Milk, the Grate of a Lemon, and Nutmeg; sweeten it to your Taste; put it in Cups, and put them in a Stew-pan of cold Water on a slow Fire: Don't put as much Water in the Pan as will come over them; put it on a slow Fire; cover the Pan with the Lid, and when the Custards are stiff, take them out: You may brown them with a Salamander. You may do any Custards in Water the same Way.

Orange

Orange Cuſtards.

TAKE the Juice of two *Seville* Oranges with a little of the Peel grated, and as much Sugar as will make
it ſweet ; give it a Boil, and ſtrain it, then boil a Mutchkin of Cream, with Nutmeg, Cinnamon, and Sugar;
thicken it with the Whites of five or ſix Eggs beaten,
then beat them all together, and put it in Cups.

Another Sort of Almond Cuſtards.

BLANCH and pound a Handful of Almonds, then
put to them a Mutchkin of Milk, preſs the Milk out,
and ſweeten it ; then beat five Eggs, but two of the
Whites, and mix them with the Milk ; put it in Cups.
You may put them in the Oven, or do them in a Pan
with Water.

To put Sweet-meats of all Colours in Jelly.

LET your Jelly be very ſtiff, and ſeaſon it and
clear it as you do other Jelly ; put a little in the Bottom of the Turks-cap ; let it ſtand to cool, then lay it
all over with different coloured whole Sweet-meats ;
then put on a little more Jelly, as much as will be
half an Inch above the Sweet-meats ; let it cool again,
and lay on more, ſo go on till the Bowl is filled,
but there muſt be an Inch of Jelly above all : When
it is very cold, turn it out on an Aſhet with the broad
Part down.

To make a Trifle.

COVER your Aſhet with Spunge Biſcuits, then
pour over them a Mutchkin of Malaga, or white Wine,
then a yellow Cream ; then lay on it Heaps of coloured Sweet-meats ; roaſt ſix or ſeven Apples, and rub
them through a Search ; put a little Sugar to them,
and mix them with four Eggs, the Whites only, and
wipe them up very high, and put this by Spoonfuls
over the reſt ; but let a little of the Cream and Sweet-
meats be ſeen. Raiſe it up as high as you can, ſo ſend
it to the Table.

S

To make Burnt Cream.

BOIL a Mutchkin of Cream, and thicken it with the Yolks of eight Eggs and a Spoonful of Flour ; boil Cinnamon and the Rind of an Orange in the Cream; take care it is not curdled ; sweeten it to your Taste ; take a Quarter of a Pound of Loaf-sugar in a Stew-pan, and pour over it half a Gill of Water ; let it boil till it ropes, and don't stir it till you take it off; then by Degrees strew it over your Ashet of Cream; brown it with a Salamander, or in the Oven.

To make Jelly of Hartshorn.

TAKE a Pound of Hartshorn, put it in a Tea Kettle with two Pints of Water, *Scots* Measure, and a Penny-worth of Isinglass ; let it boil on a very slow Fire to a Pint ; then strain it off and set it to cool ; if it is too stiff, put in a little Water, and if too limber, put in another Penny-worth of Isinglass, and boil it better ; it takes a great deal of boiling more than any other Stock for Jelly; season it with white Wine, Sugar, Lemons, and Cinnamon to your Taste ; put the Rind of a Lemon in it; beat the Whites of six Eggs, and whisk them in it : You must keep it stirring all the while it is on the Fire; have a thin Cloth tied on the Bottom of a Chair or Frame; boil it a Quarter of an Hour, and pour it up boiling hot; change the Bowl till you see it is clear. So put it in Glasses for your Use.

To make Calves Feet Jelly.

SCALD the Hair off them very clean, then slit them into, and let them lye in warm Water two Hours; put them into a closs covered Sauce-pan with a Quarter of a Pound of Hartshorn, or Two-pence worth of Isinglass ; put two Pints of Water to them, and let them boil very slow till they are all in Tavers ; then put a little of the Stock to cool, and if it is stiff, strain it off; skim it very clean, and let it stand to settle ; leave all the Settling at the Bottom ; if it is too stiff put in a little Water, if not, boil it better : The best Way to
season

feaſon Jelly is to your Taſte, but you may put a Mutchkin of Wine and four Lemons to three Mutchkins of Stock; feaſon it with Cinnamon, Sugar, and the Rind of a Lemon; clear it as you do the Hartſhorn Jelly, with Whites of Eggs.

To make Blamong.

MAKE your Stock as you do for Jelly, but a great deal ſtiffer; to a Mutchkin of Stock put a Quarter of a Pound of Almonds blanched and pounded very fine, ſix bitter ones; as you are pounding wet them with a little Cream; boil Lemon-peel and Cinnamon in your Stock; ſweeten it to your Taſte, and when it is pretty warm, rub the Almonds in it very well thro' a Cloth; ſtrain it, and if it is not white enough, put in a Gill of thick ſweet Cream; put in a little Orange-flower Water, if you have it: You may put it either in Cups, or any Thing you pleaſe, it will turn out if cold enough. Wet the Cups with Cream.

To make Leech Cream.

TAKE a Quarter of a Pound of Iſinglaſs, pull it in Pieces, and put it to boil in a cloſs covered Sauce-pan, with three Mutchkins of Water; let it boil on a very ſlow Fire, till it is all diſſolved, and the half boiled away; put it to cool, and if it be ſtiff, put to it half a Mutchkin of Cream, the Rind of a Lemon and Orange, a Stick of Cinnamon, and ſweeten it to your Taſte. You may whiten it with pounded Almonds, if you pleaſe. It is a very pretty Supper Diſh; when quite cold, ſtick Bits of Marmalade of Oranges and Almonds cut like Straws in it. It is good for any one in a Decay.

To make whipt Sillabubs.

TAKE a Mutchkin of thick Cream, put to it half a Mutchkin of white Wine, the Juice of a Lemon, and grate the Rind in it; ſweeten it to your Taſte, whiſk it up well, ſkim off the Top as you are whiſking it, and

put

put it on a Sieve; then put Wine in the Glaſs, either white or red, and a little Sugar; then ſend it to Table with Tea Spoons about it.

To make Orange Cream.

PARE the Rind of three bitter Oranges, and ſteep them in two Gills of Water, till it has a ſtrong Flavour of the Orange; then ſqueeze the Juice in it, beat the Yolks of ſix Eggs, but firſt boil your Liquor with half a Pound of fine Sugar, then mix in your Eggs by Degrees, for Fear of curdling. Let it have a Scald on the Fire, ſtirring it one Way. Put it in Cups or Glaſſes, cutting ſome of the Orange-peel like Threads, and hang them about the Rim.

To make Lemon Cream.

LEMON Cream is made the ſame Way, but with more Sugar, and two more Whites of Eggs. You muſt not whip the Whites much, or they will froth, and not thicken: When you mix your Liquor and Eggs, you muſt ſtrain it before you put it on the Fire. It muſt not boil, but be ſcalding hot, always ſtirring one Way. There muſt not be any Yolks of Eggs in this.

Maids Cream.

TAKE the Whites of five Eggs, and whiſk them to a Froth, then put them in a Sauce-pan, with very fine Sugar, three Gills of Cream, a Spoonful of Orange-flower Water, and a little pounded Cinnamon: Put it on the Fire, and keep it ſtirring one Way all the Time. Don't let it boil, but it muſt be ſcalding hot; then put it in the Aſhet, and brown it with a red hot Shovel.

To make a Rheniſh Wine Cream.

PUT on the Fire a Mutchkin of Rheniſh Wine, and a Stick of Cinnamon, and ſix Ounces of Loaf-ſugar; while it is boiling, take ſix Eggs, whiſk them very well, then whiſk in the Wine by Degrees, then put it on the
Fire,

Fire, and keep it whiſking all the Time, till it is pretty thick. It muſt not boil after the Eggs are in. Boil the Rind of a Lemon or Orange in the Wine; keep it whiſking all the Time, and when it is ſcalding hot, take it off, and put it in Cups, with as high a Froth as you can whiſk on it. You may make any Sort of white Wine the ſame Way.

To make Currant Cream.

BOIL a Mutchkin of Cream, and thicken it with two Eggs; when it is cold, put to it the Juice of a Chopin of Currants, and put the Currants in a Pan on the Fire, maſh them, and when they are thoroughly hot, ſtrain out the Juice, and ſweeten it to your Taſte; then mix it with the Cream, and put it in Cups. You may do Raſp-berry or Straw-berry Cream the ſame Way. Don't let the Cream boil after you put in the Eggs at any Time, but it muſt be ſcalding hot.

Sack Cream.

TAKE a Chopin of Cream, put it on the Fire with the Rind of a Lemon, and when it boils, take it off; beat two Eggs, and mix the Cream with them by Degrees, ſtirring them all the Time; then put it on the Fire again, and when it is ſcalding hot, take it off, and ſtir it one Way all the Time it is on the Fire; then take the China Bowl that you ſerve it to Table in, and put the Juice of half a Lemon, and nine Spoonfuls of Sack in it, and ſweeten both the Cream and Sack; then put in the Cream in the Bowl by Spoonfuls; ſend it up when quite cold, and keep it ſtirring till almoſt cold.

To make yellow Lemon Cream.

GRATE off the Peel of four Lemons, ſqueeze the Juice to it, and let it ſtand five Hours, then ſtrain it, and put to it the Whites of eight Eggs, and two Yolks well beaten and ſtrained, a Pound of double refined Sugar, and a Gill of Roſe-water; ſtir it well and ſet it

on

on the Fire, keep it ſtirring one Way, don't let it boil, when it comes to Cream it is enough.

Yellow Cream.

BOIL a Mutchkin of Cream with a Stick of Cinnamon, and the Rind of an Orange, then beat up the Yolks of eight Eggs with Roſe-water, and when the Cream is almoſt cold mix the Eggs with it by Degrees, ſweeten it to your Taſte; put it on a ſlow Fire, and keep it ſtirring one Way, till it is ſcalding hot, don't let it boil, then pour it in a Bowl, keep it ſtirring for a while, then whip up the Whites of Eggs to a Snow, and put them in the Oven, or before the Fire to harden; pour the Cream in your Diſh, but take out the Orange-peel and Cinnamon; put red Currant jelly, Marmalade of Oranges and any different coloured Sweet-meats about the Diſh, in Heaps, with the Whites of Eggs between every Heap. It is to be eaten cold.

Almond Cream.

BOIL a Chopin of Cream with Cinnamon, Lemon peel and ſliced Nutmeg; then blanch and pound ſome Almonds with Roſe-water, then take the Whites of nine Eggs well beaten, and put them into your Almonds, then rub them very well through a fine Search, ſo thicken your Cream with them; keep it ſtirring on a ſlow Fire till it is ſcalding hot; ſweeten it to your Taſte, you may put it in a Diſh, or in Cups.

Ratafia Cream.

BOIL four Laurel Leaves in a Chopin of Cream, and beat up the Yolks of five Eggs in a little cold Cream, and mix it with the reſt, put it on the Fire, and keep it ſtirring one Way; don't let it boil, but be ſcalding hot: Then take out the Leaves and ſweeten it to your Taſte, then put it in Cups. It is to be eaten cold.

To

To make Steeple Cream.

BOIL a Chopin of Cream, with two Pints of Milk, set it to cool, and skim the Cream off it, then boil it again and set it to cool; skim it, keep it boiling, and cooling and skimming till you have a Chopin of Cream that a Spoon will almost stand in it; take Care to stir it in the boiling, that no Brats come on it : Put in it, just as you are going to whisk it, half a Mutchkin of Malaga, a little fine Sugar, and the Juice of a Lemon; you must whisk it up very thick and raise it up on the Ashet in the Shape of a Sugar Loaf : Strew it all over with coloured confected Carraways, and garnish it with different coloured Sweet-meats.

To make Strawberry or Raspberry Cream.

MASH them small, and boil them with an equal Weight of Loaf-Sugar; when cold put to it a Mutchkin of Cream, or four or five Spoonfuls of either of them, and whisk them as you do Sillabubs. So fill your Glasses.

To make Coddlen or Goose-berry Cream.

CODDLE your Apples, till they are so soft that you will rub them thro' a Search with the Back of a Spoon, sweeten them to your Taste; when they are cold mix them with Cream : Goose-berries are done the same Way. Put them on an Ashet.

To make a very pretty red Cream.

TAKE a Mutchkin of Cream, and colour it with Cocheneal : Put the Grate of an Orange and Lemon in it, a little Malaga, and the White of an Egg; sweeten it to your Taste; whip it up thick and put it in Glasses. Any one may eat it, for Cocheneal is very wholesome.

To make Cream Deloutee.

TAKE a Mutchkin of Cream, the Rind of a Lemon or Orange-peel, and a Stick of Cinnamon, sweeten

ten

ten it to your Tafte ; let it ftand till it is almoft as cold
as new Milk, then take the yellow Skins that are in the
Gizzards of two Fowls, wafh them clean, cut them
fmall, and put them in the Cream ; then ftrain the
Cream through a thin Clothinto the Afhet, rubbing the
Cloth ; ftrain it two or three times, ftill keeping it rubbing: You muft be very quick in ftraining it, or it will
jelly in the Cloth ; then put it on warm Water, and cover the Afhet, then put Fire on the Cover ; when it is
jelly'd take it off gently, and fet it to cool, then ferve
it up : It muft be the Skins of the Gizzards of Hens,
Chickens or Turkies.

To make Rice Cream.

TAKE three Spoonfuls of the Flour of Rice, three
Yolks of Eggs, three Spoonfuls of Water, and two
Spoonfuls of Orange-flower Water ; mix them well
together, and put to them a Mutchkin of Cream, and
fet it on the Fire ; keep it ftirring till of a right Thick-
nefs, then difh it and eat it cold.

Clouted Cream.

TAKE an *Englifh* Gallon of good new Milk, fcald
it on a clear Fire, and keep it ftirring when it is at the
Boil ; take it off and ftir it a little, then put it in a
Milk-pan ; let it ftand twenty four Hours, then divide
the Cream with a Knife as it ftands upon the Pan, and
take it off with a Skimmer that the Milk may run from
it ; then lay it on a Difh, one Piece upon another, with
fine Sugar between each Piece till the Difh is full ;
keep it thus twenty four Hours before you fpread it :
If you pleafe beat Part of it with a little Rofe-water,
and a Lair of it, and a Lair of unbeaten Clouts, with
Sugar between; this clouted Cream beaten with a Spoon
till it is thick and light, makes *Spanifh* Cream.   It muft
be done with a little Rofe-water and Sugar.

Sack

Sack Cream.

BOIL a Bottle of white Wine, a little Cinnamon and Sugar to your Taste; then beat four Eggs with a little Nutmeg, and mix in the Wine by Degrees, keeping the Eggs beating all the Time; then put it on the Fire and keep it whisking; don't let it boil, but scalding hot; put it in Caudle Cups, send it hot to Table with a great Froth whisked on it; if you like it stiff and cold, put in the Yolks of eight Eggs, and two Whites.

To make Tablets.

WET a Pound of double refined Sugar, with two Gills of Water, it must be very finely pounded; put it on the Fire and keep it stirring all the Time till the Drop stands on the Spoon; and when it begins to candy about the Sides of the Pan, it is enough. Oil a Dish, and just as you are going to pour it out, put in it two Tea Spoonfuls of the Oil of Cinnamon, keeping it always stirring till you pour it on the Dish: When almost cold, cut it in any Shape you please. Ginger Tablets are made the same Way; but instead of the Oil of Cinnamon, put in two Drops of Ginger, beaten and sifted very fine.

To make a Crokain.

TAKE three Quarters of a Pound of fine Sugar, put it in a clear Copper-pan with two Gills of Water; put it on the Fire, let it boil flow, skim it, but don't stir it; put in the Juice of half a Lemon, then let it boil brown; then take a Spoon and try if it ropes; oil your Mold, and spin it on as neatly as you can, and let it be pretty thick at the Bottom; when it is done, take it off as gently as you can. You may put any of the Creams mentioned in this Book, or red or green preserved Apples or Oranges, under it.

T

To make a floating Island.

TAKE half a Pound of Currant Jelly, and the Whites of four Eggs ; put them in a large Bowl, and whisk it till it is as thick that you may drop it with a Spoon into any Shape you pleaſe : You muſt keep whisking all one Way, it takes a long Time to whisk it ; and it muſt be whisked from the Bottom of the Bowl ; then drop it by Spoonfuls in an Aſhet, and raiſe it up as high as you can ; put under it two Gills of Cream, a Spoonful of Roſe-water, and a little Sugar : You may make it of roaſted Apples the ſame Way, but they muſt be cold, and maſh them with the Back of a Spoon. You may put a yellow Cream under it, but don't make it too ſtiff.

Solid Sillabubs.

TAKE a Chopin of very thick Cream, put into it three Gills of Malaga, the Grate of a Lemon, the Juice of two bitter Oranges, and ſweeten it to your Taſte ; beat it well together for a Quarter of an Hour, then ſkim it with a Spoon, and put it in Glaſſes.

To make Sillabubs from the Cow.

SWEETEN either Wine, Cedar, or ſtrong Ale, put it in a Bowl, take it to the Cow, and milk her on your Liquor as faſt as you can. You may make it at home, by warming it, and pour it on the Liquor out of a Tea Pot.

A Jelly Poſſet.

TAKE twelve Eggs, leave out half the Whites, and beat them very well, put them into a large Bowl or a Soup Diſh, with a Mutchkin of Malaga or ſtrong Ale ; ſweeten it to your Taſte, and ſet it on a Pan or Pot of boiling Water, keeping it ſtirring all the Time ; then have ready a Chopin of Milk or Cream, boiled with Cinnamon and Nutmeg, and when your Wine and Eggs are ſcalding hot, put the Milk to them boiling hot, then take

take it off the Fire, and cover it for half an Hour, so send it up.

A Sack Poffet, or what is called the Snow Poffet.

BOIL a Chopin of Cream or Milk with Cinnamon and Nutmeg; then beat the Yolks of ten Eggs, and mix them with a little cold Milk; then by Degrees mix them with the Cream; stir it on the Fire till it is scalding hot; sweeten it to your Taste; put in your Dish a Mutchkin of Sack, with some Sugar and Nutmeg; set it on a Pot of boiling Water, and when the Wine is hot, let one take the Cream, and another the Whites of the Eggs, and pour them both in holding your Hands high, and stirring all together while it is on the Fire; when it is scalding hot, take it off, cover it, and let it stand a while before you send it to Table. The Whites must be beaten with a little Sack.

To make Oat-meal Flummery.

PUT three large Handfuls of Oat-meal ground small in two Chopins of Water: Let it steep a Day and a Night; then pour off the clear Water, and put two Chopins more on it, and let it stand the same Time, then stir it, and strain it through a Hair-sieve, till it is as Porridge, that is, what is called in *England* Hasty Pudding; stir it all the Time, that it may be extremely smooth before you set it on the Fire; put in a Spoonful of Sugar, and two of Orange-flower Water; when it is boiled enough, pour it in a shallow Dish; when cold, you may eat it with Wine and Sugar, Ale or Milk.

To make Scots *Flummery.*

TAKE a Mutchkin of Milk, and one of Cream; beat the Yolks of nine Eggs, with a little Rose-water, Sugar and Nutmeg; put it in a Dish, and the Dish over a Pan of boiling Water covered close; when it begins to grow thick, have ready some Currants plumped in Sack, and strew over it. It must not be stirred while it

is

is over the Fire, and when it is pretty ftiff, fend it up hot.

To make *Weft Country Flummery.*

L A Y half a Peck of Wheat Brawn in Steep, in cold Water, for three or four Days; then ftrain it, and boil it to a Jelly; Sweeten it with Sugar, and put in either Orange-flower, or Rofe-water; then fet it to cool, and eat it with Cream, Milk, Wine or Beer.

To make a *Hedge-hog.*

B L A N C H and beat a Pound of Almonds very fine, with a Spoonful of Sack or Orange-flower Water, to keep them from oiling; make it into a ftiff Pafte, then beat fix Eggs, and put two Whites, fweeten it with fine Sugar, then put in half a Mutchkin of Cream and a Quarter of a Pound of beat Butter, fet it on your Stove, and keep it ftirring till it is ftiff, that you make it into the Shape of a Hedge-hog, then ftick it full of blanch-ed Almonds cut in Straws; fet them on it like the Briftles, with two Currants plump'd for Eyes; then place it in the Middle of the Difh, and boil fome Cream; put in it the Yolks of two Eggs, and fweeten it to your Tafte; put it on a flow Fire, and when it is fcalding hot take it off; you muft keep it ftirring all the while; when it is cold put it about the Hedge-hog.

To make *Flummery Caudle.*

T A K E a Mutchkin of fine Oat-meal, put to it two Chopins of Water, let it ftand twelve Hours; then ftrain it into a Skellet with a little Mace and Nutmeg; fet it on the Fire and keep it ftirring, and let it boil a Quarter of an Hour; if it is too thick put in more Wa-ter, and let it boil longer; add to it a Mutchkin of white Wine, the Juice of a Lemon or Orange, and a Bit of Butter: Sweeten it to your Tafte; let it have one Boil. You may put in the Yolks of two Eggs, but let it boil after you put in the Eggs; let it be fcalding hot, keep it ftirring till you difh it.

To

To make Hartſhorn Flummery.

TAKE a Mutchkin of very ſtiff Hartſhorn Jelly, and put to it two Gills of Cream, Nutmeg, Cinnamon, Lemon-peel, and two Laurel Leaves, ſweeten it to your Taſte, boil all together in a clean Sauce-pan ; then ſtrain it in large Cups, and when cold turn it out in a Diſh ; put Cream, Sugar and Wine about them.

To make a Calf's Foot Flummery.

TAKE four Calf's Feet, ſplit them, and take out the long Bone, put them in three Chopins of Water, with ſome Cinnamon, Mace, Nutmeg, and Lemon-peel, let it boil gently till it is a ſtrong Jelly ; ſet it to cool, and ſkim off all the Fat, but ſtrain it firſt ; when cold take the Sediment, put it in the Pan with a Mutchkin of Cream, ſweeten it to your Taſte, put it over the Fire ; take the Yolks of eight Eggs and beat them very well, with a little cold Cream ; when the Jelly is lukewarm put in the Eggs, keep it ſtirring till the Eggs begin to be ſet, ſweeten it to your Taſte ; then run it through a Sieve, and put it in Cups. It is to be eaten cold.

A Sack or Ale Poſſet.

BOIL a Chopin of Cream, or new Milk, and grate in five or ſix fine Biſcuits, and let them boil with the Cream, ſeaſon it with Sugar and Nutmeg, let it ſtand a little to cool ; then put half a Mutchkin of Sack or ſtrong Ale in your Diſh or Bowl : Let it be a little hot, then hold up your Hand pretty high, and pour in the Cream : Let it ſtand a little, then ſend it up.

A Sack Poſſet without Cream or Eggs.

TAKE a Pound of *Jordan* Almonds, lay them all Night in Water, then blanch and beat them very fine, with a Gill of Orange-flower Water, and put them in a Chopin of Water, with the Crumbs of a Penny Loaf, beat Cinnamon, Nutmeg and Sugar ; let it boil till it be pretty thick, keep it ſtirring all the Time, then warm

two

two Gills of Sack and put to it, ſtir all together ; ſerve it up hot.

A very good Poſſet.

TAKE a Chopin of Cream, and mix it with a Mutchkin of ſtrong Ale, then beat the Yolks of eight Eggs, and three of the Whites, then put them to the Cream and Ale ; ſweeten it to your Taſte, and grate Nutmeg in it ; ſet it over the Fire, and keep it ſtirring all the while ; when it is thick, and before it boils, take it off, and put it in the Diſh very gently, ſo ſend it up ; ſtir all Things but one Way that have Eggs in them.

To make an Oat-meal Poſſet.

TAKE a Mutchkin of Milk, boil it with Nutmeg and Cinnamon, and put in it two Spoonfuls of Flour of Oat-meal, and boil it till the Rawneſs is off the Oat-meal ; then take three Spoonfuls of Sack, and three of Ale, and two of Sugar ; ſet it over the Fire till it is ſcalding hot, then put them to the Milk, give it one Stir, and let it ſtand on the Fire a Minute or two, and pour it in your Bowl ; cover it and let it ſtand a little, then ſend it up.

Egg Cheeſe.

TAKE a Chopin of Milk, a Mutchkin of Cream beat, and ten Eggs ; leave out four Whites, mix them well with the Cream, Lemon-peel, Cinnamon, Sugar, Roſe-water, and half a Mutchkin of white Wine ; then ſet it on the Fire, and keep it ſtirring all the Time till it boils ; when you ſee it broke, take it off and put it in any ſhaped Mold that has Holes in it, till the Whey runs out ; when cold, put it on the Diſh : You may put Wine and Sugar on them, or you may boil two Gills of Cream, thicken it with the Yolks of two Eggs, and pour it about it.

Cheeſe Loaves.

TAKE three Chopins of Milk, put a Spoonful of Runnet in it ; and when it is come, preſs the Whey gently

gently out of it; then put as much grated Bread as Curd, and the Yolks of twelve Eggs, six Whites, two Gills of Cream, beat Cinnamon, Mace, Nutmeg, Sugar, two Spoonfuls of Flour, a little Salt, and a Glass of Sack or Brandy; make it into a Paste, roll some of it thin to fry; make the rest in a Loaf, and bake it, then cut a Hole in the Top, pour in some beat Butter, Cream and Sugar; put the fried Cakes about it in the Dish, and send it up hot.

Almond Puffs.

BLANCH two Ounces of Almonds, then take their Weight of fine Loaf-sugar, beat them together with Orange-flower Water; then whip up the Whites of three Eggs and put to them, and add as much sifted Sugar as will make it into a Paste; then make it into little Cakes, and bake them in a very slow Oven.

Pudding Puffs.

TAKE half a Mutchkin of Cream and three well beaten Eggs, three Spoonfuls of Flour, two Spoonfuls of Rose-water, Sugar, Nutmeg, and a little Salt; mix all well together; butter some Cups, and fill them more than half full of it, and bake them ten Minutes in a slow Oven: When they are done, turn them out on a Dish, and grate Sugar on them; send them up hot.

Lemon Puffs.

BEAT and sift a Pound of Loaf-sugar, mix it with the Juice of two Lemons, and the Rind grated fine; whisk the Whites of three Eggs to a Snow; then beat all together very well; sift Sugar on Papers, and drop it on by Spoonfuls; don't let them be too near one another; put them in a very slow Oven. You may make Orange Puffs the same Way.

Orange Loaves.

CUT a Bit out of the End of the Oranges, and take out all the Inside, and grate them; boil them in
different

different Waters till they are tender, and all the Bitterness off them; let them dry, and boil them in a thin Syrup, till it has penetrated through them very well; then let them ftand in the Syrup a Day or two, then take the Yolks of fix Eggs, two Whites, a Quarter of a Pound of fine Bifcuits pounded, Butter, two Gills of Cream, fome of the Grate of the Orange, Sugar and Nutmeg; put it in a Pan, and ftir it on the Fire till it is thick, then ftir in it a little Brandy, and fill the Orange Skins; bake and ferve them up, with beat Butter, Wine, and Sugar in a Cup.

To make Wafers.

LET the Flour be very dry; make it in a thick Batter with Cream; feafon it with Sugar and Cinnamon, and a very little Salt; beat an Egg very well, and put in it; butter your Irons, and let them be very hot, then put in a Tea-fpoonful of the Batter; clap the Irons together, and hold them on the Fire for half a Minute, turning them; then take out the Wafer, and give it a Turn round your Finger, till it is in the Shape of a Funnel; as faft as you make them lay them on a Difh before the Fire.

Dutch *Wafers.*

BEAT four Eggs very well, mix with them a Pound of Flour, a Mutchkin of Cream, twelve Ounces of beat Butter; feafon it with Sugar, Nutmeg, and Rofe-water; put in two Spoonfuls of Barm, mix all well together, and bake them in your Wafer-irons; there muft be more of the Batter put in thefe than the other Wafers, and they take a longer Time on the Fire.

To make a Hen's Neft.

TAKE Calves Feet Jelly that is very ftrong, and put it in a white Bowl, or a Turks-cap; fill it near half full of the Jelly, let it be cold; take five Eggs, make a Hole

in

in the narrow End of them, that the Yolks and Whites may come out; then fill them with Blamong: Let them ftand till they are cold, then take off the Shells by Pieces, and take care not to break the Blamong; then lay them in the Middle of the Jelly, fo that they don't touch one another; then pour more Jelly on them when it is almoft cold : Cut fome Lemon-peel as Straws, and when the Jelly is ftiff, ftrew it over it; then pour a little more Jelly over it : When all is cold and very ftiff, dip the Bowl in hot Water ; have an Afhet ready, and put it on the Top of the Bowl, and turn it out quick : Don't let the Bowl be a Moment in the Water.

To make a Caudle for Sweet Pies.

TAKE two Gills of white Wine, a little Nutmeg, Sugar, and Lemon-peel ; put it on the Fire, and when it is fcalding hot, beat the Yolks of two Eggs, and mix them with a little cold Wine ; then mix all together ; keep it ftirring till it is fcalding hot, then take it up, and pour it over the Pye or Tart.

To make Fairy Butter.

TAKE the Yolks of four hard Eggs, and half a Pound of Loaf-fugar beat and fifted, half a Pound of frefh Butter; bray them in a clean Bowl with two Spoonfuls of Orange-flower Water; when it is well mixed, force it through a Corner of a thin Canvas Strainer in little Heaps on a Plate. It is a very pretty Supper Difh.

To make a Slipcoat Cheefe.

TAKE two *Englifh* Gallons of hot Milk, juft milked, and put to it twelve Spoonfuls of Runnet, and when it comes, put a thin Cloth in a Cheefe-vat; then take out the Curd with a Saucer, and lay them as gently as you can ; then pour a little Water foftly on the Curd, and let all the Whey run out ; then put on more Curd and more Water ; do this till the Vat is quite full, then put a Cloth over it, and a thin Board ; and when it falls put more Curd to it, and lay a Pound Weight on the Board : This Quantity makes two Chee-ses ; let it lye in the Vat ten Hours, then turn it with a dry Cloth, and put it in the Vat again, and let it ly ten Hours more ; then turn it on a dry Board, and sprinkle a little Salt on it ; let it ly till the Salt is melt-ed, then get Nettles, pluck off the Leaves and wipe them clean ; spread them on a dry Board, and lay the Cheese on them ; then cover it with them, and let it be kept in a warm Place : Change the Nettle Leaves twice a Day, wiping the Cheese every Time with a soft Cloth. It will be ripe in ten Days, or a Fortnight.

To make Cream Cheese, as at Newport.

GET a Vat, a Quarter and a half high, the Bottom and Top must not be fastened, it must be four Square, with Holes all over ; then take two Chopins of Cream, six Chopins of new Milk, and set it with Runnet ; when it is come, put a dry Cloth in the Vat, and lay the Curd in it with a China Saucer, and put it into the Vat ; strew a little Salt in two or three Lairs till all the Curd is in ; cover it and press it as other Cheeses ; let it stand two or three Days till all the Whey is out, but turn it with dry Cloths every Day ; then salt it lightly two Days ; let it dry without rubbing. It is to be made in *May*.

To make a good Cheese.

TAKE three Chopins of Milk hot from the Cow, and a Chopin of Cream ; put one Spoonful of Runnet in it, and when it comes, break it and put in a little Salt ; put a Cloth in the Vat, then put in the Curd, and press it as you do other Cheese ; turn it in the Vat often, and when it is wheyed, salt it, then put it to dry, wiping and turning it every Day. You must not cut it till it is a Year old.

To make a thick Cheese.

TAKE the Milk of ten Cows, and put to it three Spoonfuls of Runnet, and when it comes, break it and whey it, and let it ly for a while ; then whey it again, and when it is very well wheyed, break into it two Pounds of sweet Butter, and a little Salt ; then put it in the Vat, and press it very well; turn it very often, and change the Cloths : You may put wet Cloths at first about it, and thereafter put dry Cloths ; let it ly fourteen Hours in the Press, then take it out and salt it a little ; then dry it with a Cloth. Put it on a dry Board, and wipe and turn it every Day.

To make a Welsh *Rabbet.*

CUT Toasts, and toast them on both Sides, then toast the Cheese on the Bread, and send it up hot.

To toast Cheese.

TOAST the Bread and sock it in Wine, set it before the Fire, cut the Cheese in very thin Slices, rub Butter over the Bottom of a Plate, lay the Cheese in, pour in two or three Spoonfuls of Wine, cover it with another Plate, set it on a Chaffing dish of Coals for three Minutes ; then mix it, and when it is done, lay it on the Bread ; brown it with a Salamander, or a red hot Shovel.

To toast Cheese another Way.

TAKE a Quarter of a Pound of *Cheshire* Cheese, not too fat, two Ounces of Butter, and two Eggs ; beat all together very well, then prepare some Toasts pretty brown ; butter them on both Sides, then spread the Cheese upon them : Then brown it with a Salamander, or a red hot Fire-shovel. Serve it up hot.

To make Wigs.

TAKE a Quarter of a Peck of Flour, rub into it three Quarters of a Pound of Butter, something more
than

than Half a Pound of Sugar, a little Nutmeg and Ginger grated, three Eggs well beaten ; put to them half a Mutchkin of thick Barm, and a Glafs of Brandy, make a Hole in your Flour and pour all in, with as much warm Milk as will make it in a light Pafte ; let it ftand before the Fire to rife half an Hour, then make it into a Dozen and a Half of Wigs. Bake them half an Hour.

A Plumb-cake or Bun.

TAKE five Pounds of Flour, and put to it half an Ounce of Nutmegs, Cloves and Mace, finely beaten, and a little Salt, mix all well together, then take a Chopin of Milk, let it boil, put into it three Pounds of Butter ; when melted, and blood-warm, mix it with a Chopin of Barm, and two Gills of Brandy, twenty Eggs well beaten, ten Whites, fix Pounds of well clean'd Currants ; mix in the Flour, make a Hole in the Middle of your Flour, and put in the Milk and other Things, mixing it well with your Hands, cover it warm before the Fire to rife ; then put it in the Hoop, if the Oven is hot, two Hours will bake it ; you may put Sweetmeats in it if you pleafe.

To make Wigs another Way.

TAKE two Pounds of Flour, and a Quarter of a Pound of Butter, and as much Sugar; Nutmeg, Cloves and Mace, of each a little; pound in them a Quarter of an Ounce of Carraway feeds, a little Barm in as much Cream as will make it in Pafte, mix all together, and work them well; fet them by the Fire to rife ; when the Oven is ready they will foon bake.

To make Bath Buns.

TAKE two Pounds of Flour, a Mutchkin of Barm, put a little Brandy in the Barm, and three Eggs well beaten, a little warm Milk, Nutmeg, and a little Salt ; rub into the Flour a Pound of Butter, and a Pound of confected Carraways; mix all together, and work it with
your

your Hands; set them before the Fire to rise; bake them in a quick Oven, on flour'd Papers, in what Shape you please.

To make Shrewsbury Cakes.

TAKE one Pound of Sugar, three Pounds of Flour, a Nutmeg, and some Cinnamon beaten, the Sugar and Spice must be sifted in the Flour; wet it with three Eggs, and as much melted Butter as will make it in a good Thickness, to roll into a Paste; mould it well, and roll it and cut it into what Shape you please: Prick them before they go into the Oven.

To make Almond Cakes.

TAKE a Pound of Almonds, blanch and beat them very well, with a little Orange-flower Water, beat three Eggs, but two Whites, and put to them a Pound of Sugar sifted; and then put in your Almonds, and beat all together very well: Butter white Paper, and lay your Cakes in what Form you please, and bake them.

To make Drop Biscuit.

TAKE eight Eggs and a Pound of fine Sugar pounded and sifted, and twelve Ounces of fine Flour well dried; beat your Eggs well, then put in your Sugar and beat it, and then your Flour by Degrees, and beat it all together for an Hour without ceasing. Your Oven must be as hot as for Penny Bread. Then flour some Paper, and drop your Biscuits into what Bigness you please, and put them into the Oven as fast as you can; and when you see them rise, watch them; and if they begin to colour, take them out again, and put in more; and if the first is not enough put them in again: If they are right done they will have a white Ice on them; you may put in Carraway-seeds if you please. When they are all baked, put them into the Oven again, till they are very dry.

To

To make Marlborough *Cakes.*

TAKE eight Eggs, beat them, and put to them a Pound of Sugar, beaten and sifted, beat it three Quarters of an Hour together; then put in three Quarters of a Pound of fine dry Flour, and two Ounces of Carraway-seeds, beat it all well together, and bake it in a quick Oven in Tin Pans.

A Seed-cake.

TAKE two Pounds of fine Flour well dried, and rub in it a Pound of fresh Butter, and ten Eggs, leaving out five Whites; three Spoonfuls of Cream, four Spoonfuls of good Barm; mix all well together, and set it to the Fire, but not too near; when it is well risen, put in a Pound of confected Carraway. An Hour and a Quarter will bake it.

Another Sort of little Cakes.

TAKE a Pound of Flour, a Pound of Butter, and rub the Butter in the Flour, two Spoonfuls of Barm, and two Eggs: Make it up in a Paste buttered Paper: Roll your Paste out the Thickness of a Crown: Cut them out with the Top of a Tin Canister: Sift fine Sugar over them, and bake them in a slow Oven for an Hour.

To make Whetstone *Cakes.*

TAKE half a Pound of fine Flour, and half a Pound of Loaf-Sugar, pounded and searched, a Spoonful of Carraway Seeds, the Yolk of an Egg, and the Whites of three; a little Rose or Orange-flower Water: Mix all together, and roll it out as thin as a Wafer; cut them with a Glass, lay them on floured Papers, and bake them in a slow Oven.

A Seed-cake very rich.

TAKE a Pound of Flour dried, a Pound of Sugar beaten and sifted, a Pound of Butter work'd with your Hand to a Cream: Beat the Yolks of ten Eggs, six Whites,

Whites, and mix all together ; an Ounce of Carraway Seeds, and a Gill of Brandy. Keep it beating till you put it in the Oven.

To make a Plumb-cake.

TAKE four Pounds of fine Flour well dried, five Pounds of Currants well picked and rubbed, five Pounds of Butter beat to a Cream, two Pounds of Almonds beaten fine, thirty four Eggs, half the Whites, two Pounds of fine Sugar beaten and fifted, beaten Mace, Cloves, Ginger, Nutmeg, and two Gills of Brandy : Beat your Sugar firft in your Butter, then all the reft by Degrees. You may put in Orange, Lemon-peel candied, and Citron. Keep it beating till you put it in the Oven : Four Hours will bake it.

To ice a great Cake.

TAKE two Pounds of the fineft double refined Sugar, and beat and fift it ; beat and fift a little Starch, and mix with it ; beat fix Whites of Eggs to a Froth, and put to it fome Gum-water ; then mix and beat all this together two Hours, and put it on your Cake ; when it is baked, fet it in the Oven a Quarter of an Hour.

A rich Nun's Cake.

TAKE four Pounds of fine Flour, and three Pounds of fine Sugar pounded and fifted; dry both by the Fire, beat four Pounds of Butter with your Hands to a Cream ; then beat thirty five Eggs, leaving out half the Whites, and beat them and the Butter together, till all appears like Butter. Put in a Gill of Brandy, and beat it again ; then take your Flour and Sugar, with fix Ounces of Carraway Seeds, and ftrew it in by Degrees, beating it all the Time for two Hours together. Butter your Hoop, and let it ftand three Hours i na moderate Oven.

Sugar

Sugar Biscuits.

TAKE six Dozen of Eggs, and break them all, keep out one Dozen and a half of the Whites; then take and beat them till they drop like Water; then put in by Degrees half a Stone of Sugar well beat and search-ed; then beat it till it be extraordinary white and thick. You may know when it is enough, for there will be no red Strings through it; then put in it two Gills of Brandy, and a Quarter of a Pound of Carraway Seeds, then stir in six Fourths of Flour, then drop it upon your Papers, then glaze the Biscuits with fine Sugar before you put them in the Oven. See that the O-ven be not too hot.

A Diet Loaf.

TAKE six Eggs, beat them till they drop like Wa-ter, and put in twelve Ounces of fine Sugar, well beat and searched; then put in a Spoonful or two of Brandy, and the Grate of two Lemons; mix all together, and beat it with your Whisk well; then put in ten Ounces of Flour, then rub the Frame with Butter, let it stand an Hour in the Oven. Paper the Top, that it may not burn.

To make Saffron Cakes.

TAKE three Pounds of the finest Flour, and dry it before the Fire, mix in it, when it is cold, three Quar-ters of a Pound of fine powdered Sugar, make a Hole in the Middle of the Flour, beat six Eggs very well and pour them in the Hole, take a Quarter of an Ounce of Saffron, dry and powder it; put it in a Mutchkin of Milk, with half a Pound of Butter, warm it on the Fire; and when the Butter is melted take it off, let it be but just warm: When you pour it to the Flour, whisk among the Eggs three Gills of very good Barm, then put in the Milk and beat it together with your Hands; shake a little Flour on it, and cover it by the Fire till it rises; then mould it in Cakes the Big-ness of Bakes: They must have as slow an Oven as

Milk

Milk-bakes, and if they are too ſtiff, you muſt put in a little more Milk.

To make Ratafia Biſcuits.

POUND and ſift a Pound and three Quarters of Loaf Sugar, blanch and beat to a Paſte a Pound of bitter Almonds, mix half the Sugar with them, as you are pounding the Almonds keep them wet with Roſewater; beat the Whites of ſix Eggs to Snow, and mix the reſt of the Sugar with them: Then juſt as you are going to put them in the Oven mix all together; drop them on flour'd Papers, a Spoonful in a Place. The Oven muſt not be very hot.

To make ſhort Bread.

TAKE a Peck of Flour, make a Hole in the Middle, melt three Pounds of good Butter in a Mutchkin of Barm, put Carraway or what dry Sweet-meats you pleaſe in the Flour; then pour in your Butter and Barm, work it well with your Hands, and if too dry, put in a little warm Water; when it is well worked, roll it out in Cakes of what Shape you pleaſe. Prick it well with a Fork, and bake it on floured Papers.

To make a Seed Cake.

BEAT ſixteen Ounces of good Butter to a Cream, with your Hands; pound and ſift ſixteen Ounces of Sugar, beat twelve Eggs, the Yolks and Whites ſeparate, a Pound of fine Flour well dried, put in all theſe by Spoonfuls, keeping the Butter beating all the Time, the Yolks muſt be beat to Cream, the Whites to a Snow. Don't put in the thin that will fall to the Bottom of the Whites of the Eggs; beat in half an Ounce of Carraway Seeds; when it is beat enough it will come eaſy off your Hands; put it in your Hoop; two Hours bakes it in not too ſlow an Oven.

To make Biscuits.

TAKE fifteen Eggs, beat them till they drop like Water off the Whisk ; then beat two Pounds of Sugar, and fift it; put in your Sugar by Degrees, and the Grate of an Orange or Lemon, or Carraway Seed, a Pound and an half of Flour, ftir all together, drop them by Spoonfuls on floured Paper; don't let the Oven be too hot.

To make white Cakes.

TAKE three Chopins of fine Flour, a Pound and a half of Butter, and a Mutchkin of Cream, two Gills of good Barm, a Gill of Rofe-water and Brandy, a little Mace and Nutmegs beaten, nine Eggs, four Whites well beaten, five Ounces of fine Sugar ; mix the Sugar and Spice, and a very little Salt with your dry Flour, and keep out a Handful of the Flour, melt the Butter in a little Cream : When a little cold, put the Eggs and Barm in it ; make a Hole in the Midft, and pour in all the Flour, ftirring it round with your Hand all one Way till well mixed ; ftrew on the Flour you left out, and fet it before the Fire to rife, cover'd with a Cloth : Have three Pounds of Currants well wafh'd, pick'd and dried ; mingle them in the Flour before you wet it ; butter your Hoop, fet it in a quick Oven, or it will not rife. An Hour and a half bakes it.

To make the thin Dutch *Biscuits.*

TAKE five Pounds of Flour, and two Ounces of Carraway Seed, half a Pound of Sugar, and fome more than a Mutchkin of Milk ; put into it three Quarters of a Pound of Butter, warm the Milk, and put in a Mutchkin of good Barm ; make a Hole in the Middle of your Flour, and pour all in, and make it in a Pafte, and let it ftand a Quarter of an Hour by the Fire to rife ; then mold it, and roll it in Cakes pretty thin ; prick them all over pretty much, or they will blifter. Bake them a Quarter of an Hour.

To mak Quince Cakes.

TAKE two Pounds of dried Flour, beat fixteen Ounces of fweet Butter with your Hands till it is in a Cream;
then beat twelve Eggs, but half the Whites; pound and
fift fourteen Ounces of fine Sugar, wafh, dry, and pick
twelve Ounces of Currants; then mix them all by
Degrees, keeping them beating all the Time; put in
Nutmeg, Cinnamon and Brandy; when they are beat
enough, the Dough will come clean off your Hands;
then butter fome Tart Pans, and bake them not in too
hot an Oven, but keep the Oven-door clofs while they
are baking. You may make fmall Seed-cakes the fame
Way.

York *Cakes.*

TAKE half a Peck of Flour, a Mutchkin of Barm,
two Pound of Currants, a Pound of Butter, rub it into the Flour, grate two Nutmegs in it; mix all together
with a little Salt and fome Sugar, wet it with hot Water, it will make twelve Cakes, but let it ly before the
Fire to rife. Bake them in a quick Oven.

To make Naples *Bifcuits.*

TAKE a Pound of fine Sugar pounded and fifted,
a Pound of fine Flour, beat eight Eggs, with two Spoonfuls of Rofe-water; mix the Flour and Sugar, then
wet it with the Eggs, and as much cold Water as will
make a light Pafte; beat the Pafte very well, then put
them in Tin Pans. Bake them in a gentle Oven.

To make Macaroons.

BLANCH and beat a Pound of Almonds very
fine, keeping them wetting with Orange-flower Water:
Take an equal Quantity of fine Sugar, pounded and
fifted, then beat up the Whites of eight Eggs, and
mix them all together; place them handfomely on
Wafers, then on Tin Plates or Papers. Bake them in
a flow Oven.

To make Ginger-bread.

TAKE half a Peck of Flour well dried, five Pounds of Treacle, half a Pound of Butter, two Ounces of beaten Ginger, an Ounce of Carraway Seed; boil the Treacle and Butter together, then mix it with the Flour and Seeds: You may put candied Orange, or Lemon-peel in it: If you please put three Eggs in it, bake them in little Cakes on butter'd Papers.

To make Dutch Ginger-bread.

MIX four Pounds of Flour, two Ounces of beaten Ginger; rub in the Flour half a Pound of Butter, and add to it two Ounces of Carraway Seeds, two of O-range-peel dried and rubbed to Powder, two Pounds and a Quarter of Treacle; mix all together, and beat it with a Rolling-pin, and make it up in thirty Cakes; prick them with a Fork, and put them on double but-tered Papers.

Poor Knights of Windsor.

TAKE a Roll, and cut it into Slices; soke them in Sack, then dip them in Yolks of Eggs, and fry them; serve them up with beat Butter, Sack and Sugar.

To make Buns.

TAKE two Pounds of Flour, a Mutchkin of Barm; put a little Sack in the Barm, and three Eggs well beat, knead all these together with a little warm Milk, Nut-meg and Salt; then lay it before the Fire till it rises very light, then knead in it sixteen Ounces of sweet Butter, and a Pound of confected Carraway, and bake them in a quick Oven on floured Papers, in what Shape you please.

A Cake to eat hot.

TAKE two Pounds of Flour, rub in it half a Pound of Butter, six Ounces of Sugar, grated Nutmeg and Salt; beat up four Eggs with two Gills of Barm, put as much warm Milk as will make it in a light Dough; work it well, and put it to the Fire to rise: An Hour
and

and a half bakes it. You may put half a Pound of Currants, and half a Pound of ſton'd Raiſins in it, if you pleaſe.

A common Breakfaſt Cake.

TAKE three Quarters of a Pound of Flour, eight Ounces of Butter, four Eggs, half an Ounce of Carraway Seeds; beat it well with your Hands, and bake it in a quick Oven.

Bath *Cakes.*

TAKE a Quart of Flour, a Pound of Butter, ten Ounces of confected Carraways, ſix Eggs, and but three Whites, ſix Spoonfuls of Barm, and a little Cream; mix all together, then put them in the Flour, the Butter and Cream muſt be melted; don't let it be too hot, then put it to the Barm and Eggs; work the Dough well, and ſet it to the Fire to riſe; then ſhake in the Carraways, and make it into little Cakes, and bake them on floured Papers in a quick Oven.

CHAP. V.

Of PICKLING, *&c.*

RULES to be obſerved.

ALWAYS uſe Stone Jars for all Sorts of Pickles that require hot Pickle; for Vinegar and Salt will penetrate through all earthen Veſſels: Stone and Glaſs are the only Things to keep Pickles in: Don't put your Hands in them, but take them up with a Spoon: Let your Braſs Pan for any Pickles be very bright and clean, and your Pan for white Pickles well tinned: Uſe the very beſt Vinegar, and when they are in the Jars, and cold, melt Sewet, and when it is as cold that it will but juſt pour on them, put it over them, then cover them with wet Bladders.

To

To pickle Samphire.

IF it is frefh pulled, put it in a Pickle of Salt and
Water, that will bear an Egg, changing the Water every four Days, till the Samphire is yellow ; then drain
it well, and put it in a Brafs Kettle, with green Cabbage Leaves over and under them, and as much Water
as will cover them, and the Bignefs of a Walnut of
Roche Allum : Put it on a Fire that will only keep it in
a moderate Heat till it is green ; then drain it off and
dry it with a Cloth ; put it in a Jar, and pour on it as
much Vinegar boiling hot, with Cloves, Mace, Pepper and fliced Ginger, as will cover it ; ftop it clofs ; if
the Samphire is yellow, and has been in Pickle before,
green it the fame Way. Obferve, that all Sorts of Spices are to be put on Pickles whole, except Nutmeg and
Ginger.

To pickle Elder Flowers when they are green, and before they are blown.

LET them ly in a ftrong Pickle of Salt and Water
two Days, then drain them, and put them in a Pan to
green, with as much Water as will cover them, and two
Gills of Vinegar ; put them on a very flow Fire, and
put green Blades over and under them ; when they are
green, dry them with a Cloth, then put them in a Jar,
and pour on them as much boiling Vinegar, with Cloves, Mace, Pepper and Ginger in it, as will cover them:
Potatoe-apples, and Nafturtian Buds are pickled the
fame Way.

To pickle Walnuts.

TAKE the Walnuts before the Shells are hard, and
make a Pickle of Salt and Water, ftrong enough to
bear an Egg ; boil and fkim it, and pour it on your
Walnuts : Let them ly twenty Days, changing the Pickle every five Days, and boiling it every Time ; then
take them out, and wipe them with a Cloth : Boil as
much white Wine Vinegar as will cover them, with
Pepper, Cloves, Mace, Ginger and Nutmeg quartered ;

flice

flice the Ginger, and let all the reft be whole : To
a hundred of Walnuts, put fix Spoonfuls of Muftard-
feed, and fix Cloves of Garlick : When your Walnuts,
Muftard, and Garlick are in the Jar, pour your Vinegar
and Spice boiling hot on them; prick them full of
Holes before you put them in the Salt and Water.

To pickle Walnuts green.

TAKE the largeft and cleareft you can get before
the Shells are hard ; pare them very thin, and as you
pare them, throw them in Spring-water ; put into the
Water a Pound of Bay-falt ; let them ly in it Twenty-
four Hours ; take them out and put them in a Jar, and
between every Lair of Walnuts lay a Lair of Vine-
leaves, and alfo at the Top and Bottom ; then fill it up
with cold Vinegar; let them ftand all Night, then pour
the Vinegar from them into a Bell-metal Sauce-pan,
with a Pound of Bay-falt, and let it boil ; pour it hot
on your Nuts, cover them clofs, and let them ftand a
Week ; pour off that Pickle, and rub them with a Piece
of Flannel ; then put them in the Jar with Vine-leaves,
as before, and boil frefh Vinegar with Cloves, Mace,
Ginger, Nutmeg, and Pepper ; pour it boiling hot on
them every Day for four Days, then put in with them
a little Muftard-feed, and either Garlick or Shalots.

To pickle Mufhrooms.

TAKE the fmall hard white Buttons, put them in
Water, and wipe them with a Bit of clean white Flannel till all the Spots or black is off them, and as you
wipe them throw them in clean Water; then put them
in a Pan of clean cold Water, with the Bignefs of a Nut
of Allum, and put them on the Fire ; don't let them
boil, but coming to it ; take them off, and fpread them
on a Cloth, and cover them with another ; have ready
boiled as much white Wine Vinegar as will cover them,
white Pepper, Cloves, Mace, Ginger in it ; they muft
be all whole : Don't put on the Vinegar till cold;
put

put a little fweet Oil on the Top of the Bottle you put them in. Obferve, that all the Water you put them in muft be cold.

To pickle Onions.

TAKE fmall Onions, put them in a Pan of cold Water on the Fire, and when they are coming to boil, take them off, and take off all the brown Skins; lay them between two Cloths till cold, then put them in Bottles, and boil white Wine Vinegar, Pepper, Mace, Cloves, Ginger, and pour it on them.

To pickle red Cabbage.

CUT the Cabbage in thin Shaves; put it in a Goblet with a Gill of Vinegar, and a little Salt; put it on the Fire clofs covered, and let it ly for ten Minutes, fhaking the Goblet very often; then put it in a well glazed Can, and boil as much Vinegar as will cover it, with whole Pepper, Cloves, Mace, and fliced Ginger; pour it on boiling hot; cover it clofs. It will be fit for eating in four Days.

To pickle Cucumbers, or Kidney-beans.

PUT them in a ftrong Pickle of Salt and Water for four Days; then drain them off, and dry them in a Cloth; put them in a Brafs Pan with green Cabbage-leaves under and over them, with as much Water as will cover them, and a little Bit of Roche Allum; put them on a very flow Fire, and change the Blades when they turn yellow; when they are very hot, take off the Pan till they are cold, then put it on again; put it on and off till they are green, then put them in a Cloth and dry them; boil white Wine Vinegar, whole Pepper, *Jamaica* Pepper, Cloves, and fliced Ginger, and when they are in the Jar, pour it on them boiling hot; cover them clofs. You may pickle any green Pickles the fame Way.

To pickle Cucumbers in Slices.

CUT large green Cucumbers in Slices, not too thin, put them in a broad Pan with some small peeled Onions ; let them stand twenty-four Hours close cover'd ; then put them in a Sieve to drain : Boil as much Vinegar as will cover them, whole Pepper, Mace, Ginger, and a little Salt ; and when they are in the Jar pour it boiling hot on them : Cover them close, boil the Vinegar every Day for four or five Days, then they will be fit for Use.

To pickle Mangoes.

TAKE the largest green Cucumbers you can get, and cut a Piece out of the Side, and take out all the Seeds ; fill them with Mustard, whole Pepper, Cloves, Mace, and Ginger sliced ; put in them Garlick, or Rockambole or Shalots ; then put in the Piece you cut out of the Side, and tye it fast : Green them as you do Cucumbers ; dry them, put them in a Jar, pour over them Vinegar boiling hot. Let all Sorts of Spice be boil'd in it.

To pickle Colliflowers.

TAKE Colliflowers, when then they are as big as an Egg, close and white, and just give them a Scald in boiling Water, then spread them on a Cloth, and cover them with it, boil the best Vinegar with whole white Pepper, Mace and Cloves ; and when they are dry put them in a Jar, and pour the Vinegar when cold on them. You may pickle white Cabbage Stalks and young Turneps the same Way, but pare the Turneps, and cut them the Bigness of Mushrooms.

To pickle Colliflowers red.

CUT them in small Pieces, but leave on them a short Stalk, put in a Chopin of Vinegar, three Pennyworth of Cocheneal, a little *Jamaica* and black Pepper, and a little Salt, boil it, and pour it hot over the Colliflowers : Let it stand two or three Days close covered ;

Y   scald

scald it every three Days till it is red. The Cocheneal must be very finely pounded.

To pickle Asparagus.

TAKE the largest Asparagus that is very green, cut off the White, and scrape them lightly to the Head, then put them in a Jar, and throw over them some Salt, and a few Cloves and Mace, and pour on them as much Vinegar as will cover them : Let them lye nine Days, then put the Vinegar in a Brass Kettle, and put the Asparagus into it, stow them down closs ; let them stand a little, then set them on the Fire until they are green ; then put them in a Jar, and tye them close.

To pickle Plumbs like Olives.

MAKE a Pickle of Water, Vinegar, white Wine and Fennel-seed ; boil it, put in as much of each as will give the Pickle a Taste ; then put in the Plumbs, and take them off the Fire presently. Let them stand till they are cold, and put them in Bottles

To pickle Sellery.

CUT Sellery two Inches long, put them in Salt and Water when it boils, and let them boil two or three Minutes ; let them cool, and boil Vinegar, Pepper, Cloves and Ginger ; and when cold pour it on them.

To pickle Codlins like Mangoes.

GET Codlins full grown, but not full ripe, put them in Salt and Water that will bear an Egg, let them lye in it nine Days, shift the Pickles every two Days, then dry them ; take out the Stalk so whole that it may fit again ; and scoop out the Core, but leave the Eye in them ; fill in the Room of the Core, with whole Mustard, a Clove of Garlick, Pepper, Mace and Cloves : Put in your Piece and tye it up tight, boil as much Vinegar as will cover them, whole Pepper, Cloves, Mace,

and

and fliced Ginger ; pour it boiling hot upon them every Day for a Fortnight.   Cover them clofe.

To make Goofeberry Vinegar.

BRUISE the Goofeberries with your Hand when
they are full ripe, and to every Chopin of Goofeberries put three Chopins of Water boil'd, and let it be
put cold on them, and let it ftand twenty-four Hours,
then ftrain it through Canvas, or Flannel ; to four
Chopins of it put a Pound of brown Sugar, ftir it well
and put it in a Barrel ; let it lye three Quarters of a
Year, but the longer the better : It is good for Pickling.

Muſhroom Powder.

TAKE a Fourth-part of large Mufhrooms, rub them
clean, but don't take out the Infide or Skins ; put to
them fixteen Blades of Mace, forty Cloves, a Spoonful of Pepper, and a Handful of Salt, the Bignefs of
an Egg of Butter, two Gills of Vinegar ; let all ftew faft
on the Fire, keep them ftirring till they have fpent
their Liquor ; keep the Liquor for any favoury Difhes,
and dry the Mufhrooms firft on a Difh in the Oven,
then on Sieves, till they are dry enough to pound. It
will keep four or five Years, and a little of it will re-
lifh any Meat Difh.

To codle the right Codlin with Cream.

PUT the Codlins in a Stew-pan, with as much
Water as will cover them ; fet them on a flow Fire till
the Skin peels off them, then take them up and peel
them ; put them in a very thin Syrup, with fome of
the Leaves of Apple Trees: Cover them clofs, and put
them on the Fire again, and let them fimmer, but not
boil : When they are green and tender, clarify half a
Pound of Sugar, and boil the Codlins in it : Set them
to fimmer on a very flow Fire, then fet them to cool, and
boil half a Mutchkin of Cream ; thicken it with the Yolks
of three Eggs : Put in it two Spoonfuls of Rofe-water,
fweeten

sweeten it to your Taste, and when it is cold, pour it over the Apples.

To keep Fruit for Tarts.

PULL the Goose-berries before they are full ripe, pick off the black Eyes and the Stems; get wide mouth-ed Bottles, that are very dry and sweet, put your Goose-berries in them, cork the Bottles well, put them in an Oven almost cold, and let them ly in it till they turn white; then take out the Bottles, and when they are cold, rosin the Corks, and put them in a cold, but not a damp Place. You may bottle red, white and black Currants, but they must be ripe.

To keep Damsons or small Plumbs for Tarts.

PUT them in a Lime Can: To six Pounds of Dam-sons put three Pounds of *Lisbon* Sugar, then put coarse Paste on the Can, and put it in the Oven for an Hour; when you are going to make Use of them, take them up with a Horn or Wooden Spoon: Never put your Hand in any preserved Fruit, for it will spoil them.

To make a Pupton of Apples.

PARE some Apples, take out the Cores, put them in a Sauce-pan, and chop them grosly; to three Mutchkins of these Apples put in a Quarter of a Pound of Sugar, and two Spoonfuls of Water: Put them on a slow Fire, keep them stirring, grate the Rind of an Orange and Lemon in it: When it is quite thick as Marmalade, let it stand till cold; then beat up the Yolks of four Eggs, and stir in a Handful of grated Bread, and a Quarter of a Pound of sweet Butter: Mix them all together, form it into what Shape you please, and bake it in a slow Oven; then put it on a Plate up-side down, for a second Course or Supper.

To make black Caps.

CUT twelve large Apples in Halves, and take out the Cores; place them on a white Iron Patty-pan with their Skins on; put to them four Spoonfuls of Rofe-water, and grate fine Sugar over them; fet them in a hot Oven till the Skins are black a little, and the Apples tender, fo ferve them up; and when you difh them, grate more Sugar over them.

To bake Apples.

PUT your Apples in an Earthen Can, with a few Cloves, a little Lemon-peel, coarfe Sugar, and a Glafs of red Wine; cover them clofs; they will take an Hour's Baking in a quick Oven. You may do Pears the fame Way, but they will take two Hours Baking.

To ftew Apples in Halves.

PARE them, and cut them in Halves, and take out the Cores: To eight Apples, put a Chopin of Water, a Quarter of a Pound of Sugar, the Rind of a Lemon and Orange cut in fmall Strings; put them in a Pan, cover them, and put them over the Fire; when they are foft, ferve them up with Lemon and Orange-peel about them, and the Syrup. You may do them the fame Way, without taking off the Skin.

To preferve Apples for Tarts, or Torts, for a Year.

PULL the right Sort of white Codlins, when they are no bigger than large Walnuts, and fome of the Leaves; put them in a Pan of cold Water, and put them on a flow Fire; when they turn white, take them up one by one, lay them on a Cloth, don't let them touch one another; cover them till both them and their Liquor is cold, then put them in a well glaz'd Can, and pour the Liquor over them; pour fome render'd Sewet over them, and tye them up clofs with a Bladder: When you are going to ufe them, take off their Skin, and put them, a little of their own

Liquor,

Liquor, and a Bit of fine Loaf-fugar in a preferving Pan ; cover them with Water, put green Kail-leaves over them, and fet them on a flow Fire till they are green, then boil up a Syrup of fine Sugar, and put them in it, and let them fimmer in it for an Hour. You may fend them when cold to Table, in the Syrup with Rofe-water in it, or bake them in Tarts, or Torts.

To make a Caudle for Apple or Goofe-berry Torts.

B O I L a half Mutchkin of Cream, with a Stick of Cinnamon, the Rind of a Lemon, and a little Sugar; thicken it with the Yolks of two Eggs : When your Tort is cold, and your Cream, put in it two or three Spoonfuls of Rofe-water, and pour it over the Tort.

To preferve Goofe-berries green.

T A K E the faireft green Goofe-berries and largeft, pick off the black Tops, and caudle them in fair Water ; then peel them, and put them into the warm Water as you peel them : When they are all done, fet them over a very flow Fire not to boil, and cover them clofs till they look very clear and green ; have ready fome Jelly of Goofe-berries made of the greeneft Gaskins, boil it uncovered very faft till they are to Pieces ; ftrain out the Jelly and the Goofe-berries into it, and the fame Weight of fine Sugar ; boil and skim them till they are enough, then glafs them up.

To preferve Pears.

T A K E the beft preferving Pears frefh pulled, make a fmall Hole at the black End, and pick out the Seeds with a Needle-head ; then put them in fcalding Water, and take the Skin off them ; then take their equal Weight of fine Sugar, and take the fame Water your Pears were boiled in, and mix the Sugar with as much of the Water as will cover the Pears ; then let it come a-boiling, and fkim it ; put in your Pears, and let them boil till they be foft, then take them out, and boil up
your

your Syrup ; and when they are both cold, lay in your
Pears in Gallypots ; pour the Syrup over them before
you boil them, put a Clove in every Hole, pour Jelly
of Apples over them, and they will keep a great while.

To preserve Rafpberries whole.

TAKE the faireſt and largeſt Raſp-berries you can
get, and to every Pound of Raſps, add a Pound and
a half of fine Sugar ; clarify it and boil it till it blows
very ſtrong, put in the Raſps, and let them boil as
quick as poſſible, ſtrewing ſome fine beat Sugar on
them as they boil : When the Sugar boils over them,
take them off, and let them ſtand to cool, then put
them on the Fire again ; put to every Pound of Raſps
two Gills of Currant Jelly ; then boil it till the Syrup
hangs in Flax from the Spoon, keep them well ſkimmed, then put them in Glaſſes when they are almoſt
cold.

To make Rafpberry Jam.

PICK them clean, and to every Pound of Raſps
put two Gills of Currant Juice, and a Pound and a half
of Sugar ; boil them on a quick Fire, and when they
fall to the Bottom, they are enough.

To preserve the green admirable Plumb.

TAKE theſe Plumbs when full grown, and juſt on
the Turn ; prick them with a large Needle, and ſet
them on the Fire with as much Water as will cover
them, with green Kail-leaves under and over them ;
let them green very gradually, they muſt not boil ;
then drain them, and boil them in clarified Sugar, let
them cool a little, and give them another Boil if they
ſhrink ; prick them with a Fork in the Syrup, and give
them another Boil ; put a Sheet of clean white Paper
over them, and ſet them by ; next Day boil ſome Sugar till it blows, and put it to them, and give them a
good Boil, then put them by for Uſe.

To

To preserve Goose-berries whole.

TAKE the largeſt preſerving Gooſe-berries, and pick off the black Eye, but not the Stalk; ſet them over the Fire in a Pot of Water to ſcald; cover them very cloſs, and let them ſcald, but not boil, or break, and when they are tender, take them up in cold Water; then take a Pound and a Half of double refined Sugar to a Pound of Gooſe berries; clarify the Sugar with Water, and when the Syrup is cold, put your Gooſe-berries into your preſerving Pan, and put the Syrup to them; ſet them on a gentle Fire, and let them boil, but not too faſt, left they break; when you perceive the Sugar has entered them, take them off; cover them with white Pepper, and ſet them by till the next Day, then take them out of the Syrup, and boil the Syrup till it begins to rope; ſkim it and put it to them again, and ſet them on a gentle Fire till you perceive the Syrup will rope; then take them off, and when cold cover them with Paper; boil ſome Gooſe-berries to Jelly, and put them in Glaſſes, and cover them with it.

To ſcald Fruit for preſent Uſe.

PUT your Fruit in boiling Water, as much as will cover them; ſet them on a ſlow Fire till they are tender, turning them often; lay a Paper cloſs on them; let them ſtand till cold. To a Pound of Fruit put half a Pound of Sugar; let it boil, but not faſt, till it looks clear: If you do whole Pipins, you muſt cut Orange and Lemon-peel as ſmall as Straw, and put them and the Juice of Lemon in them.

To make white Quince Marmalade.

SCALD your Quinces tender, take off the Skin, and pulp them from the Core very fine: To every Pound of Quinces put a Pound and a half of fine Sugar in Lumps, and two Gills of Water; dip your Sugar in Water, and boil and ſkim it till it is a thick Syrup;

Syrup, then put in your Quinces. Boil it on a quick Fire.

To preserve Apricocks.

PULL the faireſt Apricocks before they are too ripe, wipe them, and put them in a Pan of cold Water; ſet them on the Fire, and when the Water is juſt ſcalding hot, take them off and ſkin them, and as you ſkin them, grate Sugar on them : If there are any Bits that want Skin pare it off very thin with a Pen-knife ; then take out the Stones on the Side that has a Creſs in it, but don't break the Apricock : If there are any very hard to come out, let them alone till they are boiled in the Syrup. To every Pound of them put a Pound of very fine Loaf-ſugar ; dip it in Water, and boil it ; ſkim it, and then put in the Apricocks ; let them ly in it till the Syrup is cold, then put them on a ſlow Fire, and let them ſimmer, cover them with a clean Sheet of Paper ; take them off again, and let them cool ; break the Stones, and take out your Kernels whole, put them in with the Apricocks ; put them on and off the Fire three or four times, ſtill letting them cool till the Syrup penetrates into them, then let them boil till they are clear, take care they don't break ; never let them boil till the laſt Time, only ſimmer ; then put them in Gallypots, and when cold, paper them. Take the Skins off the Kernels.

To preserve red or white Currants whole.

PULL the largeſt Branches and biggeſt Kernels you can get ; make a very ſmall Slit in the Side of them with a Needle, and pick out the Seeds ; hold them very gently in your Fingers, for Fear of bruiſing or pulling them off the Stems : To every Pound of Currants, you muſt have two Pounds of clarified double refined Sugar, and put the Currants in it on a clear Fire : The red muſt have half a Mutchkin of the Juice of red Currants in it, and you muſt boil both till they are quite clear on a quick Fire.

Z

To preserve Pears red.

TAKE the large Pound Pears, when full ripe, pare them, and put them in as much Water as will cover them, then put in a Penny-worth of pounded Cocheneal, and let them boil till they are tender ; then put in the Weight of your Pears of Sugar, and let it boil to a thick Syrup ; cover your Pears till you boil and fkim your Syrup ; then put in your Pears, and let them boil till they are red and clear : put the Rind of a Lemon and Orange cut in Strings, and fqueeze in the Juice in the Syrup before it comes to boil : Put them in Gallypots, and put on them the Jelly of red Goofe-berries, it is made as the Jelly of green Goofe-berries.

To make Marmalade of Oranges.

TAKE your Oranges, grate them, cut them in Quarters, take the Skins off them, and take the Pulp from the Strings and Seeds ; put the Skins in a Pan of Spring-water, boil them till they are very tender, then take them out of the Water, and cut them in very thin Slices ; beat fome in a Marble Mortar, and leave the thin Slices to boil by themfelves. To every Pound of Oranges put a Pound of fine Sugar ; firft wet the Sugar in Water, boil it a good while, then put in Half of the Pulp, keep the other Half for the fliced Oranges ; to every Mutchkin of the Pulp you muft put in a Pound of Sugar likeways, then put in the grated Rind, boil it till it is very clear, then put it in Gallypots ; when cold, paper them. Boil your Chips the fame Way, but don't mix the pounded with them.

To preserve Goose-berries for Tarts.

PICK them clean, and to every ten Pounds of Goofe-berries put eight Pounds of fine powdered Sugar, and two Gills of Water ; put them on a flow Fire till the Sugar is well fimmered among them ; fkim them, and then let them boil as faft as you pleafe : Boil them till they are very clear and will jelly. You may preferve
green

green Gafkens, and red and white Goofeberries for Tarts, the fame Way.

To preferve white Plumbs.

TAKE your Plumbs before they are too ripe, give them a Slit in the Seam, and prick them behind, make your Water almoft fcalding hot, and put a little Sugar into it, and put in your Plumbs, and cover them clofs, fet them on the Fire to coddle, and take them off a little and fet them on again ; take care they do not break ; boil to a Height as much refined Sugar as will cover them ; and when they are coddled pretty tender, take them out of the Liquor, and put them into your preferving Pan to your Syrup, which muft be Blood-warm : Let them boil till they are clear, fkim them, and take them off, and let them ftand two Hours, then fet them on, and boil them again ; when they are clear put them in Glaffes, boil your Syrup till it is thick, and when cold pour it on your Plumbs. Put Jelly of Pipins over them.

To preferve Damfons.

TAKE fome Damfons, and cut them in Pieces, and put them in in a Skellet over the Fire, with as much Water as will cover them ; when they boil, and the Liquor pretty ftrong, ftrain it out : Add for every Pound of your whole Damfons a Pound of dou-ble refined Sugar, put the third Part of the Sugar in the Liquor, and fet it on the Fire, and when it fim-mers put in your whole Damfons, wipe them clean, let them have one good Boil, take them off for half an Hour, and cover them up clofe; then fet them on again, and let them fimmer over the Fire, often turning them : Take them out, and put them in a Bafon, and ftrew all the Sugar you left on them, and pour the hot Liquor over them, and cover them up, and let them ftand till next Day; then boil them up again till they are e-nough, take them up and put them in Pots ; boil the
Liquor

Liquor till it jellies, and pour it on them when it is almoſt cold, ſo paper them.

To preſerve green Plumbs.

TAKE green Plumbs before they begin to ripen, let them be carefully gathered, with their Stalks and Leaves, put them in cold Spring-water over a Fire, and let them boil very gently; when they will peel take off the Skins, and put the Plumbs in other cold Water, and let them ſtand over a very gentle Fire till they are ſoft; put two Pounds of double refined Sugar to every Pound of Plumbs, and make the Sugar with ſome Water into a very thick Syrup. Before the Plumbs are put in it, the Stones of the Plumbs muſt be as ſoft as you may thruſt a Pin in them. After the ſame Manner do green Apricocks.

To preſerve Mulberries.

SET ſome Mulberries on the Fire, and draw from them a Mutchkin of Juice, put to it three Pounds of Sugar; boil your Syrup and ſkim it, and put into it two Pounds of ripe Mulberries, and let them ſtand in the Syrup till they are thoroughly warm, then ſet them on the Fire, and let them boil gently, then put them by till next Day, then boil them; and when the Syrup is pretty thick, and the Drop ſtands, they are enough; ſo put them in Glaſſes, and paper them when cold.

Jelly of Gooſe berries.

TAKE your Gooſe-berries when they are at full Growth, but not ripe; fill a Pint-ſtoup, and ſtop the Mouth of it, and put it in a Pot of Water, and let it boil till they are tender; then put them in a Search, and let the Juice drain from them; then fill up the Stoup again, and do ſo till you have ſtewed all you have a-mind to do; to every Mutchkin of Juice put a Pound and a Quarter of fine Sugar, and when diſſolved, boil it as you did the Apple Jelly.

To

To preserve golden Pipins red.

PARE them, and make a Hole in them through the Heart with a Skewer; put them in a Pan with as much Water as will cover them; put a Penny-worth of Cocheneal in a Bit of Musling, and put it in; cut the Rind of a Lemon and Orange in long small Strings, and put that and the Juice in them; let them simmer till they are a little tender, then put in two Pounds of fine Loaf-sugar to a Dozen, and let it diffolve; then put them on a quick Fire, and let them boil very fast till they are a clear red, and very tender; the faster they boil, the wholler they will be. You must not cover them at all, but stand and keep them under the Syrup with a Silver-spoon, they take a long Time to boil. You may do them clear the same Way, leaving out the Cocheneal. A Bath-metal Skellet is the best to do them in.

To make Marmalade of Plumbs, or any Fruit.

PUT them in a Stoup, and put the Stoup in a Pot of Water; let it stew till they are very tender, then rub them through a Search; put to them their e-qual Weight of fine Sugar, and boil them to a Marmalade; break the Sugar very small before you put it in the Marmalade.

To make a Syrup of Nettles.

PICK the young red Nettles in *April*, and put them in a Pint-stoup; put the Stoup in a Pot of Water, and let them simmer for twelve Hours, then squeeze out the Tincture, and put it in a clean Pan, beat the Whites of two Eggs and mix with it; and when it boils, skim it, and to every Mutchkin of Tincture put a Pound of brown Sugar-candy: When it is diffolved, set it on the Fire and boil it up to a Syrup, then let it cool, and bottle it, put no Water to the Nettles. —— They are good for Confumptions.

Syrup of Maiden-hair.

FILL a Pint-ftoup as much as it will hold, and put as much Water as will cover it, and fet it on the Side of the Fire, and let it ftand twenty four Hours, then try if all the Tafte be from it, if not, fet it nearer the Fire, and let it boil, then ftrain it, and to every Mutchkin of the Tincture put a Pound of white Sugar-candy, and two Drops of Cinnamon, and a Drop of Mace, they muft be whole, boil all together to a Syrup, and when cold, bottle it. You may make any Herb-fyrup the fame Way.

To make Jelly of Apples the Colour of Amber.

TAKE big Pipins, pare them, and take out the Cores, and boil them in a Chopin of Water till it comes to a Mutchkin ; put in it two Spoonfuls of Rofe-water, a Pound of fine Sugar, boil it uncovered till it comes to the right Colour ; drop a little on a Piece of Glafs, and if it ftands upright, it is enough ; put it in Glaffes or Gally-pots. You may make red Jelly the fame Way, but colour the Water with a little Cocheneal.

Goofe-berry Jam.

TAKE the green Goofe-berries full ripe, top and tail them, and weigh them ; put a Pound of Fruit to three Quarters of a Pound of fine Sugar, and two Gills of Water ; boil the Sugar and Water together, fkim it, and put in your Goofe-berries, and boil them till they are clear and tender, then put them in Pots.

To preferve Cherries.

TAKE the beft Morello Cherries when full ripe, either ftone them, or clip off Part of the Stalks ; to every Pound take a Pound of Sugar, and boil it till it blows very ftrong ; then put in your Cherries, and by Degrees bring them to boil as faft as you can, that the Sugar may come over them ; skim them, and fet them by, next Day boil a Mutchkin of the Juice of
red

red Currants, and a Pound of Sugar, and skim it, and put it in the Cherries, then give all a Boil together : When almoft cold, place them in Glaffes, and pour the Syrup on them.

To make Currant Jelly.

MASH the Currants, and put them on the Fire, then fqueeze out all the Juice, and to every *Englifh* Quart, put two Pounds of Sugar ; put it on the Fire and boil it, keep it well fkimmed, and ftir it till the Sugar diffolves : When it boils twelve Minutes, drop a little on a Plate, and if it jellies, take it off and put it in Glaffes, the finer the Sugar is, the better for all Sweet-meats : If it is white Currants, clarify the Sugar, and ftrain the Juice.

To make Conferve of Rofes.

TAKE the Scarlet Buds before they are ripe, and cut off all the Whites, then weigh all the Rofes, and put them into a Mortar, and beat them extraordinary well, till they be like Powder ; then take the triple Weight of your Rofes in Sugar, well fearched, and put it in by Degrees, always beating them ; and as it diffolves, put in more, till your Sugar be all made Ufe of ; and when it is all well mixed, put it up in your Gallypots, and fet it againft the Sun ; ftir them once in two or three Days for a Fortnight, then it is fit for Ufe : After this Manner you may make Conferve of Violets or Gilliflowers.

Clear Pipin Jelly.

TAKE fourteen good Pipins, and throw them into cold Water ; fet them on the Fire till they are diffolved, then ftrain them, and to a Mutchkin of it put a Pound of double refined Sugar ; let it boil very faft, and keep it clean fkimmed ; then put in it the Juice of two large Lemons : As it is boiling, try it on a Plate,

and

and when you find it jellies, it is enough. You may put a Chopin of Water in it.

Jelly of Pipins with Slices.

BOIL a Mutchkin of Water, and a Pound of Sugar, with six Pipins, the Juice of a Lemon and Orange, to a clear Jelly; then pare and core three Pipins, and cut them in Slices, and put them in your Jelly, and boil them very quick, till they are clear, but don't let them break, so put them in Glasses.

To colour Jellies.

JELLIES made of Hartshorn or Calves Feet, may be made of what Colour you please. If white, use Almonds pounded and strained after the usual Manner; if yellow, put in Yolks of Eggs, or a little Saffron steeped and squeezed; if red, some Juice of Beet-root or Cocheneal; if Purple, Turnsole or Powder of Violets; if green, Juice of Beets or Spinage.

A very fine Way to dry Cherries.

TO every five Pound of ston'd Cherries, take a Pound of double refined Sugar; put the Cherries into the preserving Pan, with a very little Water: Make both but just scalding hot, take them immediately out of this Liquor, and dry them; then put them a-gain into the Pan, and strew on Sugar between every Lair of Cherries; let it stand to melt, and then set it on the Fire, and make it scalding hot, as before; which must be done twice or thrice with the Sugar; then drain them from the Syrup, and lay them sing-ly to dry in the Sun, or in the Stove. When they are dry, throw them into a Bason of cold Water, and take them immediately out, and dry them with a Cloth; set them again in the hot Sun, or in the Stove, and keep them in a dry Place all the Year. This is

not

not only the beſt Way to give them a good Taſte, but
alſo the moſt certain Way for Colour and Plumpneſs.

Currants preſerved in Bunches.

STONE your Currants, and tye them up in ſmall
Bunches: To every Pound of Currants, boil two Pounds
of Sugar, till it blows very ſtrong; then ſlip in the
Currants, and give them a quick Boil, till the Sugar
covers them; let them ſettle a Quarter of an Hour,
then let them boil till the Sugar riſes almoſt to
the Top of the Pan; then let them ſettle, ſkim
them, and ſet them by till next Day, then drain them,
and lay them out, taking Care to ſpread out the Sprigs,
that they may not ſtick together; then duſt them well,
and dry them in a hot Stove.

Currants in Jelly.

STRIP the Currants, and put them in an Earthen
Pot, tye them cloſs down, and ſet them in a Kettle of
boiling Water, and let them ſtand three Hours, the
Kettle ſtill boiling; then take a clean flaxen Cloth, and
ſtrain out the Juice; and when it is ſettled, take a Pound
of double refined Sugar beaten and ſifted, and put to
it a Mutchkin of clear Juice: Have ready ſome whole
Currants ſton'd, and put them in when the Juice boils,
and let them boil till the Syrup jellies, which you may
know by trying it in a Spoon, then put it in Glaſſes.
Make Jelly of Currants the ſame Way, only leave out
the whole Currants. When cold, paper them up

To preſerve Raſp-berries liquid.

TAKE the faireſt and largeſt Raſp-berries you can
get, and to every Pound of Raſps, take a Pound and a
half of Sugar, clarify it, and boil it till it blows very
ſtrong: Put in the Raſps, and let them boil as quick
as poſſible, ſtrewing ſome fine beat Sugar on them as
they boil: When they have had a good Boil, and that
the Sugar riſes all over them, take them off, and let

them settle a little ; then give them another Boil, and put to every Pound of Rasps half a Pint of Currant Jelly ; give them a good Boil, till you perceive the Syrup hangs in Flaiks from your Skimmer, then take them from the Fire, take off the Scum, and put them into Glasses or Pots. Take the Scum clean off the Top ; when cold, make a Jelly of Currants, and fill up your Glasses ; cover them with Paper, first wet in Water, and dried a little betwixt two Cloths, which Paper you must put close to the Jelly, then wipe the Glasses clean, and cover the Tops with the dry Paper.

Raspberry Cakes.

PICK away all the Stems and spotted Raspberries, then bruise the rest through a Hair-sieve into an earthen Pan, and put on a Board or Weight to press out all the Water you can ; then pour the Paste into the Preserving-pan, and dry it over the Fire till there is no Moisture in it, that is, no Juice that will run from it, stirring it close to keep it from burning : To every Pound take a Pound and two Ounces of Sugar finely beat, and put it in gradually : When all is in put it on the Fire, and let it incorporate well together ; then take it off and scrape it all to one Side of the Pan, let it cool a very little, and put it into Moulds ; when quite cold, put them into the Stove without dusting, and dry it as other Paste. Take care the Paste does not boil after the Sugar is in, for it will make it greasy, and hinder it to dry.

Raspberry clear Cakes.

TAKE two Quarts of ripe Goose-berries, and a Quart of red Raspberries ; put them into a Stone Jug, and stop them close ; then set them into a Pot of cold Water, as much as covers the Neck of the Jug, and let it boil till it comes to a Paste ; then put them into a Hair-sieve, and press out all the Jelly into a Pan, and strain it through a Jelly-bag. To every Pound
put

put twenty Ounces of double refined Sugar, and boil it till it crack in the Water; then take it off, and put in the Jelly, and ſtir it over a ſlow Fire till all the Sugar is melted; then give it a good Fleet till it is well incorporated; then take it off and ſkim it well, and fill your clear Cake Glaſſes; take off the Skim, and put it into the Stove to dry. When they begin to cruſt on the upper Side, turn them out upon ſquare Glaſ-ſes, and ſet them to dry again. When they begin to have a tender Candy, cut them into Quarters, or as you pleaſe, and ſet them to dry till hard; then turn them on Sieves, and when thoroughly dry, put them into Boxes. In filling up your clear Cakes and clear Paſte, you muſt be as expeditious as poſſible; for if it cools, it will be a Jelly before you can get it in. White Raſpberry clear Cakes are made the ſame Way, only mixing them with the Gooſe-berries in the Infuſion.

To preſerve green Amber Plumbs.

TAKE green Amber Plumbs when full grown, prick them in two or three Places, and put them in cold Water; ſet them over the Fire to ſcald, and take care not to let the Water become too hot, leſt it ſpoil them: When they are very tender, put them into a very thin Sugar, that is to ſay, one Part Sugar and two Parts Water; give them a little Warm in it, and ſet them by covered: Next Day give them another Warm, and the third Day drain them, and boil up the Syrup, adding a little more Sugar; then put the Syrup to the Plumbs, and give them a Warm. Next Day do the ſame; the Day following boil the Syrup till it is a little ſmooth, put in the Plumbs, and give them a Boil; the next Day boil the Syrup till very ſmooth, put it to the Plumbs and cover them, and put them in the Stove; next Day boil ſome Sugar to blow very ſtrong; put it to the Fruit, and give all a Boil, then put it into the Stove for two Days; then drain them, and lay them

ou

out to dry; firſt duſting them very well, and manage them in the drying as any other Fruit.

To preſerve the green Mogul Plumb.

LET it be juſt upon the turning ripe, prick it into the Stone on that Side where the Clift is with a Pen-knife, and as you do them throw them into cold Water, and ſet them over a very ſlow Fire to ſcald; when they are very tender take them carefully out of the Water, and put them into a thin Sugar, half Sugar, half Water; warm them gently, cover them and ſet them by: The next Day drain off the Syrup and boil it ſmooth, adding a little freſh Sugar, and give them a gentle Boil; the Day following boil the Sugar very ſmooth, and pour it on them, and ſet them in the Stove for two Days; then drain them, and boil freſh Sugar very ſmooth, juſt to blow a little; put in your Plumbs, and give them a good covered Boiling; ſkim them and put them into the Stove for two Days; drain them and lay them out to dry, duſt-ing them very well.

To preſerve yellow Amber Plumbs.

TAKE them when full ripe, put them into the preſerving Pan with as much Sugar as will cover them, and give them a good Boil; let them ſettle a litttle, and give them another Boil three or four times round the Fire, ſkim them, and next Day drain off the Sy-rup; put them again into the Pan, and boil as much freſh Sugar as will cover them to blow. Give them a thorough Boiling, and ſkim them, and ſet them in the Stove Twenty-four Hours; then drain them, and lay them out to dry. Duſt them firſt.

To preſerve green Grapes.

TAKE the largeſt and fineſt Grapes before they are thorough ripe, ſtone them and ſcald them, and let them ly two Days in the Water they are ſcalded in;
then

then drain them and put them into a thin Syrup, and
give them a Heat over a flow Fire : Next Day turn
them in the Pan, and warm them again : Next Day
drain them, and give them a good Boil in clarified
Sugar, and skim them and set them by : The Day following boil some Sugar to blow, and put in the Grapes,
and give them a good Boil ; skim them, and set them
in a warm Stove all Night ; drain them next Day, and
lay them out to dry, having dufted them well.

Green Apricocks.

T A K E them before the Stones are hard, wet them
and lay them in a coarfe Cloth with two or three Handfuls of Salt, and rub them till the Roughnefs is off;
then put them in fcalding Water, and let them be almoft boiled ; then set them off till almoft cold, do this
two or three Times : After this let them be clofs covered, and when they look green, let them boil till
they begin to be tender; take their Weight of double
refined Sugar, and to a Pound of Sugar two Gills of
Water ; make the Syrup, and when it is almoft cold,
put in the Apricocks, boil them till they are clear ;
warm your Syrup three or four Times till it is thick.
You may put them in cold Jelly, or dry them as you
ufe them.

Apricock Chips.

S L I C E the Apricocks the long Way, but not pare
them ; take their Weight of double refined Sugar, boil
it to a thin Candy, put in the Apricocks and let them
ftand on the Fire till they are fcalding hot ; let them
ly a Night in the Liquor, then lay them on thin Plates,
and set them in the Sun to dry.

Jam Apricocks.

P A R E them and take out the Stones, break them
and take out the Kernels, and blanch them ; to every
Pound of Apricocks boil a Pound of Sugar till it blows
very ftrong, put in the Apricocks and give them a
quick

quick Boil till they are broke, then take them off and bruiſe them well; put in the Kernels and ſtir all together on the Fire, and fill your Pots or Glaſſes with them. If it is too ſweet, ſharpen it with a little white Currant Jelly to your Taſte.

To preſerve green Walnuts.

GATHER them in fair Weather, and before the Shell grows hard; boil them in Water to take off the Bitterneſs, then put them into cold Water; peel off the Rind, and lay them in a Pan with a Lair of Sugar equal to the Weight of the Nuts, and as much Water as will wet it. When they are boiled up over a moderate Fire and cooled, do the ſame Thing again, and ſet them by for Uſe.

To preſerve Mulberries liquid.

TAKE two Quarts of Mulberry Juice, ſtrain it, boil it over a gentle Fire, with a Pound and a half of Sugar till it become a Kind of Syrup; then ſlip into the Pan three Quarts of Mulberries not over ripe: Give them a Boil, then pour all into an Earthen Veſſel, ſtop it cloſs, and keep it for Uſe.

Another Way.

BOIL the Sugar till a little pearled, allowing three Pounds to four Pounds of Mulberries, and give them a light covered Boiling in the ſame Sugar, ſhaking the Pan gently, then ſet it by till next Day, then drain off the Syrup in order to bring it to its pearled Quality; then ſlip in the Fruit, adding a little more pearled Sugar if needful: When cold enough, put it into Pots.

To preſerve Seville Oranges in Quarters, or in Sticks.

EITHER zeaſt or turn your Oranges according as you deſign to do them, whether in Zeaſts, Chips or Faggots *Turning*, in this Senſe, is a Term of Art which denotes a particular Manner of paring Oranges
and

and Lemons, when the outer Rind or Peel is pared off
very thin and narrow with a Knife for the Purpose,
winding it about the Fruit, so as the Peel may extend
to a very great Length without breaking. To *zeaſt,*
is to cut the Peel from Top to Bottom in ſmall Slips
as thin as poſſible. The Orange thus prepared may
be cut into Quarters, or into Sticks as you pleaſe. You
muſt take away the inſide Skin and the Juice ; ſet them
over the Fire in Water, do not put them in till the
Water begins to boil, and when they are done enough,
(which you will know by their ſlipping of a Pin when
ſtuck into them) let them cool, and put them into
freſh Water, and next into clarified Sugar ; let them
have ſeven or eight covered Boilings before you ſet
them by to cool. Boil them over again till the Syrup
is almoſt ſmooth ; drain them next Day and put them
into Pots, let your Syrup be pearled, and pour it on
them. Keep them in that Way till you think fit to
dry them.

Oranges preſerved in Slips.

WHEN the Fruit is zeaſted, cut the Pulp into
Slips, which are to be ſlit again in their Thickneſs to
make them very thin ; ſcald theſe Slips in Water till
they are very ſoft, then throw them into clarified Sugar newly paſſed thro' the ſtraining Bag when it is ready
to boil, and give it twenty Boilings : Next Day having
brought your Sugar to the ſmooth Quality, put the
Slips into it, and give them ſeven or eight Boilings :
The third Day boil your Sugar till pearled, and give
them a covered Boiling. Some Time after put them
into Pots, and you may dry them as Occaſion ſerves.
Lemons, Limes and Citrons are preſerved much the
ſame Way, either intire, or in Sticks, Faggots, Zeaſts,
Slips, &c.

Red criſp Almonds, or Prawlings.

MELT a Pound of Loaf or powdered Sugar with
a little Water, and let a Pound of Almonds be boiled
in

in it till they crackle ; add as much Cocheneal as will give it a right red, let it boil again to its cracked Qua-lity, and at that inftant tofs in your Almonds ; and re-moving the Pan from the Fire, ftir them clofs till they are dry. The Cocheneal may be prepared by boiling it with Allum and Cream of Tartar, which Liquor is generally ufed for every Thing that is to be brought to a fine Colour, as Marmalades, Jellies, Paftes, Creams, &c.

To preferve white Citrons.

CUT them in Pieces of what Size you pleafe, put them in Salt and Water for four or five Hours ; wafh them and boil them tender, then drain them and put them into as much clarified Sugar as will cover them, and fet them by till next Day ; drain them and boil the Syrup a little fmooth, when cool, put it on the Citrons ; next Day boil your Syrup quite fmooth, and pour it on the Citrons ; the Day after boil all together, and put it into a Pot to be candied, or put in Jelly or Compofts as you pleafe. You muft look over thefe Fruits fo kept in Syrup, and if you perceive any Froth on them, give them a Boil ; and if they fhould become very frothy and four, boil firft the Syrup, and then all together.

To make clear Quince Cakes.

BOIL and clarify over a Fire a Pint of the Syrup of Quinces, with a Quart or two of Rafpberries ; fkim it well from time to time, add a Pound and a half of Sugar, and boil up the fame Quantity of Sugar to a Candy Height, and pour it in hot ; ftir all together, and keep it clofs ftirring till it is almoft cold, then fpread it upon Plates, and cut it into Cakes of what Shape you pleafe.

Marmalade of Apricocks.

TAKE full ripe Apricocks, pare and quarter them, and take out the Strings ; put three Quarters of a Pound of Loaf-fugar to every Pound of Apricocks, and
put

put them into a pretty broad Pan ; set the Apricocks
on the Fire without either Water or Sugar, keep them
stirring that they may not burn : When they are melted and boiled a pretty while, strew in the Sugar as
quick as you can, and let them boil quick till the Syrup is thick, and they look clear, then put them in
Pots or Glasses.

Marmalade of Apples.

SCALD them in Water, and when tender take them
out and drain them, and strain them through a Sieve ;
boil your Sugar till it is well feathered, allowing three
Quarters of a Pound of Sugar to every Pound of Apples ; temper and dry the whole over the Fire as usual,
and let them simmer together ; strew it over with fine
Sugar, and put it into Pots or Glasses.

Marmalade of Raspberries.

MAKE the Body of this Marmalade of very ripe
Currants, to which add a Handful of Raspberries, that
it may look as it were all of Raspberries.

Marmalade of Quinces, after the Italian Manner.

PARE about thirty Quinces as thin as possible, and
take out the Cores, and put them into a Quart of Water with two Pounds of Sugar, let all boil together till
they are soft ; then strain the Juice and Pulp, and put
to it four Pounds of Sugar, and boil it up to a right
Consistence.

To make Quiddany of Pipins, of an Amber or Ruby Colour.

PARE the Pipins, and cut them into Quarters, and
boil them in as much Water as will cover them, till they
are soft, and sink in the Water, then strain the Pulp.
Take a Pint of the Liquor, and boil it with half a Pound
of Sugar, till it appears a quaking Jelly on the Moulds.
When the Quiddany is cold, turn it on a wet Trencher,

B b   and

and slide it into Boxes. If you would have it of a red Colour, let it boil leisurely, close covered, till it is red like Claret.

Quiddany of all Sorts of Plumbs.

BOIL the Plumbs in Apple Water till they are red as Claret; when you have made the Liquor strong of the Fruit, put to every Mutchkin half a Pound of Sugar, and let it boil till a Drop of it will hang on the Back of a Spoon like a quaking Jelly. If you would have it of an Amber Colour, you must boil it on a quick Fire.

Paste of ripe Apricocks.

APRICOCK Paste is made the same Way as the Marmalade, or you may scald the Apricocks without Sugar; but if they are not thoroughly ripe, bruise them well, or pound them in a Mortar. Then slip in the Fruit into an equal Quantity of cracked Sugar, and incorporated with it, when well dried over the Fire; then let all simmer, and dress your Paste as usual. You may dry it at the same Time if you please.

Goose-berry Paste.

TAKE them when full grown, wash them and put them into the preserving Pan, with as much Water as covers them; boil them very thick all to a Pommish; then strain them through a Hair Sieve into a Pan, and press out all the Juice; and, to every Pound of this Paste take one Pound and two Ounces of Sugar, boil it till it cracks; then mix in your Paste, and let it incorporate with Sugar over a slow Fire: When it is well incorporate, skim it, and fill your Pots, then skim it again, and when cold put it into the Stove. When it is crusted on the Top, turn them and set them in the Stove again, and when a little dry, cut them in long Pieces, and set them to dry quite; and when they are so crusted as to bear touching, turn them on Sieves, and dry the other Side, and put them into Boxes. You may make them
red

red or green, by putting the Colour, when the Sugar and Paſte is all mixed, giving it a Warm all together.

To make Ketchup.

GET the largeſt Muſhrooms, wipe them clean, and maſh them with your Hand; ſtrew on them a Handful of Salt; let them lye all Night, then put them on the Fire ten Minutes, keep them ſtirring all the while, then ſqueeze them through a Canvas, and let them ſettle; pour it from the Sediment, then put it on the Fire, and clarify it with the Whites of two Eggs; then put in it whole Pepper, Cloves, Mace, Ginger and *Jamaica* Pepper, and Salt; it muſt be very high ſeaſoned: Boil one Part of it away, and when cold bottle it, putting the Spices in the Bottles with it.

To keep *Artichoke Bottoms the whole Year.*

PUT them in a Pot, and put as much Water about them as will cover them, ſalt them, let them boil till the Leaves come eaſily from them; then take off every thing of the Bottoms; put them in a ſlow Oven on or before the Fire; keep them in a dry Place, when they are thoroughly dry.

Syrup of Lemons and Oranges.

TO a Mutchkin of Juice put a Pound and a Half of fine Loaf Sugar; put it on the Fire and let it ſimmer, ſkim it, and ſtir it often, then let it ſettle; and when it is cold bottle it, but don't put the Sediment in it.

To preſerve whole Oranges.

GRATE off the Rind very gently, cut a Bit out of the Top where the Stem is, and ſcoop out all that is in them; put them in a very clean Kettle of cold Water, cover it cloſs, boil them as tender that you may thruſt a Straw in them, ſhifting the Water three or four Times; then put them between two Cloaths to drain, and to every Pound of them put two Pounds of Loaf
Sugar

Sugar, with two Gills of Water, and boil it till it blows; ſkim it clean; then put in the Oranges, and boil them till they are very clear, keeping them down in the Syrup with a Spoon whil they are boiling: Then put them in Cans.

To preſerve Angelica.

BOIL the Stalks of Angelica in Water till they are very tender, then peel them and put them into other warm Water, and cover them till they are green'd on a gentle Fire: When they are green lay them on a Cloth to dry, and take their Weight of fine Sugar, and boil it to a Syrup; tye up the Stalks in any Shape you pleaſe, and boil them in the Syrup very quick; if you dry them, you muſt ſhake Sugar on them, and put them in a ſlow Oven.

To preſerve Peaches in Brandy.

PUT your Peaches in boiling Water, but don't let them boil; take them out and put them in Water, dry them between two Cloths, then put them in wide mouth'd Bottles; to ſix Peaches put a Quarter of a Pound of Sugar, clarify it, and put it on the Peaches, then fill up the Bottles with Brandy; ſtop them cloſs, and keep them in a cold Place.

To dry Pears or Apples.

TAKE preſerving Pears, and thruſt a wooden Skewer into the Head of them beyond the Core, then pare them the long Way, and ſcald them, but not too tender; then take their Weight of Sugar, and to every Pound of Sugar put two Gills of Water; clarify it, and put in your Pears; ſet them on the Fire, and let them boil very quick half an Hour, cover them with white Paper, and ſet them by till next Day. Then take them out of the Syrup, and boil it till it is thick and ropy; then put in the Pears, and put it on the Fire, and let the Syrup boil very faſt over them: Then cover them with Paper, and ſet them in the Oven, or

Stove

Stove for twenty-four Hours; then take it out, and put them on a Sieve; then lay them on White-iron Plates, and duft them with fine Sugar, then put them in the Oven; and when one Side is dry lay them on Papers, and turn them, and duft the other with Sugar; fqueeze the Pears by Degrees. If you do Apples, fqueeze the Eyes to the Stalks: When they are dry put them in Boxes, with Papers between. You may do Apricocks, Peaches and Nectarines the fame Way; but when they are fcalded take out the Stones.

CHAP. VI.

Of WINES, *&c.*

To make Orange Wine.

TO fix Gallons of Water, put twelve Pounds of fingle refined Sugar, the Whites of four Eggs well beaten, put them in the cold Water; then let it boil three Quarters of an Hour, taking off the Scum as it rifes; when it is cold put in two Spoonfuls of Barm, and fix Ounces of Syrup of Lemons beaten together; put in alfo the Juice and Rinds of fifty Oranges thin pared, that no white Part, or any of the Seeds go in with the Juice which fhould be ftrained: Let all ftand two Days in an open Veffel, or large Pan, then put it in a clofs Veffel, and in three or four Days ftop it down. When it has ftood three Weeks then draw it off into another Veffel, and add to it two Quarts of Rhenifh or white Wine. Then ftop it clofs again, and in fix Weeks it will be fine to bottle, and to drink in a Month after. Obferve, that an *Englifh* Gallon is two *Scots* Pints, and, if the Barm be not very good, to put in thirteen or fourteen Spoonfuls.

A

To make Raiſin Wine.

TO each five Pounds of Raiſins picked clean from the Stalks, take one *Engliſh* Gallon of cold Water ; chop the Raiſins ſmall, and put them into a Veſſel, fit for the Quantity ; then pour on the cold Water, ſtir them about, and cover the Veſſel with a Cloth, ſo let them ſtand ten Days, ſtirring them about twice a-day : At the End of ten Days, ſtrain out the Liquor through a Search, ſqueezing the Raiſins very well ; then put the Liquor into a Barrel that will juſt hold the Quantity you make. After a hiſſing Noiſe, which is commonly about three Weeks after, bung up the Barrel, and let it ſtand a Year, then bottle it for Uſe.

To make Vinegar.

TAKE half the Quantity of the above Water, let it be boiling hot, and pour it upon the Raiſins : After you have ſqueezed them out of the firſt Liquor, and after ſtanding, (till it is as cold as Wort, when Barm is put to it) take a Mutchkin of good Barm and put to it, and let it work two Weeks, ſtirring it once or twice a-day ; then ſqueeze it through a Search into a Barrel, and ſet it by a Fire : When it has wrought a Fortnight in the Barrel, bung it up, and let it ſtand till ſour enough, which will be according to the Degree of Heat ; and in eight or ten Months it is commonly done.

To make Balm Wine.

TO every Chopin of Honey, put three Chopins of Water ; boil it on a quick Fire, till one Chopin is boiled away ; take Care to keep it cloſs ſkimmed, then put it to cool, and put in it a large Handful of Balm ; when almoſt cold, put in it half a Gill of the beſt Barm, and let it ſtand till the Head is flat, and done working, which will be in four or five Days ; then ſkim it, and ſtrain it through a very fine Search in a Can, but take Care that the Grounds at the Bottom do not mix with it ; put it in a Jar, and ſtop it cloſs, and when

clear,

clear, bottle it; it will keep feven or eight Years; the older the better. You may make Elder Wine the fame Way of the white Bloffom, but take Care that none of the Stems or green be among them. They both are very wholefome. Meath is made the fame Way, leaving out the Balm and Elder Flowers.

To make Metheglin.

GET fome good ftrong Wort, and to every four Chopins of it, put a Chopin of Honey; boil one Chopin away on a quick Fire, keep it well fkimmed, and when cold, put a Gill of Barm to it, and let it work two or three Days, then put it in your Cafk; a Brandy one is beft for all Wines, if you make a Quantity of them: Get a Bag of Linen, and to every *Englifh* Gallon, put in it two Nutmegs; cut in Quarters a Quarter of an Ounce of Ginger, one Dram of Mace, one of Cloves grofly pounded; put the Bag with thefe in it, in the Cafk; bottle it in fix Months, or you may not till twelve.

To make Currant Wine, white or red.

TAKE the Currants when they are full ripe, and fqueeze them through a coarfe Cloth, and put to every *Englifh* Gallon of Juice, two Gallons of boiled foft Water, and three Pounds of Sugar; ftir it very well together, then barrel it up, filling up the Barrel every Day, till it has done working; then bung it up clofs, and let it ftand fix Months, and bottle it. Brandy Cafks are beft for all Sorts of made Wine.

To make Goofe-berry Wine.

GATHER the Goofe-berries in dry Weather when they are half ripe, bruife them in a Tub with a wooden Mallet or Peftle; then put them in a coarfe Canvas Bag, and prefs out all the Juice; to every *Englifh* Gallon put three Pounds of powdered Sugar, ftir the Sugar in it till it diffolves, then put it in a Cafk; and if you make but

but a fmall Quantity, put it in a fmall Cafk, for it muft be full; let it ftand three Weeks, then draw it off, and pour out the Lees; then put it again in the Cafk and ftop it clofs, then let it ftand three Months and bottle it: If you make a large Quantity, let it ftand longer in the Cafk; if you fqueeze a Dozen of bitter Oranges in it, and put fome of the Rinds pared thin in it, they will give it a fine Tafte.

Elder-berry *Wine*.

GATHER the Elder-berries when they are full ripe, when it is a very dry Day; then bruife them with your Hands and ftrain them, then fet the Liquor by in a Gray-beard for twelve Hours to fettle; then put to every Pint of the Juice, a Pint and a half of Water; and to every *Englifh* Gallon of this Liquor, put three Pounds of *Lisbon* Sugar; put it in a Kettle on the Fire, and when it is almoft boiling, clarify it with the Whites of four Eggs; let it boil an Hour, and when it is almoft cold, put in it a little ftrong Ale Barm, and then ton it; and as it works out, fill up the Veffel with fome of the fame Liquor; in a Month's Time it will be fit to be bottled; and after it is bottled, it will be fit to drink in two Months; but remember that all Liquors muft be fine before they are bottled: When it is fine, it will be the better to put in it a Bottle of Mountain Wine.

To make purging Ale.

TAKE Polypody of the Oak and Senna, of each two Ounces, of Sarfaparilla an Ounce, Anife-feeds and Carraway Seeds, of each half an Ounce; fix Handfuls of Scurvy-grafs, three of Ground-ivy, one of Agrimony, and one of Maiden-hair; beat all thefe eafily, and put them in a coarfe Canvas Bag, and hang them in a Gallon of ftrong Ale that is juft working, and it will be fit to drink in five or fix Days.

To brew strong Ale and small Beer.

BOIL the Water, and put some of the Malt in the Vat, and stir it and the boiling Water very well together; then put in more Malt and more Water mashed pretty thin; then cover the Vat and let it stand three Hours; then let some of the Wort run, and throw it up again once or twice till it is clear; strew some dry Malt on the Top of the Vat; put your Hops in the Tub that the Wort runs in, and then put them in the brewing Pan on the Fire with the Wort; let it boil till it curdles, and then clears; put boiling Water on the Vat by Degrees. Twenty *English* Bushels of Malt will make two Hogsheads of strong Ale, and four Hogsheads of small Beer, but it will take ten Pounds of Hops. This Ale will keep two or three Years; when it is almost as cold as Water, barm it, but strain the Hops out of it when it is warm, and boil them in the small Beer: Let it work three Days, then skim it and barrel it, and when it is done working stop it up close, but keep the Barrel always filling while it is working. *October* or *March* is the best Time to brew.

To make Syder.

WHEN the Apples are ripe, pull them on a dry Day, and pound them in a Trough with wooden Pounders, then put them in a Hair Bag, and press the Juice out of them; put it in a Brandy or white Wine Cask that is very sweet: Put in the Cask some Slices of Apples, and two Penny-worth of Isinglass; stop the Bung close, and bottle it in ten Months.

To make Ratafia.

TAKE three Gallons of Brandy, or good Whisky, and blanch and pound half a Pound of bitter Almonds, and put them in the Spirits, with the Rind of Lemons. Let them infuse a Fortnight, then filter off

C e   the

the Spirits, and cork the Bottles clofs you put it in ;
it is good for any Puddings.

To diſtill cold Surfeit Water.

TAKE two Handfuls of Spearmint, two of Balm,
one of Angelica, one of Wormwood, one of Carduus,
and one of Marigold Flowers ; cut them, and put them
in Water, then wring them out, and put them in the
Still. Keep wet Cloths about it, and a flow Fire under
it.

To make Plague Water.

TAKE Rue, Carduus, Balm, Spearmint, Wormwood, Penny-royal, Dragon, Marigold Flowers, Angelica and Rofemary, of each two Handfuls ; cut them
fmall, and put them in the Still with Anife-feeds, Carraway, Coriander, and fweet Fennel Seeds ; then cover them with Spirits, and diftill it off.

To make Shrub.

TAKE five *Engliſh* Gallons of Rum, three Chopins
of Orange and Lemon-juice, and four Pounds of double refined Sugar ; mix all together, but firft pare the
Rind of fome of the Lemons and Oranges, and let them
infufe in the Rum for fix Hours : Let all run through
a Jelly bag, then cafk it till it is fine, and bottle it.

A very fine Waſh for Ladies that have the Scurvy, or any Redneſs in the Face.

BOIL two Ounces of fine Barley, a Chopin of
Water to four Gills, beat two Ounces of Almonds to
a Pafte, mixing them with a little of the Barley Water;
when cold, warm them, and fqueeze them through a
Cloth ; then diffolve one Penny-worth of Camphire
in a Spoonful of Brandy, or any ftrong Spirits : Mix
them and wafh the Face every Night when you are going

ing to Bed : It is the beſt Waſh ever was made for the Face.

The beſt Pomatum for the Lips.

TAKE an Ounce of Sperma-cete, and mix it with an Ounce of the Oil of bitter Almonds, and a little pounded Cocheneal ; melt them all together and ſtrain it through a Cloth in a little Roſe-water, and rub your Lips going to Bed at Night.

To make Eye-Water.

GET two Gills of white Roſe-water, put in it the Bigneſs of a Nut of white Vitriol, and the ſame Quantity of the fineſt Loaf-ſugar ; when it is diſſolved ſhake the Bottle, and waſh the Eyes going to Bed with it, and a ſoft clean Cloth : It is as good an Eye-Water as ever was made.

To make the Sacred Tincture.

PUT in a Mutchkin Bottle five Penny-worth of Hiera Picra, one of Cocheneal pounded ; then fill the Bottle with Half *Lisbon* Wine, and Half Brandy, tye a Bit of clean Cloth on the Bottle, and put it in a Pan of cold Water, as full that it won't go into the Bottle ; put it on a very ſlow Fire, and don't let it boil but ſimmer ; then take off the Pan, and let the Bottle ſtand till the Water is cold : It is a very ſafe gentle Phyſick, and good for a Cholick.

To make Stoughton's Drops.

INFUSE in a Chopin of *French* Brandy a Pennyworth of Cocheneal, a Penny-worth of Snake-root, half an Ounce of *Jamaica* Oranges, two Ounces of bitter Orange-peel, one Ounce of Gentian-root, two Drachms of *Turkey* Rhubarb ; pound the Rhubarb, Cocheneal, and *Jamaica* Oranges, ſlice the Gentian ; put them near the Fire for two Days in a ſtrong Glaſs Bottle ; then put the Bottle in a Pan of cold Water, on a

ſlow

ſlow Fire : And when it ſimmers take off the Pan.
and when the Water is cold take out the Bottle, let it
ſtand two Days ; then pour off all that is clear, and you
may put ſtrong Whiſkey to the reſt, and it will be
good for preſent Uſe.

To make Daffy's *Elixir.*

TAKE a Mutchkin of Brandy, and a Mutchkin of
Liſbon; infuſe in it half an Ounce of Carraway, half an
Ounce of Aniſe-ſeed, half an Ounce of ſweet Fennel-
ſeeds, one Ounce of Hiera-picra, one Ounce of bitter
Alloways, two Drachms of Saffron, two Ounces of
bitter Orange-peel, and one of Snake root ; let theſe
ly near the Fire for a Fortnight, then put the Bottle
in a Pan of cold Water, and when it ſimmers take it
off ; when cold filter it off : You may take two Spoonfuls of it at Night, it is good for a Cholick, and is a
gentle Phyſick.

To make the yellow *Balſam.*

TAKE four Pounds of *May* Butter, and gather in a
dry Day a Pound of Elder Flowers, let none of the
Stems or Green be in them ; mix them with the
Butter in a cloſs well glazed Can ; put it in the
Sun by Day, and near the Fire by Night ; keep them
that Way till the green Broom bloſſoms ; then get a
Pound of the Bloſſoms, and mix them very well together,
keep them as above for five or ſix Weeks ; then warm
it well, but don't boil it, and wring it all out in a
Cloth as well as you can. It is good for any Inflam-
mation, Pain or Stitch, rubbing the Part affected before
the Fire with a very little of it ; and if inwardly, ſwal-
low five or ſix Pills roll'd in Sugar : It is as wholeſome
and ſafe a Thing as ever was taken.

F I N I S.

INDEX

This index is to recipe titles and any personal and place names in the text. Spelling has been modernized throughout, except for Scots words &c, the meanings of which are explained in the introduction.

Abbotsford x
Adam, J. xiii, xxx
Adam, W. xiii
Ainslie, J. xi
ale
    posset 149
    purging 200
    strong 201
almond
    cakes 157
    cheesecakes 135
    cream 142
    custard 136, 137
    pudding 112, 113
    puffs 151
    red crisp 191
    soup 9
amulet (omelette) 129
angelica 196
apple
    for tarts 173
    in halves 173
    jelly 182
    marmalade 193
    pie 81
        with chestnuts & almonds 85
        with potatoes 85
    pudding 115
    pupton 172
    tart 132, 174
    to bake 173
    to dry 196
    see also codlins, pippins
apricot
    chips 189
    jam 189

apricot *contd.*
    marmalade 193
    paste of, 194
    preserved 177
    preserved green 189
Arniston xiii
artichoke
    & kernel pie 84
    bottoms, to keep 195
asparagus
    pickle 170
    soup 12
Auchendinny xii
bacon
    & eggs 129
    to make 42
Baillie, Lady Grisell xxii
bake xxiv
balm wine 198
balsam, yellow, 204
barley
    broth 8
    Scots 7
    pottage 4
Bath
    buns 156
    cakes 165
Bath metal xvi
beef
    à la daube 49
    boiled rump of 52
    cakes 56
    to collar 50
    collops 60
    Dutch 51
    escarlet of 50

beef *contd.*
    forced sirloin 56
    hams 44
    hung 52
    la vinaigre 50
    ollops 58
    to pot 57, 109, 110
    steak pie 28
    stewed rump, 51, 53
    stuffed round or rump 62
biscuits 162
    ratafia 161
    sugar 160
    thin Dutch 162
black caps 173
blade xxiv
blamong 139
blood puddings 112
brain cakes 75
brander xvi
brawn, pork 66
    imitation of 66
    souse for 96
bread pudding 116
breakfast cakes 165
broth 8
    barley 8
    calves' feet 15
    fish 14
    jelly 5
    mutton 7
    roots 15
    Scots barley 7
Bruce, Sir W. xii
Buccleuch, Duke of xi
buns 164
    Bath 156
butter, fairy 153
cabbolow xxiv
    to dress 32
cake
    almond 157
    Bath 165
    gingerbread 164
        Dutch 164

cake *contd.*
    little 158
    Marlborough 158
    nun's 159
    plumb 158, 159
    saffron 160
    seed 158, 161
    Shrewsbury 157
    to eat hot 164
    to ice 159
    whetstone 158
    white 162
    York 163
cake soup 16
calf's feet
    broth 15
    flummery 149
    jelly 138
    pie 79
    to dress 56
    to ragout 73
calf's head
    with oysters 55
    soup 7
    surprise 49
    to boil 49
    to hash 63
    to roast 49
cans xiv
carp
    to boil 28
    to stew 18
    to stew à la Royale 28
caudle
    flummery 148
    for apple or gooseberry tarts 174
    for sweet pies 153
cauliflower, to pickle 169
celery, to pickle 170
chafing dishes xv
cheesecake 134
    almond 135
    egg 135
    orange 134
    potato 134

cheese
  a good 154
  cream 154
  slipcoat 153
  thick 155
  to toast 155
  Welsh rabbet 155
chestnut tarts 133
cherries
  to dry 184
  to preserve 182
chervil pottage 5
chicken
  forced, with gravy 92
  forced, with oysters 91
  fricassée
    brown 87
    white 86
    sauce for 90
  in paste 91
  pie 79
  royal 92
  sauce for 90
  to boil 97
    with asparagus 92
  to stew, with peas and lettuce 89
    & celery 91
    & tongues &c. 92
chopin xxi
cider 201
citron
  pudding 113
  to preserve white 192
clouted cream 144
cockles
  fried with eggs 130
  to pickle 34
cod
  head 19
  roast 27
  tail 28
  to broil 27
  to crimp 22
codlins
  coddled with cream 171

codlins *contd.*
  cream 143
  pickled like mangoes 170
collops
  beef 60
  minced 60
  white Scots 62
cow heel
  to collar 106
  fricassee of 86
Cowdray House xvi
crab
  to butter 33
  to dress 37
  to stew 38
crayfish soup 2
cream
  almond 142
  burnt 138
  clouted 144
  codlin 143
  currant 141
  deloute 143
  gooseberry 143
  lemon 140
    yellow 141
  maids 140
  orange 140
  raspberry 143
  ratafia 142
  red 143
  rice 144
  sack 141, 145
  steeple 143
  strawberry 143
    yellow 142
crokain 145
cucumber
  to pickle 168, 169
  ragout of stuffed 73
  soup 8
curlew 101
currants
  cream 141
  jelly 183

currants *contd.*
    preserved in bunches 185
    preserved in jelly 185
    red or white, preserved 177
    wine, red or white 199
custard 136
    almond 136, 137
    orange 137
    pudding 118
    rice 136
Daffy's Elixir 204
damsons
    for tarts 172
    to preserve 179
deloute cream 143
diet loaf 160
Digby, Sir K. xxii
Dods, Meg xxiii
drop biscuits 57
Drops, Staughton's 203
Drumlanrig xi
draught xv
duck
    à la braise 72
    to boil 89
    to dress
        with oysters 94
        with lemon juice 93
    to stew 94
    to stove the Dutch way 93
duckling à la mode 93
dumplings
    apple 121, 123
    barm 123
    hard 123
Edinburgh ix, x, xi
eel
    à la daube 29
    with brown sauce 28
    soup 9
    to fry 29
    to pot 32
    to roast 30
    to stew 35
    with white sauce 28

eggs
    & bacon, fried 129
    & the juice of sorrel 129
    cheese 150
    cheesecakes 135
    fried with oysters & cockles 130
    poached in cream 130
    whites of 130
elder flowers, to pickle 166
elderberry wine 200
Elixir, Daffy's 204
eye water 203
eyes, ox or cow, to ragout
    with palates 74
eyes, ox or cow 74, 107, 109
Fenton, Professor A. xii
fish
    broth 14
    collar of 40
    cullis for 10
    forcemeat of 35
    water sokey 37
    see also names of particular fish
Fleming, R. & Gray, W. ix
Floating Island 146
Florence, J. xi
flounder
    to boil 31
    to broil 31
    to stew 32
    with sorrel 31
flour pudding 117
flummery
    calves' feet 149
    caudle 148
    hartshorn 149
    oatmeal 147
    Scots 147
    West country 147
forced meat balls 59
Foulis of Ravelston xxii
fowl
    to boil with celery 89
    to mince 89
    white fricassee sauce for 90

frames xiv
fritters
    apple 122
    currant 123
    French 122
    potato 123
fruit, to keep for tarts 172
gammon, to roast 64
giblets
    pie 82
    pottage 16
    to boil 95
gigot xxi, xxii
gill xxi
gingerbread, 164
    Dutch 164
Glasgow ix
Glasse, H. xxiii, xxvii
goblets xv
goose
    giblet pottage 16
    green
        to ragoo 72
        to roast 94
    pie 80
    to boil 95
    to dress with onions or
        cabbage 94
    to dry 95
    to roast 95
    to souse 94
gooseberry
    cream 143
    jam 182
    jelly 180
    paste 194
    preserved 176
    preserved for tarts 133, 178
    pudding 115
    tarts 132, 174
    vinegar 171
    wine 199
Gordon, W. ix
grapes, green, to preserve 188
grouse, to roast 100

gurnards, to boil 40
haddock, to stew 34
haggis xxi, xxii
ham
    beef 44
    mutton 93
    veal 42
    to boil 42
    to make 42
    to roast 64
hare
    jugged 102
    pie 28
    soup 18
    to hash 103
    to mince 103
    to pot 109
    to roast 102-0
haricles xxiv
hartshorn
    flummery 149
    jelly of 138
haslet, pig's, to roast 69
heart, ox or sheep, to roast 44
hedgehog, to make a 148
hen's nest (jelly) 148
    sauce for 90
herring, potted 34
hodge podge 13
hog's head, cheese fashion 66
Home, P. xiii
hoops xiv
Hopetoun, Earl of xi, xvi
Hopetoun House xi, xvi
Howard, H. xxii
ice a great cake, to 159
James V xxi
jelly
    bags xix
    broth 5
    calves' feet 138
    clear pippin 183
    currant 183
    currants in 185
    gooseberry 180

jelly *contd.*
    hartshorn 138
    hen's nest 152
    posset 146
    sweetmeats, of all colours in 137
Johnstone, Mrs C.I. xxiii
Kent, Countess of xxii
kettles xvi, xviii
ketchup, to make 195
kidney beans, to pickle 168
kidneys, to ragout 70
La Chapelle, V. xxiii
La Varenne, F.P. de xxiii
lamb
    hash 60
    minced 75
    pie 78
    to collar a fore quarter 105
    white fricassee of 85
    with rice 62
lamb's head
    to hash 63, 64
    to stew 64
lamb's stones & sweetbreads
    to ragout 71
    white fricassee of 88
lark
    pie 83
    to roast 101
    to stew 101
leech cream 139
lemon
    cream 140
        yellow 141
    puffs 151
    syrup of 195
liver
    to dress 64
    to ragout 72
lobster
    pie 80
    sauce 19
    soup 2
    the Italian way 36
    to butter 33

lobster *contd.*
    to dress 36
    to fry 37
    to pot 33
    to scallop 35
London ix, x
McLintock, Mrs ix
McNeill, F.M. xii, xxiv
macaroons 163
mackerel
    to boil 39
    to broil 39
    to pickle 39
maids (skate or thornback)
    to fry 39
maids cream 140
mangoes, to pickle 169
Marlborough cakes 158
marmalade
    apple 182
    apricot 193
    in the Italian manner 193
    orange 178
    plumb 181
    quince, white 176
    raspberry 193
Marnette, M. xxiii
Markham, G. xxii
marrow
    pasties 111
    pudding 116
Mary of Lorraine xxi
Massialot, F. xxii
May, R. xxii, xxvii
metheglin 199
midriffs, to broil 77
midrit xxiv
minced pies 81
Montrose, Duke of xvi
morels, to ragout 75
mould, with holes in 150
muirfowl
    to roast 100
    pie 83

mulberries
    preserved 180
    in liquid 190
mushrooms
    powder 171
    to pickle 167
    to ragout 70
    white fricassee of 85
mussel soup 17
mutchkin xxi
mutton
    & potato pie 84
    breast, grillando 53
    broth 7
    carbonaded 53
    collar, to roast 54
    cutlets 53
    hams 43
    leg, roast 54, 57
        forced 60
    pastry, as venison 78
    shoulder, in epigramme 54
    steak pie 80
    to haricot 91
    to hash 60
Naples biscuits 163
nettles, syrup of 181
nun's cake 159
oatmeal
    flummery 147
    posset 150
    pudding 116, 117
offal, see the various cuts
onions
    soup 9, 12
    to pickle 168
    to ragout 73
orange
    cheesecakes 134
    cream 140
    in chips 191
    loaves 151
    marmalade 178
    syrup of 195
    tarts 134

orange *contd.*
    to preserve 190
    whole 195
    wine 197
ovens xiii, xiv
ox cheek, to bake 57
Oxford sausages 68
oyster
    fricassee with kernels 87
    fried with eggs 130
    loaves 24
    pie 80
    sauce 19
    sausages 68
    soup 15
    to fricassee 33, 35, 88
    to pickle 34
    to scallop 35
    white 88
palates
    to ragout with eyes 74
    white fricassee of 87
pancakes 121, 122
    common 126
    custard 121
    Irish 127
    oatmeal 127
    rice 127
    royal 126
    with chopped apple 127
pans xiv
partridge
    à la braise 96
    & oysters 97
    hash 97
    pie 83
    roast 96
    to boil 97
    white fricassee of 88
paste
    cold water for pasties 131
    for raised pies 131
    for tarts 132
    of dripping 131
    puff 130

patty pans xxv
Paxton House xiii, xxx
peach tarts 133
pears
    to dry 196
    to preserve 174
    to preserve red 178
pease
    pudding 113
    soup 3, 12, 13, 17
petticoat tails xxi, xxii
pettitoes, pigs' 69
pheasant
    to boil 97
    to stew 100
pickles
    asparagus 170
    cauliflower 169
    celery 170
    codlins like mangoes 170
    cucumbers 168
    elder flowers 166
    kidney beans 168
    mangoes 169
    mushrooms 167
    onions 168
    plumbs like olives 176
    red cabbage 168
    samphire 166
    walnuts 166
        green 167
pig
    feet & ears, to dress 70
    in jelly 66
    rolliand 67
    the French way 65
    to collar 105
    to roast 90
        in quarters 67
pigeon
    à la daube 99
    disguised 100
    pie 78
    pottage 4
    pupton of 98

pigeon *contd.*
    ragout of 72
    to boil 99
        with rice 98
    to fry 99
    to pot 101
    to stew with cabbage
        & lettuce 100
pike
    to bake or roast 23
    to boil 25
    to fry 25
    to pot 111
    to souse 25
    to stew 41
pippins
    gold, to preserve red 181
    jelly of 184
    quiddany of 193
plague water 202
plaice
    to bake 26
    to boil 31
    to broil 31
    to stew 32
plovers 102
    to stew 102
plumb
    broth 5
    cake 156
    for tarts 172
    green admirable 175
    preserve green 180
    pudding 112
    quiddany of 194
    to pickle like olives 170
    white 179
pomatum, for the lips 203
Poor Knights of Windsor 164
pork
    loin with onions 67
    roast breast 65
    to broil steaks 65
    to collar 105

without the skin 65
possets
    ale 149
    jelly 146
    oatmeal 150
    sack 147, 149
    very good 150
    without cream or eggs 149
potato
    cheesecakes 135
    pudding 114
pottage
    barley 4
    brown royal 3
    chervil 5
    chopped herbs 14
    French 14
    goose giblets 16
    summer 6
prawlongs 191
Prestonpans xiv
prune tarts 132
pudding
    almond 112, 113
    apple 115, 119
    barley 119
    black caps 173
    blood 112
    bread 116
    carrot 118
    citron 113
    custard 118
    flour 117
    four-hour 116
    fried pan 122
    gooseberry 115
    lemon 118, 120
    liver 108
    marrow 116
    oatmeal 116, 117
    orange 118
        custard 120
    pease 113
    pippin tansy 125
    plumb 112

potato 114
pudding *contd.*
    rice 114, 117, 120
    sago 115
    suet 117
    tansey 115, 124, 126
    white pot 126
    yellow 119
    Yorkshire 112
puffs
    almond 151
    lemon 152
    pudding 151
purslane soup 8
quail
    to boil 97
    to roast 101
quiddany
    of pippins 193
    of plumbs 194
quince
    cakes 163, 192
    marmalade, white 176
rabbits
    fricassee of
        brown 87
        white 87
    to boil 104
        with sausages 104
    to stew the French way 104
raisin wine 198
raspberry
    cakes 186
    cream 143
    jam 175
    marmalade 143
    preserved 185
        whole 174
    tarts 134
ratafia 201
    cream 142
red cabbage, to pickle 168
red cream 143
Rhenish wine cream 140
rice

cream 144
rice *contd.*
    custard 136
    pudding 114
        baked 117
    soup 4
roasting range xvii
roots, broth of 15
roses, conserve of 183
Roxburgh, Duke of xi, xvi
Rozea, J. xi, xvi
Rutherford, Anne x
sack
    cream 141, 145
    posset 147, 149
        without cream or eggs 149
sacred tincture 203
saffron cakes 160
sago pudding 160
salamander xviii
salmon
    to bake or roast 19
    to broil 20
    to caper 33
    to collar 104
    to force slices 20
    to fry 21
    to pickle 19, 34
    to pot 32
        Newcastle way 111
samphire, to pickle 166
saucepans xv
sausages, 69
    Bologna 68
        fried with apples
            or potatoes 68
    Oxford 68
    oyster 68
scallops
    to pickle 34
    to pot 33
    to stew 40
Scots
    barley broth 7
    flummery 147

white collops 62
Scott, Sir Walter x, xi, xxiii
searce xix
seed cake 158, 161
shortbread 161
Shrewsbury cakes 157
shrimp
    pie 80
    sauce 19
shrub 202
skate, to crimp 31
skillets xvi
skimmer xviii
skink xxii
skirret pie 81
    white fricassee of 88
smelts, to pickle 26
Smith, E. xxiii, xxvii
Smith, J. xii
snipe
    to pot 108
    to roast 100
snow posset 147
sole
    to fry 36
    to stew 22, 26
soups, broths & pottages
    almond 9
    barley 4, 8
        Scots 7
    brown 11
    brown pottage royal 3
    cake 16
    calf's head 7
    calves' feet 15
    chervil 5
    crayfish 2
    cucumber 8
    de santé 6
    eel 9
    fish, broth 14
        cullis 10
        stock 2
    French pottage 14
    goose giblet 16

gravy, brown 1
soups, broths & pottages *contd.*
    gravy, white 2
    green cullis 10
    hare 18
    herb 14
    hodge podge 13
    jelly 5
    lobster 2
    meagre 8
        with herbs 7
    mussel 17
    mutton 7
    onion 9, 12
    oyster 15
    pease 3, 12, 13, 17
    pigeon & onion 4
    plumb 5
    purslain 8
    rice 4
    roots 15
    Scots barley 7
    strong 1
    summer 6
    turnip 17
    veal
        cullis 10
        soup 3
    vermicelli 2
    white 11
sperling (smelts) xxiv
    to fry 39
    to stew 39
steeple cream 143
stewpans xv
Stoughton's drops 203
stoves xiii, xv, xvi
strawberry cream 143
strainers xix
Stuart, Mary xxi
sturgeon
    to boil 38
    to fry 38
    to roast 38
suet pudding 117

surfeit water 202
sweetbreads, sheep, ragout of 74
sweetmeat tarts 133
syllabub
    from the cow 146
    solid 146
    whipt 139
tablets 145
tansey pudding 115
tavers xix
tench
    to bake 30
    to fry 30
    to roast 30
    to stew 18
tincture, sacred 203
tongues, neat's
    the Polish way 56
    to fry 57
    to stew 57
tongues, ox, à la mode 50
tongues, sheep's,
    boiled with oysters 55
    to ragout 74
trifle 137
tripe
    the Polish way 74
    to boil 74
    to fricassee 86
    to ragout 70, 73
    to roast 74
trotters, sheep's, entrée of 61
trout
    pie 80
    to pot 32
    to souse 37
    to stew 37
truffles, ragout of 75
turbot
    to bake 21
    to boil 23
    to fry 22
    to souse 22
    to stew 22
turkey

to boil with celery 89
turkey *contd.*
to roast young 93
white fricassee sauce for 90
Turk's-cap xv
udder, to roast 50
veal
breast, to collar 105
to ragout 70
collops 58
cullis 10
cutlets 75
fillet, roast 47
florendines 78
fricandoes 59
rolled 77
hams 43
knuckle, to stew 48
minced 75
neck, to ragout 71
shoulder, to broil 48
to roast 48
soup 3
venison
civet of 46
haunch
to boil 47
to roast 44
in avet 46
in blood 45, 46
pastry 77
shoulder 44
sokay 47
to broil 47
to keep all year 46
to pot 110
to ragout 72
to recover 46

to souse 45
venison *contd.*
to stew 45
vermicelli soup 2
vinegar 198
gooseberry 171
wafer-irons xvi
wafers 152
Dutch 152
wash, for scurvy or redness 202
water
eye 203
plague 202
surfeit 202
Wedderburn Castle x
weights & measures xx
West Country flummery 147
Whetstone cakes 158
white biscuits 162
whiting
to fry 40
to stew 40
wigs, to make, 155, 156
wild fowl, sauces for 108
wine
balm 198
currant, red or white 199
elderberry 200
gooseberry 199
orange 197
raisin 198
woodcock
to pot 108
to roast 100
Wright C. & Co. ix
yellow
balsam 204
cream 142
York cakes 163
Yorkshire pudding 112